NEB

WE HAVE A DREAM

WE HAVE A DREAM

AFRICAN-AMERICAN VISIONS OF FREEDOM

Compiled by Diana Wells

Carroll & Graf Publishers/Richard Gallen
New York

Collection copyright © 1993 by Diana Wells

The permissions listed on pages 7 to 8 constitute an
extension of this copyright page.

First Carroll & Graf/Richard Gallen edition 1993

Carroll & Graf Publishers, Inc.
260 Fifth Avenue
New York, NY 10001

Library of Congress Cataloging-in-Publication Data

Wells, Diana.
    We have a dream : African-American visions of
freedom / compiled by Diana Wells.
      p.   cm.
    ISBN 0-88184-941-3 : $21.95.
    ISBN 0-88184-957-X : $11.95
    1. Afro-Americans—Civil rights.   I. Title.
E185.61.W44   1993
323.1′196073—dc20   93-20000
                                                    CIP

Manufactured in the United States of America

Contents

Acknowledgments   7
Introduction   9

I
Acts of Definition

Langston Hughes, "Montage of a Dream Deferred" 17
Booker T. Washington, from *Up From Slavery*
    "The Struggle for an Education"   19
Richard Wright, from *Black Boy*   27
Maya Angelou, from *I Know Why the Caged Bird*
    Sings   37
James Farmer, from *Lay Bare the Heart*
    "I'll Keep My Soul"   51
James Baldwin, from *Notes of a Native Son*
    "Autobiographical Notes"   69
bell hooks, from *Talking Back*   75

II
The World Remade

Langston Hughes, "Question and Answer"   85
David Walker, from *An Appeal to the*
   Coloured Citizens of the World
      "Our Wretchedness in Consequence of the
      Preachers of the Religion of Jesus Christ"   87
Jane Johnson, "The Rescue of Jane Johnson"   92
James Madison Bell, "The Day and the War"   95
Frederick Douglass, "Reconstruction"   116
Booker T. Washington, "An Address Delivered
   at the Opening of the Cotton States Exposition
   in Atlanta, Georgia, September 1895"   122
W. E. B. Du Bois, from *The Souls of Black Folk*
      "Of the Sons of Master and Man"   128
Ida B. Wells-Barnett, from *Crusade for Justice*
      "Illinois Lynchings"   147
Mary McLeod Bethune, "A College on a
   Garbage Dump"   158
Martin Luther King, Jr., "I Have a Dream"   167

III
A Different Image

Dudley Randall, "A Different Image"   175
Marcus Garvey, from *The Philosophy and*
   Opinions of Marcus Garvey

"Speech Delivered on Emancipation Day at
Liberty Hall, New York City, N.Y.U.S.A." 177
"The Future As I See It" 180
Malcolm X, from *The Autobiography of
Malcolm X,* "1965" 186
James Baldwin, "The American Dream
and the American Negro" 196
Adam Clayton Powell, Jr., from *Adam by Adam*
"Black Power and the Future of America" 202
Shirley Chisholm, "The 51% Minority" 213
Alex Haley, from *Roots* 218

IV
The Promised Land

Robert Hayden, "Runagate Runagate" 239
Harriet Tubman, "On Liberty or Death" 243
Richard Wright, from *Black Boy* 245
Claude Brown, from *Manchild in the
Promised Land* 252

V
A Vision of the World United

Zora Neale Hurston, from *Dust Tracks on the Road*
"Looking Things Over" 267
Paul Robeson, from *Here I Stand*
"Love Will Find Out the Way" 273

Martin Luther King, Jr., "A Christmas
  Sermon on Peace"   288
Bayard Rustin, from *Down the Line*
    "Reflections on the Death of
    Martin Luther King, Jr."   296
Alice Walker, from *In Search of
  Our Mothers' Gardens*
    "Saving the Life That Is Your Own: The
    Importance of Models in the Artist's Life" 307

Acknowledgments

I would like to thank Richard Gallen for the opportunity to work on this project, David Gallen for his helping to make it a reality, and Peter Skutches for his masterful midwifery.

To Mom, Dad, Aileen, Christine, Paul, and unnamed friends and mentors, thanks for the love and guidance.

Most importantly, my debt is to those included here, and the many more who are not, who have acted on their visions for a more just world.

The Publisher gratefully acknowledges the following for permission to reprint from previously published material:

AFL-CIO Federationist, for "Reflections on the Death of Martin Luther King, Jr." by Bayard Rustin.

Alfred A. Knopf, Inc., for "Montage of a Dream Deferred" from *Montage of a Dream Deferred* by Langston Hughes. Copyright © 1951 by Langston Hughes.

Alfred A. Knopf, Inc., for "Question and Answer" from *The Panther and the Lash* by Langston Hughes. Copyright © 1967 by Langston Hughes.

Atheneum Publishers, an imprint of Macmillan Publishing Company, for excerpts from *Philosophy and Opinions of Marcus Garvey* by Amy Jacque-Garvey, editor. Copyright © 1923, 1925 by Amy Jacque-Garvey.

Estate of James Baldwin, for "The American Dream and the American Negro" by James Baldwin, first published in *The New York Times Magazine* (March 7, 1965).

Beacon Press, for excerpt from *Notes of A Native Son* by James Baldwin. Copyright © 1955, 1983 by James Baldwin.

Beacon Press, for excerpt from *Here I Stand* by Paul Robeson. Copyright © 1958, 1971, 1988 by Paul Robeson.

Broadside Press, for "A Different Image" from *Cities Burning* by Dudley Randall. Copyright © 1968 by Dudley Randall.

Doubleday, a division of Bantam Doubleday Dell Publishing Group, Inc., for excerpts from *Roots* by Alex Haley. Copyright © 1976 by Alex Haley.

Harcourt Brace Jovanovich, Inc., for "Saving the Life That Is Your Own" from *In Search of Our Mothers' Gardens* by Alice Walker (Harcourt Brace Jovanovich, 1983).

HarperCollins Publishers, Inc., for selection from *Dust Tracks on the Road* by Zora Neale Hurston. Copyright © 1942 by Zora Neale Hurston; copyright © renewed 1970 by John C. Hurston.

HarperCollins Publishers, Inc., for "A Christmas Service on Peace" from *The Trumpet of Conscience: Writings by Martin Luther King, Jr.,* edited by James M. Johnson. Copyright © 1967 by Martin Luther King, Jr.

HarperCollins Publishers, Inc., for selections from *Black Boy* by Richard Wright. Copyright © 1937, 1942, 1944, 1945 by Richard Wright; copyright © renewed by Ellen Wright.

The Joan Daves Agency, for "I Have a Dream" and "A Christmas Sermon on Peace" by Martin Luther King, Jr.

Macmillan Publishing Company, for excerpts from *Manchild in the Promised Land* by Claude Brown. Copyright © 1965 by Claude Brown.

The New York Times Company, for "The American Dream and the American Negro" by James Baldwin. Copyright © 1965.

Adam Clayton Powell, III, for excerpt from *Adam by Adam* by Adam Clayton Powell, Jr. (Dial Press, 1971).

Random House, Inc., for excerpt from *I Know Why the Caged Bird Sings* by Maya Angelou. Copyright © 1969 by Maya Angelou.

Random House, Inc., for excerpt from *The Autobiography of Malcolm X* by Malcolm X, with Alex Haley. Copyright © 1964 by Alex Haley and Malcolm X; copyright © 1965 by Alex Haley and Betty Shabazz.

South End Press, for "Talking Back" from *Talking Back* by bell hooks.

University of Chicago Press, for excerpt from *Crusade for Justice* by Ida B. Wells-Barnett.

William Morrow and Company, Inc., for excerpt from *Lay Bare the Heart* by James Farmer. Copyright © 1985 by James Farmer.

Introduction

On August 28, 1963, at the March on Washington, in one of the most famous public addresses in our nation's history, Martin Luther King, Jr., told us that he had a dream. He eloquently shared that dream of a more just world—a world without color barriers, a nation delivered from racist prejudice, a land truly of the free, and equal—with more than two hundred thousand people who had gathered that brilliant summer day in front of the Lincoln Memorial, and he inspired Americans everywhere with a faith in human possibility. The power of King's speech on that occasion lay not only in its moving rhetoric. Nor did it lie only in the passionate spirit of the man who spoke the words and had dreamt the dream. Its power lay in the voice it gave to a people's hope—to the hope of twenty-two million African Americans inside a nation and to the hope of the nation itself.

King did not dream alone. The African-American dream of a better world and more just tomorrow belongs to a literary tradition as old as the nation in which it grew. In her essay "Saving the Life That Is Your Own," Alice Walker links the African-American vision of a better future to the historical past:

> . . . Black writers seem always involved in a moral and/or physical struggle, the result of which is expected to be some kind of larger freedom. Perhaps this is because our literary tradition is based on the slave narratives, where escape for the body and freedom for the soul

went together, or perhaps this is because black people have never felt themselves guilty of global, cosmic sins.

Those early slave narratives that storied freedom fostered dreams that would in time be variously articulated in letters, diaries, autobiography, essays, speeches, and poetry. The dream might offer hope in the face of despair, or cry for justice against the oppressor. It might divine an apocalypse. It might stay for a moment the nightmare of history. To dream, the act itself, can often be its own triumph. The thirty-four selections in this anthology of African-American writing range from dreams of personal achievement to visions of mass political mobilization, the shape of each as distinctive as the intelligence that informs it. Still, in each can be heard the call, cry, plea, or prayer for a more regenerate world, for "some kind of larger freedom."

Freedom has first to be imagined to be achieved. As does justice, as does equality. In vision lie the seeds of change, and our social reality has in fact often proved to be altered by the dreams it would appear most adamantly to resist. The dream, though, must find its means. Social change is wrought by strategy. In the past hundred years Ida B. Wells-Barnett launched her anti-lynching campaign, Marcus Garvey instituted the Back to Africa movement, Alex Haley painstakingly reconstructed his family's—and a people's—lost history, King redefined civil disobedience, and Zora Neale Hurston pleaded for human unity. Strategies have varied as widely as the experience and ideology of the women and men who devised them. Some of the twenty-eight writers included in this volume emerge from the urban ghettos of the industrial North, others from rural communities in the agrarian South, and their strategies may bear the intellectual stamp of Marx, Gandhi, Islam, the Baptist church, or feminism. Yet, however diverse their individual histories, all twenty-eight share a vision of justice. Furthermore, while any single strategy may have effected but a small advance in its time, or even occasioned a major setback, every battle, march, rebellion, riot, protest, and outcry for that justice have made change possible. And collectively, cumulatively, they have significantly altered the currents in American society in this century.

The writers in this volume, then, have more than embraced the African-American dream of a better, more equitable world. They have enlarged it. At the same time, too, their personal vision and brave, inspiring words have helped to create a history for their people and shape an identity for their race. A dream, however, begins with a dreamer. Behind the African-American dream of freedom and the hope for future justice, for instance, stand the slave narratives that together compose a history of the African experience in eighteenth century America, and inside the words of those solemn, old autobiographical tales still stir the woes and the pride of black men and women who, in the course of recording their experience in an alien, often cruel land, were also in effect collaborating in the creation of a racial identity. The process continues; the history, the identity, and the vision that African Americans share continue to grow with each new dream, with each new act of self-definition. "Acts of Definition," the first part of this anthology, focuses on the dream as autobiography. Looking back upon their earlier years, the writers in these selections see themselves at sometimes painful odds with the world outside the private imagination—with their peers, the family, the black community, a white society—in their youthful attempts to make of a personal dream a reality. They see, too, that in their struggle toward achievement they were at the same time defining their emerging selves as individuals and as African Americans.

Vision is dynamic. Whether it is a defining act of the individual imagination or radically transforms our perception of social destiny, whether it provides a young boy with an epiphany into his essential blackness or offers African Americans a reconstruction of their political reality, perhaps imperceptibly and perhaps only eventually, but on some occasions with dramatic immediacy, vision alters what it reflects: an individual's history, a particular time and place, an ideology, cultural identity, the collective experience of a people. The translation of personal vision directly into public action redefines and reshapes the larger world. In the past one hundred fifty years of our national history slavery has been abolished, lynching has been outlawed, African-American citizens have been enfranchised, schools have been integrated, civil rights have been legislated

—because some have dared to act upon their dreams of a
world remade. "The World Remade," the second part of this
volume, includes now historical letters, speeches, essays, and
addresses that championed the cause of African Americans in
their struggle for justice and illuminates the more public di-
mensions of a people's dream.

For four hundred years African Americans served another
people's dream. For four hundred years white America excluded from its dream of national success the very people
whose lives and labor for generation after generation after generation made it possible, and in 1965, as James Baldwin pointed
out in a debate at England's Cambridge University, despite civil
rights legislation white America was still denying the African
one-ninth of the population its liberty and justice, its humanity
and pride. Baldwin was not the first to argue that African Americans needed a dream—and a history—of their own to free
them from the shackles of a slave mentality and to image more
positively their racial identity. All the writers represented in the
third part of this volume, "A Different Image," envisioned for
African Americans a vitally new role for themselves as a people
—not as slaves or coloreds or boys or mammies but as Negroes, and later as blacks, as people of color, and as African
Americans. To establish a more actively political consciousness
among African Americans and a more powerful racial image,
Marcus Garvey founded the Universal Negro Improvment Association, Malcolm X advocated black nationalism, W.E.B. Du
Bois espoused Pan-Africanism. With less manifestly political
purpose Alex Haley traveled two continents in an untiring
search for his family's roots. His journey—his discovery of a
long unrecorded African heritage that redeemed his people
from historical anonymity and substantially redefined their racial identity—made a difference for all African Americans.

From the beginning travel figured significantly in the literature and history of African Americans. An ocean voyage
brought the first generation of native Africans in chains to the
new American continent. Their freedom lost, their body weight
the measure of a commodity, only in their dreams could they
journey home again. Their children and their children's children, born in bondage, dreamed a journey, too; it took them
northward to a better place, across muddy rivers and state

lines to a land where, they had heard, they could be free. Like the old slave narratives Alice Walker speaks of, their dreams linked "escape for the body" with "freedom for the soul." Then, at the outset of the nineteenth century, the Underground Railroad began to make of some of those dreams a reality. Stealthy night journeys, secret messages, narrow escapes, and dark borders were written into African-American history as thousands of fugitive slaves found in the free states and Canada their Canaan or, as they also called it, their Promised Land. History birthed a mythic North that continued long after the Emancipation Proclamation to lure black Americans from their impoverished, meager lives on the fringes of a segregated, southern, agrarian-based, and white-dominated society. Spurred by economic hopes, dreaming of an opportunity to be more than merely nominally free, they braved a journey that more often than not led to a dead-end menial job and a tenement in an urban ghetto. Reality increasingly failed to support the myth of northern prosperity so that by the 1950s the dream of "The Promised Land," as the fourth part of the book is titled, reverberated with cruel irony.

The irony was not lost on Malcolm X. That the promise of economic parity for black Americans or their hope for social justice in the cities of the industrial North had been unremittingly blighted into urban despair roused the Muslim leader's indignation, scorn, anger, and rage. Rallying blacks against the inhumanity that they had suffered for four hundred years, Malcolm X strove to restore his people's pride. He also opened an entire nation's eyes to its own ignominy. When he observed, on the assassination of America's thirty-fifth president, that Kennedy "never foresaw that the chickens would come home to roost so soon," whatever else Malcolm X may have intended, he pointed up that injustice cannot be contained inside the city ghetto or within any single community, class, or race. Injustice affects us all; it kills black kids in the projects, it kills civil rights volunteers in Mississippi, it kills presidents. To continue living together in a world whose ethnically diverse peoples have become increasingly more interdependent and to begin living together in multicultural harmony demand a vision beyond the reach of irony. In the last part of this anthology, "A Vision of the World United"—a vision that crosses color lines, overrides international boundaries, and breaks down cultural barriers—African Americans identify themselves and the audience they address as members, first and foremost, of the human race. They call upon their brothers and sisters of all colors to transcend their differences and forge new bonds that will establish and ensure global harmony. They dream of peace. Here, then, is the apogee of the African-American dream, for once it is achieved dreams of of freedom and equality and justice shall have been rendered obsolete.

Who can imagine peace, who can imagine freedom and equality in a world regenerate and just, stands among the millions who share the African-American dream. The dream was born in the consciousness of a people oppressed; it was nurtured by vision and hope and rhetoric and fire. In tin-roofed shanties, in dusty fields at planting time, on buses and at lunch counters and inside prison cells, in a laboratory at Tuskegee Institute and on the campus of Howard University, on the steps of the national Capitol and in the streets of Harlem or Watts, in Birmingham and Paris, in Accra and Brooklyn, by fits and starts, with advances and setbacks, out of rage and legislation and chaos and poetry, it grew. It changed minds. It found new words, and in new words it continues to grow. This volume seeks to explore the African-American dream as it was dreamed by some of the people to whom the dream belongs. We trust that it does not belong to them alone.

—Diana Wells and Peter Skutches

I

Acts of Definition

*A dream begins with a dreamer . . .
and with each new dream,
with each new act of self-definition,
the history, the identity, and the vision that
African Americans share
continue to grow.*

Langston Hughes

(1902–1967)

Montage of a Dream Deferred

Langston Hughes was born in Joplin, Missouri. Educated first in engineering and then in the law, he went on to become one of the leading artists in the Harlem Renaissance as a prolific writer of poetry, novels, short stories, plays, nonfiction, and autobiography.

"Montage of a Dream Deferred" originally appeared in a volume of poetry by the same name.

What happens to a dream deferred?
Does it dry up
Like a raisin in the sun?
Or fester like a sore—
And then run?
Does it stink like rotten meat?

Or crust and sugar over—
Like a syrupy sweet?

Maybe it just sags
Like a heavy load.

Or does it explode?

Booker T. Washington

(1856?–1915)

---

from *Up From Slavery*
The Struggle for an Education

*Born in Hales Ford, Virginia, the son of a slave
mother and white father, Booker T. Washington
worked at odd jobs to earn the money that eventually
took him to the Hampton Normal and Agricultural Institute in Hampton, Virginia. After being graduated he
taught for several years in Malden, Virginia, and
when, in 1881, he was sent to the backwoods of Alabama, with two thousand dollars he founded the now
famous Tuskegee Institute.*

*In "The Struggle for an Education" Washington re-
calls a time he worked for one very demanding Mrs.
Ruffner—at a salary of five dollars a month—so that
he could pursue his personal dream and travel the five
hundred miles to the institute at Hampton. Out of that
dream grew Washington's vision to improve the lot of
all African Americans, not by political wrangling but*

through self-help and education—a position much crit-icized by his contemporary W.E.B. Du Bois.

One day, while at work in the coal-mine, I happened to over-hear two miners talking about a great school for coloured peo-ple somewhere in Virginia. This was the first time that I had ever heard anything about any kind of school or college that was more pretentious than the little coloured school in our town.

In the darkness of the mine I noiselessly crept as close as I could to the two men who were talking. I heard one tell the other that not only was the school established for the members of my race, but that opportunities were provided by which poor but worthy students could work out all or a part of the cost of board, and at the same time be taught some trade or industry.

As they went on describing the school, it seemed to me that it must be the greatest place on earth, and not even Heaven presented more attractions for me at that time than did the Hampton Normal and Agricultural Institute in Virginia, about which these men were talking. I resolved at once to go to that school, although I had no idea where it was, or how many miles away, or how I was going to reach it; I remembered only that I was on fire constantly with one ambition, and that was to go to Hampton. This thought was with me day and night.

After hearing of the Hampton Institute, I continued to work for a few months longer in the coal-mine. While at work there, I heard of a vacant position in the household of General Lewis Ruffner, the owner of the salt-furnace and coal-mine. Mrs. Vi-ola Ruffner, the wife of General Ruffner, was a "Yankee" woman from Vermont. Mrs. Ruffner had a reputation all through the vicinity for being very strict with her servants, and especially with the boys who tried to serve her. Few of them had remained with her more than two or three weeks. They all left with the same excuse: she was too strict. I decided, how-ever, that I would rather try Mrs. Ruffner's house than remain in the coal-mine, and so my mother applied to her for the vacant position. I was hired at a salary of $5 per month.

I had heard so much about Mrs. Ruffner's severity that I was almost afraid to see her, and trembled when I went into her presence. I had not lived with her many weeks, however, before I began to understand her. I soon began to learn that, first of all, she wanted everything kept clean about her, that she wanted things done promptly and systematically, and that at the bottom of everything she wanted absolute honesty and frankness. Nothing must be sloven or slipshod; every door, every fence, must be kept in repair.

I cannot now recall how long I lived with Mrs. Ruffner before going to Hampton, but I think it must have been a year and a half. At any rate, I here repeat what I have said more than once before, that the lessons that I learned in the home of Mrs. Ruffner were as valuable to me as any education I have ever gotten anywhere since. Even to this day I never see bits of paper scattered around a house or in the street that I do not want to pick them up at once. I never see a filthy yard that I do not want to clean it, a paling off of a fence that I do not want to put it on, an unpainted or unwhitewashed house that I do not want to paint or whitewash it, or a button off one's clothes, or a grease-spot on them or on a floor, that I do not want to call attention to it.

From fearing Mrs. Ruffner I soon learned to look upon her as one of my best friends. When she found that she could trust me she did so implicitly. During the one or two winters that I was with her she gave me an opportunity to go to school for an hour in the day during a portion of the winter months, but most of my studying was done at night, sometimes alone, sometimes under someone whom I could hire to teach me. Mrs. Ruffner always encouraged and sympathized with me in all my efforts to get an education. It was while living with her that I began to get together my first library. I secured a dry-goods box, knocked out one side of it, put some shelves in it, and began putting into it every kind of book that I could get my hands upon, and called it my "library."

Notwithstanding my success at Mrs. Ruffner's I did not give up the idea of going to the Hampton Institute. In the fall of 1872 I determined to make an effort to get there, although, as I have stated, I had no definite idea of the direction in which Hampton was, or of what it would cost to go there. I do not think that any one thoroughly sympathized with me in my ambition to go to Hampton unless it was my mother, and she was troubled with a grave fear that I was starting out on a "wild-goose chase." At any rate, I got only a half-hearted consent from her that I might start. The small amount of money that I had earned had been consumed by my stepfather and the remainder of the family, with the exception of a very few dollars, and so I had very little with which to buy clothes and pay my travelling expenses. My brother John helped me all that he could, but of course that was not a great deal, for his work was in the coal-mine, where he did not earn much, and most of what he did earn went in the direction of paying the household expenses.

Perhaps the thing that touched and pleased me most in connection with my starting for Hampton was the interest that many of the older coloured people took in the matter. They had spent the best days of their lives in slavery, and hardly expected to live to see the time when they would see a member of their race leave home to attend a boarding school. Some of these older people would give me a nickel, others a quarter, or a handkerchief.

Finally the great day came, and I started for Hampton. I had only a small, cheap satchel that contained what few articles of clothing I could get. My mother at the time was rather weak and broken in health. I hardly expected to see her again, and thus our parting was all the more sad. She, however, was very brave through it all. At that time there were no through trains connecting that part of West Virginia with eastern Virginia. Trains ran only a portion of the way, and the remainder of the distance was travelled by stage-coaches.

The distance from Malden to Hampton is about five hundred miles. I had not been away from home many hours before it began to grow painfully evident that I did not have enough money to pay my fare to Hampton. One experience I shall long remember. I had been travelling over the mountains most of the afternoon in an old-fashioned stage-coach, when, late in the evening, the coach stopped for the night at a common, unpainted house called a hotel. All the other passengers except myself were whites. In my ignorance I supposed that the little hotel existed for the purpose of accommodating the passengers who travelled on the stage-coach. The difference that the colour of one's skin would make I had not thought anything about. After all the other passengers had been shown rooms and were getting ready for supper, I shyly presented myself before the man at the desk. It is true I had practically no money in my pocket with which to pay for bed or food, but I had hoped in some way to beg my way into the good graces of the landlord, for at that season in the mountains of Virginia the weather was cold, and I wanted to get indoors for the night. Without asking as to whether I had any money, the man at the desk firmly refused to even consider the matter of providing me with food or lodging. This was my first experience in finding out what the colour of my skin meant. In some way I managed to keep warm by walking about, and so got through the night. My whole soul was so bent upon reaching Hampton that I did not have time to cherish any bitterness toward the hotel-keeper.

By walking, begging rides both in wagons and in the cars, in some way, after a number of days, I reached the city of Richmond, Virginia, about eighty-two miles from Hampton. When I reached there, tired, hungry, and dirty, it was late in the night. I had never been in a large city, and this rather added to my misery. When I reached Richmond, I was completely out of money. I had not a single acquaintance in the place; and, being unused to city ways, I did not know where to go. I applied at several places for lodging, but they all wanted money, and that was what I did not have. Knowing nothing else better to do, I walked the streets. In doing this I passed by many food-stands where fried chicken and half-moon apple pies were piled high and made to present a most tempting appearance. At that time it seemed to me that I would have promised all that I expected to possess in the future to have gotten hold of one of those chicken legs or one of those pies. But I could not get either of these, nor anything else to eat.

I must have walked the streets till after midnight. At last I became so exhausted that I could walk no longer. I was tired, I was hungry, I was everything but discouraged. Just about the time when I reached extreme physical exhaustion, I came upon a portion of a street where the board sidewalk was considerably elevated. I waited for a few minutes, till I was sure that no

passers-by could see me, and then crept under the sidewalk
and lay for the night upon the ground, with my satchel of clothing for a pillow. Nearly all night I could hear the tramp of feet
over my head. The next morning I found myself somewhat
refreshed, but I was extremely hungry, because it had been a
long time since I had had sufficient food. As soon as it became
light enough for me to see my surroundings I noticed that I
was near a large ship, and that this ship seemed to be unload-
ing a cargo of pig iron. I went at once to the vessel and asked
the captain to permit me to help unload the vessel in order to
get money for food. The captain, a white man, who seemed to
be kind-hearted, consented. I worked long enough to earn
money for my breakfast, and it seems to me, as I remember it
now, to have been about the best breakfast that I have ever
eaten.

My work pleased the captain so well that he told me if I
desired I could continue working for a small amount per day.
This I was very glad to do. I continued working on this vessel
for a number of days. After buying food with the small wages I
received there was not much left to add to the amount I must
get to pay my way to Hampton. In order to economize in every
way possible, so as to be sure to reach Hampton in a reasonable time, I continued to sleep under the same sidewalk that
gave me shelter the first night I was in Richmond. Many years
after that the coloured citizens of Richmond very kindly ten-
dered me a reception at which there must have been two thousand people present. This reception was held not far from the
spot where I slept the first night I spent in that city, and I must
confess that my mind was more upon the sidewalk that first
gave me shelter than upon the reception, agreeable and cordial
as it was.

When I had saved what I considered enough money with
which to reach Hampton, I thanked the captain of the vessel for
his kindness, and started again. Without any unusual occurrence I reached Hampton, with a surplus of exactly fifty cents
with which to begin my education. To me it had been a long,
eventful journey; but the first sight of the large, three-story,
brick school building seemed to have rewarded me for all that I
had undergone in order to reach the place. If the people who
gave the money to provide that building could appreciate the

influence the sight of it had upon me, as well as upon thousands of other youths, they would feel all the more encouraged to make such gifts. It seemed to me to be the largest and most beautiful building I had ever seen. The sight of it seemed to give me new life. I felt that a new kind of existence had now begun—that life would now have a new meaning. I felt that I had reached the promised land, and I resolved to let no obstacle prevent me from putting forth the highest effort to fit myself to accomplish the most good in the world.

As soon as possible after reaching the grounds of the Hampton Institute, I presented myself before the head teacher for assignment to a class. Having been so long without proper food, a bath, and change of clothing, I did not, of course, make a very favourable impression upon her, and I could see at once that there were doubts in her mind about the wisdom of admitting me as a student. I felt that I could hardly blame her if she got the idea that I was a worthless loafer or tramp. For some time she did not refuse to admit me, neither did she decide in my favour, and I continued to linger about her, and to impress her in all the ways I could with my worthiness. In the meantime I saw her admitting other students, and that added greatly to my discomfort, for I felt, deep down in my heart, that I could do as well as they, if I could only get a chance to show what was in me.

After some hours had passed, the head teacher said to me: "The adjoining recitation-room needs sweeping. Take the broom and sweep it."

It occurred to me at once that here was my chance. Never did I receive an order with more delight. I knew that I could sweep, for Mrs. Ruffner had thoroughly taught me how to do that when I lived with her.

I swept the recitation-room three times. Then I got a dusting-cloth and I dusted it four times. All the woodwork around the walls, every bench, table, and desk, I went over four times with my dusting-cloth. Besides, every piece of furniture had been moved and every closet and corner in the room had been thoroughly cleaned. I had the feeling that in a large measure my future depended upon the impression I made upon the teacher in the cleaning of that room. When I was through, I reported to the head teacher. She was a "Yankee" woman who knew just where to look for dirt. She went into the room and inspected the floor and closets; then she took her handkerchief and rubbed it on the woodwork about the walls, and over the table and benches. When she was unable to find one bit of dirt on the floor, or a particle of dust on any of the furniture, she quietly remarked, "I guess you will do to enter this institution."

I was one of the happiest souls on earth. The sweeping of that room was my college examination, and never did any youth pass an examination for entrance into Harvard or Yale that gave him more genuine satisfaction. I have passed several examinations since then, but I have always felt that this was the best one I ever passed. . . .

Richard Wright

(1908–1960)

from *Black Boy*

Inquisitive, rebellious, independent-minded, Richard Wright left his native Tennessee, and the Jim Crow South, at the age of fifteen. He traveled first to Chicago and later moved to New York. A self-educated man and outspoken social critic, author of the powerful novel Native Son *and a Guggenheim Fellow, Wright left America in 1947 for Paris, where he died in 1960.*

The following excerpt from Wright's autobiography recounts his first attempt as a teenager to realize his dream of becoming a writer, a desire and effort that were greeted by his family with disapproval, disbelief, and dismay.

SUMMER. Bright hot days. Hunger still a vital part of my consciousness. Passing relatives in the hallways of the crowded home and not speaking. Eating in silence at a table where prayers are said. My mother recovering slowly, but now definitely crippled for life. Will I be able to enter school in September? Loneliness. Reading. Job hunting. Vague hopes of going north. But what would become of my mother if I left her in this queer house? And how would I fare in a strange city? Doubt. Fear. My friends are buying long-pants suits that cost from seventeen to twenty dollars, a sum as huge to me as the Alps! This was my reality in 1924.

Word came that a near-by brickyard was hiring and I went to investigate. I was frail, not weighing a hundred pounds. At noon I sneaked into the yard and walked among the aisles of damp, clean-smelling clay and came to a barrow full of wet bricks just taken from the machine that shaped them. I caught hold of the handles of the barrow and was barely able to lift it; it weighed perhaps four times as much as I did. If I were only stronger and heavier!

Later I asked questions and found that the water boy was missing; I ran to the office and was hired. I walked in the hot sun lugging a big zinc pail from one laboring gang of black men to another for a dollar a day; a man would lift the tin dipper to his lips, take a swallow, rinse out his mouth, spit, and then drink in long, slow gulps as sweat dripped into the dipper. And off again I would go, chanting:

"Water!"

And somebody would yell:

"Here, boy!"

Deep into wet pits of clay, into sticky ditches, up slippery slopes I would struggle with the pail. I stuck it out, reeling at times from hunger, pausing to get my breath before clambering up a hill. At the end of the week the money sank into the endless expenses at home. Later I got a job in the yard that paid a dollar and a half a day, that of bat boy. I went between the walls of clay and picked up bricks that had cracked open; when my barrow was full, I would wheel it out onto a wooden scaffold and dump it into a pond.

I had but one fear here: a dog. He was owned by the boss of the brickyard and he haunted the clay aisles, snapping, growling. The dog had been wounded many times, for the black workers were always hurling bricks at it. Whenever I saw the animal, I would take a brick from my load and toss it at him; he would slink away, only to appear again, showing his teeth. Several of the Negroes had been bitten and had been ill; the boss had been asked to leash the dog, but he had refused. One afternoon I was wheeling my barrow toward the pond when something sharp sank into my thigh. I whirled; the dog crouched a few feet away, snarling. I had been bitten. I drove the dog away and opened my trousers; teeth marks showed deep and red.

I did not mind the stinging hurt, but I was afraid of an infection. When I went to the office to report that the boss's dog had bitten me, I was met by a tall blonde white girl.

"What do you want?" she asked.

"I want to see the boss, ma'am."

"For what?"

"His dog bit me, ma'am, and I'm afraid I might get an infection."

"Where did he bite you?"

"On my leg," I lied, shying from telling her where the bite was.

"Let's see," she said.

"No, ma'am. Can't I see the boss?"

"He isn't here now," she said, and went back to her typing.

I returned to work, stopping occasionally to examine the teeth marks; they were swelling. Later in the afternoon a tall white man wearing a cool white suit, a Panama hat, and white shoes came toward me.

"Is this the nigger?" he asked a black boy as he pointed at me.

"Yes, sir," the black boy answered.

"Come here, nigger," he called me.

I went to him.

"They tell me my dog bit you," he said.

"Yes, sir."

I pulled down my trousers and he looked.

"Humnnn," he grunted, then laughed. "A dog bite can't hurt a nigger."

"It's swelling and it hurts," I said.

"If it bothers you, let me know," he said. "But I never saw a dog yet that could really hurt a nigger."

He turned and walked away and the black boys gathered to watch his tall form disappear down the aisles of wet bricks.

"Sonofabitch!"

"He'll get his someday!"

"Boy, their hearts are hard!"

"Lawd, a white man'll do anything!"

"Break up that prayer meeting!" the white straw boss yelled. The wheelbarrows rolled again. A boy came close to me.

"You better see a doctor," he whispered.

"I ain't got no money," I said.

Two days passed and luckily the redness and swelling went away.

Summer wore on and the brickyard closed; again I was out of work. I heard that caddies were wanted and I tramped five miles to the golf links. I was hired by a florid-faced white man at the rate of fifty cents for nine holes. I did not know the game and I lost three balls in as many minutes; it seemed that my eyes could not trace the flight of the balls. The man dismissed me. I watched the other boys do their jobs and within half an hour I had another golf bag and was following a ball. I made a dollar. I returned home, disgusted, tired, hungry, hating the sight of a golf course.

School opened and, though I had not prepared myself, I enrolled. The school was far across town and the walking distance alone consumed my breakfast of mush and lard gravy. I attended classes without books for a month, then got a job working mornings and evenings for three dollars a week.

I grew silent and reserved as the nature of the world in which I lived became plain and undeniable; the bleakness of the future affected my will to study. Granny had already thrown out hints that it was time for me to be on my own. But what had I learned so far that would help me to make a living?

Nothing. I could be a porter like my father before me, but what else? And the problem of living as a Negro was cold and hard. What was it that made the hate of whites for blacks so steady, seemingly so woven into the texture of things? What kind of life was possible under that hate? How had this hate come to be? Nothing about the problems of Negroes was ever taught in the classrooms at school; and whenever I would raise these questions with the boys, they would either remain silent or turn the subject into a joke. They were vocal about the petty individual wrongs they suffered, but they possessed no desire for a knowledge of the picture as a whole. Then why was I worried about it?

Was I really as bad as my uncles and aunts and Granny repeatedly said? Why was it considered wrong to ask questions? Was I right when I resisted punishment? It was inconceivable to me that one should surrender to what seemed wrong, and most of the people I had met seemed wrong. Ought one to surrender to authority even if one believed that that authority was wrong? If the answer was yes, then I knew that I would always be wrong, because I could never do it. Then how could one live in a world in which one's mind and perceptions meant nothing and authority and tradition meant everything? There were no answers.

The eighth grade days flowed in their hungry path and I grew more conscious of myself; I sat in classes, bored, wondering, dreaming. One long dry afternoon I took out my composition book and told myself that I would write a story; it was sheer idleness that led me to it. What would the story be about? It resolved itself into a plot about a villain who wanted a widow's home and I called it *The Voodoo of Hell's Half-Acre*. It was crudely atmospheric, emotional, intuitively psychological, and stemmed from pure feeling. I finished it in three days and then wondered what to do with it.

The local Negro newspaper! That's it . . . I sailed into the office and shoved my ragged composition book under the nose of the man who called himself the editor.

"What is that?" he asked.

"A story," I said.

"A news story?"

"No, fiction."

"All right. I'll read it," he said.

He pushed my composition book back on his desk and looked at me curiously, sucking at his pipe.

"But I want you to read it *now,*" I said.

He blinked. I had no idea how newspapers were run. I thought that one took a story to an editor and he sat down then and there and read it and said yes or no.

"I'll read this and let you know about it tomorrow," he said.

I was disappointed; I had taken time to write it and he seemed distant and uninterested.

"Give me the story," I said, reaching for it.

He turned from me, took up the book and read ten pages or more.

"Won't you come in tomorrow?" he asked. "I'll have it finished then."

I honestly relented.

"All right," I said. "I'll stop in tomorrow."

I left with the conviction that he would not read it. Now, where else could I take it after he had turned it down? The next afternoon, en route to my job, I stepped into the newspaper office.

"Where's my story?" I asked.

"It's in galleys," he said.

"What's that?" I asked; I did not know what galleys were.

"It's set up in type," he said. "We're publishing it."

"How much money will I get?" I asked, excited.

"We can't pay for manuscript," he said.

"But you sell your papers for money," I said with logic.

"Yes, but we're young in business," he explained.

"But you're asking me to *give* you my story, but you don't *give* your papers away," I said.

He laughed.

"Look, you're just starting. This story will put your name before our readers. Now, that's something," he said.

"But if the story is good enough to sell to your readers, then you ought to give me some of the money you get from it," I insisted.

He laughed again and I sensed that I was amusing him.

"I'm going to offer you something more valuable than money," he said. "I'll give you a chance to learn to write."

I was pleased, but I still thought he was taking advantage of me.

"When will you publish my story?"

"I'm dividing it into three installments," he said. "The first installment appears this week. But the main thing is this: Will you get news for me on a space rate basis?"

"I work mornings and evenings for three dollars a week," I said.

"Oh," he said. "Then you better keep that. But what are you doing this summer?"

"Nothing."

"Then come to see me before you take another job," he said. "And write some more stories."

A few days later my classmates came to me with baffled eyes, holding copies of the *Southern Register* in their hands.

"Did you really write that story?" they asked me.

"Yes."

"Why?"

"Because I wanted to."

"Where did you get it from?"

"I made it up."

"You didn't. You copied it out of a book."

"If I had, no one would publish it."

"But what are they publishing it for?"

"So people can read it."

"Who told you to do that?"

"Nobody."

"Then why did you do it?"

"Because I wanted to," I said again.

They were convinced that I had not told them the truth. We had never had any instruction in literary matters at school; the literature of the nation or the Negro had never been mentioned. My schoolmates could not understand why anyone would want to write a story; and, above all, they could not understand why I had called it *The Voodoo of Hell's Half-Acre*. The mood out of which a story was written was the most alien thing conceivable to them. They looked at me with new eyes, and a distance, a suspiciousness came between us. If I had thought anything in writing the story, I had thought that perhaps it would make me more acceptable to them, and now it was cutting me off from them more completely than ever.

At home the effects were no less disturbing. Granny came into my room early one morning and sat on the edge of my bed.

"Richard, what is this you're putting in the papers?" she asked.

"A story," I said.

"About what?"

"It's just a story, granny."

"But they tell me it's been in three times."

"It's the same story. It's in three parts."

"But what is it about?" she insisted.

I hedged, fearful of getting into a religious argument.

"It's just a story I made up," I said.

"Then it's a lie," she said.

"Oh, Christ," I said.

"You must get out of this house if you take the name of the Lord in vain," she said.

"Granny, please . . . I'm sorry," I pleaded. "But it's hard to tell you about the story. You see, granny, everybody knows that the story isn't true, but . . ."

"Then why write it?" she asked.

"Because people might want to read it."

"That's the Devil's work," she said and left.

My mother also was worried.

"Son, you ought to be more serious," she said. "You're growing up now and you won't be able to get jobs if you let people think that you're weak-minded. Suppose the superintendent of schools would ask you to teach here in Jackson, and he found out that you had been writing stories?"

I could not answer her.

"I'll be all right, mama," I said.

Uncle Tom, though surprised, was highly critical and contemptuous. The story had no point, he said. And whoever heard of a story by the title of *The Voodoo of Hell's Half-Acre?* Aunt Addie said that it was a sin for anyone to use the word "hell" and that what was wrong with me was that I had nobody to guide me. She blamed the whole thing upon my upbringing.

In the end I was so angry that I refused to talk about the story. From no quarter, with the exception of the Negro newspaper editor, had there come a single encouraging word. It was rumored that the principal wanted to know why I had used the word "hell." I felt that I had committed a crime. Had I been conscious of the full extent to which I was pushing against the current of my environment, I would have been frightened altogether out of my attempts at writing. But my reactions were limited to the attitude of the people about me, and I did not speculate or generalize.

I dreamed of going north and writing books, novels. The North symbolized to me all that I had not felt and seen; it had no relation whatever to what actually existed. Yet, by imagining a place where everything was possible, I kept hope alive in me. But where had I got this notion of doing something in the future, of going away from home and accomplishing something that would be recognized by others? I had, of course, read my Horatio Alger stories, my pulp stories, and I knew my Get-Rich-Quick Wallingford series from cover to cover, though I had sense enough not to hope to get rich; even to my naïve imagination that possibility was too remote. I knew that I lived in a country in which the aspirations of black people were limited, marked-off. Yet I felt that I had to go somewhere and do something to redeem my being alive.

I was building up in me a dream which the entire educational system of the South had been rigged to stifle. I was feeling the very thing that the state of Mississippi had spent millions of dollars to make sure that I would never feel; I was becoming aware of the thing that the Jim Crow laws had been drafted and passed to keep out of my consciousness; I was acting on impulses that southern senators in the nation's capital had striven to keep out of Negro life; I was beginning to dream the dreams that the state had said were wrong, that the schools had said were taboo.

Had I been articulate about my ultimate aspirations, no doubt someone would have told me what I was bargaining for; but nobody seemed to know, and least of all did I. My classmates felt that I was doing something that was vaguely wrong, but they did not know how to express it. As the outside world grew more meaningful, I became more concerned, tense; and my classmates and my teachers would say: "Why do you ask so many questions?" Or: "Keep quiet."

I was in my fifteenth year; in terms of schooling I was far behind the average youth of the nation, but I did not know that. In me was shaping a yearning for a kind of consciousness, a mode of being that the way of life about me had said could not be, must not be, and upon which the penalty of death had been placed. Somewhere in the dead of the southern night my life had switched onto the wrong track and, without my knowing it, the locomotive of my heart was rushing down a dangerously steep slope, heading for a collision, heedless of the warning red lights that blinked all about me, the sirens and the bells and the screams that filled the air.

Maya Angelou

(b. 1928)

---

from *I Know Why the Caged Bird Sings*

Novelist, essayist, dancer, actress, teacher, Maya Angelou was born in St. Louis, Missouri. She has toured Europe and Africa in Porgy *and* Bess. *She danced with Martha Graham. Fluent in six languages, she has taught theater in Rome, Tel Aviv, Chicago, and New York. Currently she is a professor at Wake Forest University in North Carolina.*

In the autobiographical selection that follows Angelou's quest for personal identity is realized in a moment of epiphany. For the first time defining herself clearly not just as her own woman but as a black woman, she further envisions herself as the heritor to all the black poets, women and men, unknown and known, who have come before her, for, as she herself says, "we survive in the exact relationship to the dedication of our poets."

The children in Stamps trembled visibly with anticipation. Some adults were excited too, but to be certain the whole young population had come down with graduation epidemic. Large classes were graduating from both the grammar school and the high school. Even those who were years removed from their own day of glorious release were anxious to help with preparations as a kind of dry run. The junior students who were moving into the vacating classes' chairs were tradition-bound to show their talents for leadership and management. They strutted through the school and around the campus exerting pressure on the lower grades. Their authority was so new that occasionally if they pressed a little too hard it had to be overlooked. After all, next term was coming, and it never hurt a sixth grader to have a play sister in the eighth grade, or a tenth-year student to be able to call a twelfth grader Bubba. So all was endured in a spirit of shared understanding. But the graduating classes themselves were the nobility. Like travelers with exotic destinations on their minds, the graduates were remarkably forgetful. They came to school without their books, or tablets or even pencils. Volunteers fell over themselves to secure replacements for the missing equipment. When accepted the willing workers might or might not be thanked, and it was of no importance to the pregraduation rites. Even teachers were respectful of the now quiet and aging seniors, and tended to speak to them, if not as equals, as beings only slightly lower than themselves. After tests were returned and grades given, the student body, which acted like an extended family, knew who did well, who excelled, and what piteous ones had failed.

Unlike the white high school, Lafayette County Training School distinguished itself by having neither lawn, nor hedges, nor tennis court, nor climbing ivy. Its two buildings (main classrooms, the grade school and home economics) were set on a dirt hill with no fence to limit either its boundaries or

those of bordering farms. There was a large expanse to the left
of the school which was used alternately as a baseball diamond
or a basketball court. Rusty hoops on the swaying poles represented the permanent recreational equipment, although bats
and balls could be borrowed from the P. E. teacher if the bor-
rower was qualified and if the diamond wasn't occupied.

Over this rocky area relieved by a few shady tall persimmon
trees the graduating class walked. The girls often held hands
and no longer bothered to speak to the lower students. There
was a sadness about them, as if this old world was not their
home and they were bound for higher ground. The boys, on
the other hand, had become more friendly, more outgoing. A
decided change from the closed attitude they projected while
studying for finals. Now they seemed not ready to give up the
old school, the familiar paths and classrooms. Only a small
percentage would be continuing on to college—one of the
South's A & M (agricultural and mechanical) schools, which
trained Negro youths to be carpenters, farmers, handymen,
masons, maids, cooks and baby nurses. Their future rode heavily on their shoulders, and blinded them to the collective joy
that had pervaded the lives of the boys and girls in the grammar school graduating class.

Parents who could afford it had ordered new shoes and
ready-made clothes for themselves from Sears and Roebuck or
Montgomery Ward. They also engaged the best seamstresses
to make the floating graduating dresses and to cut down
secondhand pants which would be pressed to a military slick-
ness for the important event.

Oh, it was important, all right. Whitefolks would attend the
ceremony, and two or three would speak of God and home, and
the Southern way of life, and Mrs. Parsons, the principal's wife,
would play the graduation march while the lower-grade graduates paraded down the aisles and took their seats below the
platform. The high school seniors would wait in empty classrooms to make their dramatic entrance.

In the Store I was the person of the moment. The birthday
girl. The center. Bailey had graduated the year before, although to do so he had had to forfeit all pleasures to make up
for his time lost in Baton Rouge.

My class was wearing butter-yellow piqué dresses, and Momma launched out on mine. She smocked the yoke into tiny crisscrossing puckers, then shirred the rest of the bodice. Her dark fingers ducked in and out of the lemony cloth as she embroidered raised daisies around the hem. Before she considered herself finished she had added a crocheted cuff on the puff sleeves, and a pointy crocheted collar.

I was going to be lovely. A walking model of all the various styles of fine hand sewing and it didn't worry me that I was only twelve years old and merely graduating from the eighth grade. Besides, many teachers in Arkansas Negro schools had only that diploma and were licensed to impart wisdom.

The days had become longer and more noticeable. The faded beige of former times had been replaced with strong and sure colors. I began to see my classmates' clothes, their skin tones, and the dust that waved off pussy willows. Clouds that lazed across the sky were objects of great concern to me. Their shiftier shapes might have held a message that in my new happiness and with a little bit of time I'd soon decipher. During that period I looked at the arch of heaven so religiously my neck kept a steady ache. I had taken to smiling more often, and my jaws hurt from the unaccustomed activity. Between the two physical sore spots, I suppose I could have been uncomfortable, but that was not the case. As a member of the winning team (the graduating class of 1940) I had outdistanced unpleasant sensations by miles. I was headed for the freedom of open fields.

Youth and social approval allied themselves with me and we trammeled memories of slights and insults. The wind of our swift passage remodeled my features. Lost tears were pounded to mud and then to dust. Years of withdrawal were brushed aside and left behind, as hanging ropes of parasitic moss.

My work alone had awarded me a top place and I was going to be one of the first called in the graduating ceremonies. On the classroom blackboard, as well as on the bulletin board in the auditorium, there were blue stars and white stars and red stars. No absences, no tardinesses, and my academic work was among the best of the year. I could say the preamble to the Constitution even faster than Bailey. We timed ourselves often: "WethepeopleoftheUnitedStatesinoordertoformamoreperfectunion . . ." I had memorized the Presidents of the United States from Washington to Roosevelt in chronological as well as alphabetical order.

My hair pleased me too. Gradually the black mass had lengthened and thickened, so that it kept at last to its braided pattern, and I didn't have to yank my scalp off when I tried to comb it.

Louise and I had rehearsed the exercises until we tired out ourselves. Henry Reed was class valedictorian. He was a small, very black boy with hooded eyes, a long, broad nose and an oddly shaped head. I had admired him for years because each term he and I vied for the best grades in our class. Most often he bested me, but instead of being disappointed I was pleased that we shared top places between us. Like many Southern Black children, he lived with his grandmother, who was as strict as Momma and as kind as she knew how to be. He was courteous, respectful and soft-spoken to elders, but on the playground he chose to play the roughest games. I admired him. Anyone, I reckoned, sufficiently afraid or sufficiently dull could be polite. But to be able to operate at a top level with both adults and children was admirable.

His valedictory speech was entitled "To Be or Not to Be." The rigid tenth-grade teacher had helped him write it. He'd been working on the dramatic stresses for months.

The weeks until graduation were filled with heady activities. A group of small children were to be presented in a play about buttercups and daisies and bunny rabbits. They could be heard throughout the building practicing their hops and their little songs that sounded like silver bells. The older girls (nongraduates, of course) were assigned the task of making refreshments for the night's festivities. A tangy scent of ginger, cinnamon, nutmeg and chocolate wafted around the home economics building as the budding cooks made samples for themselves and their teachers.

In every corner of the workshop, axes and saws split fresh timber as the woodshop boys made sets and stage scenery. Only the graduates were left out of the general bustle. We were free to sit in the library at the back of the building or look in quite detachedly, naturally, on the measures being taken for our event.

Even the minister preached on graduation the Sunday before. His subject was, "Let your light so shine that men will see
your good works and praise your Father, Who is in Heaven."
Although the sermon was purported to be addressed to us, he
used the occasion to speak to backsliders, gamblers and general ne'er-do-wells. But since he had called our names at the
beginning of the service we were mollified.

Among Negroes the tradition was to give presents to children going only from one grade to another. How much more
important this was when the person was graduating at the top
of the class. Uncle Willie and Momma had sent away for a
Mickey Mouse watch like Bailey's. Louise gave me four embroidered handkerchiefs. (I gave her three crocheted doilies.)
Mrs. Sneed, the minister's wife, made me an underskirt to
wear for graduation, and nearly every customer gave me a
nickel or maybe even a dime with the instruction "Keep on
moving to higher ground," or some such encouragement.

Amazingly the great day finally dawned and I was out of bed
before I knew it. I threw open the back door to see it more
clearly, but Momma said, "Sister, come away from that door
and put your robe on."

I hoped the memory of that morning would never leave me.
Sunlight was itself still young, and the day had none of the
insistence maturity would bring it in a few hours. In my robe
and barefoot in the backyard, under cover of going to see about
my new beans, I gave myself up to the gentle warmth and
thanked God that no matter what evil I had done in my life He
had allowed me to live to see this day. Somewhere in my fatal-
ism I had expected to die, accidentally, and never have the
chance to walk up the stairs in the auditorium and gracefully
receive my hard-earned diploma. Out of God's merciful bosom
I had won reprieve.

Bailey came out in his robe and gave me a box wrapped in
Christmas paper. He said he had saved his money for months
to pay for it. It felt like a box of chocolates, but I knew Bailey
wouldn't save money to buy candy when we had all we could
want under our noses.

He was as proud of the gift as I. It was a soft-leatherbound
copy of a collection of poems by Edgar Allan Poe, or, as Bailey
and I called him, "Eap." I turned to "Annabel Lee" and we

walked up and down the garden rows, the cool dirt between our toes, reciting the beautifully sad lines.

Momma made a Sunday breakfast although it was only Friday. After we finished the blessing, I opened my eyes to find the watch on my plate. It was a dream of a day. Everything went smoothly and to my credit. I didn't have to be reminded or scolded for anything. Near evening I was too jittery to attend to chores, so Bailey volunteered to do all before his bath.

Days before, we had made a sign for the Store, and as we turned out the lights Momma hung the cardboard over the doorknob. It read clearly: CLOSED. GRADUATION.

My dress fitted perfectly and everyone said that I looked like a sunbeam in it. On the hill, going toward the school, Bailey walked behind with Uncle Willie, who muttered, "Go on, Ju." He wanted him to walk ahead with us because it embarrassed him to have to walk so slowly. Bailey said he'd let the ladies walk together, and the men would bring up the rear. We all laughed, nicely.

Little children dashed by out of the dark like fireflies. Their crepe-paper dresses and butterfly wings were not made for running and we heard more than one rip, dryly, and the regretful "uh uh" that followed.

The school blazed without gaiety. The windows seemed cold and unfriendly from the lower hill. A sense of ill-fated timing crept over me, and if Momma hadn't reached for my hand I would have drifted back to Bailey and Uncle Willie, and possibly beyond. She made a few slow jokes about my feet getting cold, and tugged me along to the now-strange building.

Around the front steps, assurance came back. There were my fellow "greats," the graduating class. Hair brushed back, legs oiled, new dresses and pressed pleats, fresh pocket handkerchiefs and little handbags, all homesewn. Oh, we were up to snuff, all right. I joined my comrades and didn't even see my family go in to find seats in the crowded auditorium.

The school band struck up a march and all classes filed in as had been rehearsed. We stood in front of our seats, as assigned, and on a signal from the choir director, we sat. No sooner had this been accomplished than the band started to play the national anthem. We rose again and sang the song, after which we recited the pledge of allegiance. We remained

standing for a brief minute before the choir director and the
principal signaled to us, rather desperately I thought, to take
our seats. The command was so unusual that our carefully rehearsed and smooth-running machine was thrown off. For a
full minute we fumbled for our chairs and bumped into each
other awkwardly. Habits change or solidify under pressure, so
in our state of nervous tension we had been ready to follow our
usual assembly pattern: the American national anthem, then
the pledge of allegiance, then the song every Black person I
knew called the Negro National Anthem. All done in the same
key, with the same passion and most often standing on the
same foot.

Finding my seat at last, I was overcome with a presentiment
of worse things to come. Something unrehearsed, unplanned,
was going to happen, and we were going to be made to look
bad. I distinctly remember being explicit in the choice of pro-
noun. It was "we," the graduating class, the unit, that concerned me then.

The principal welcomed "parents and friends" and asked the
Baptist minister to lead us in prayer. His invocation was brief
and punchy, and for a second I thought we were getting back
on the high road to right action. When the principal came back
to the dais, however, his voice had changed. Sounds always
affected me profoundly and the principal's voice was one of my
favorites. During assembly it melted and lowed weakly into the
audience. It had not been in my plan to listen to him, but my
curiosity was piqued and I straightened up to give him my
attention.

He was talking about Booker T. Washington, our "late great
leader," who said we can be as close as the fingers on the hand,
etc. . . . Then he said a few vague things about friendship and
the friendship of kindly people to those less fortunate than
themselves. With that his voice nearly faded, thin, away. Like a
river diminishing to a stream and then to a trickle. But he
cleared his throat and said, "Our speaker tonight, who is also
our friend, came from Texarkana to deliver the commence-
ment address, but due to the irregularity of the train schedule,
he's going to, as they say, 'speak and run.' " He said that we
understood and wanted the man to know that we were most
grateful for the time he was able to give us and then something

about how we were willing always to adjust to another's program, and without more ado—"I give you Mr. Edward Donleavy."

Not one but two white men came through the door offstage. The shorter one walked to the speaker's platform, and the tall one moved over to the center seat and sat down. But that was our principal's seat, and already occupied. The dislodged gentleman bounced around for a long breath or two before the Baptist minister gave him his chair, then with more dignity than the situation deserved, the minister walked off the stage.

Donleavy looked at the audience once (on reflection, I'm sure that he wanted only to reassure himself that we were really there), adjusted his glasses and began to read from a sheaf of papers.

He was glad "to be here and to see the work going on just as it was in the other schools."

At the first "Amen" from the audience I willed the offender to immediate death by choking on the word. But Amens and Yes, sir's began to fall around the room like rain through a ragged umbrella.

He told us of the wonderful changes we children in Stamps had in store. The Central School (naturally, the white school was Central) had already been granted improvements that would be in use in the fall. A well-known artist was coming from Little Rock to teach art to them. They were going to have the newest microscopes and chemistry equipment for their laboratory. Mr. Donleavy didn't leave us long in the dark over who made these improvements available to Central High. Nor were we to be ignored in the general betterment scheme he had in mind.

He said that he had pointed out to people at a very high level that one of the first-line football tacklers at Arkansas Agricultural and Mechanical College had graduated from good old Lafayette County Training School. Here fewer Amen's were heard. Those few that did break through lay dully in the air with the heaviness of habit.

He went on to praise us. He went on to say how he had bragged that "one of the best basketball players at Fisk sank his first ball right here at Lafayette County Training School."

The white kids were going to have a chance to become

Galileos and Madame Curies and Edisons and Gauguins, and our boys (the girls weren't even in on it) would try to be Jesse Owenses and Joe Louises.

Owens and the Brown Bomber were great heroes in our world, but what school official in the white-goddom of Little Rock had the right to decide that those two men must be our only heroes? Who decided that for Henry Reed to become a scientist he had to work like George Washington Carver, as a bootblack, to buy a lousy microscope? Bailey was obviously always going to be too small to be an athlete, so which concrete angel glued to what country seat had decided that if my brother wanted to become a lawyer he had to first pay penance for his skin by picking cotton and hoeing corn and studying correspondence books at night for twenty years?

The man's dead words fell like bricks around the auditorium and too many settled in my belly. Constrained by hard-learned manners I couldn't look behind me, but to my left and right the proud graduating class of 1940 had dropped their heads. Every girl in my row had found something new to do with her handkerchief. Some folded the tiny squares into love knots, some into triangles, but most were wadding them, then pressing them flat on their yellow laps.

On the dais, the ancient tragedy was being replayed. Professor Parsons sat, a sculptor's reject, rigid. His large, heavy body seemed devoid of will or willingness, and his eyes said he was no longer with us. The other teachers examined the flag (which was draped stage right) or their notes, or the windows which opened on our now-famous playing diamond.

Graduation, the hush-hush magic time of frills and gifts and congratulations and diplomas, was finished for me before my name was called. The accomplishment was nothing. The meticulous maps, drawn in three colors of ink, learning and spelling decasyllabic words, memorizing the whole of *The Rape of Lucrece*—it was for nothing. Donleavy had exposed us.

We were maids and farmers, handymen and washerwomen, and anything higher that we aspired to was farcical and presumptuous.

Then I wished that Gabriel Prosser and Nat Turner had killed all whitefolks in their beds and that Abraham Lincoln had been assassinated before the signing of the Emancipation

Proclamation, and that Harriet Tubman had been killed by that blow on her head and Christopher Columbus had drowned in the *Santa María.*

It was awful to be Negro and have no control over my life. It was brutal to be young and already trained to sit quietly and listen to charges brought against my color with no chance of defense. We should all be dead. I thought I should like to see us all dead, one on top of the other. A pyramid of flesh with the whitefolks on the bottom, as the broad base, then the Indians with their silly tomahawks and teepees and wigwams and treaties, the Negroes with their mops and recipes and cotton sacks and spirituals sticking out of their mouths. The Dutch children should all stumble in their wooden shoes and break their necks. The French should choke to death on the Louisiana Purchase (1803) while silkworms ate all the Chinese with their stupid pigtails. As a species, we were an abomination. All of us.

Donleavy was running for election, and assured our parents that if he won we could count on having the only colored paved playing field in that part of Arkansas. Also—he never looked up to acknowledge the grunts of acceptance—also, we were bound to get some new equipment for the home economics, building and the workshop.

He finished, and since there was no need to give any more than the most perfunctory thank-you's, he nodded to the men on the stage, and the tall white man who was never introduced joined him at the door. They left with the attitude that now they were off to something really important. (The graduation ceremonies at Lafayette County Training School had been a mere preliminary.)

The ugliness they left was palpable. An uninvited guest who wouldn't leave. The choir was summoned and sang a modern arrangement of "Onward, Christian Soldiers," with new words pertaining to graduates seeking their place in the world. But it didn't work. Elouise, the daughter of the Baptist minister, recited "Invictus," and I could have cried at the impertinence of "I am the master of my fate, I am the captain of my soul."

My name had lost its ring of familiarity and I had to be nudged to go and receive my diploma. All my preparations had fled. I neither marched up to the stage like a conquering Amazon, nor did I look in the audience for Bailey's nod of approval.

Marguerite Johnson, I heard the name again, my honors were read, there were noises in the audience of appreciation, and I took my place on the stage as rehearsed.

I thought about colors I hated: ecru, puce, lavender, beige and black.

There was shuffling and rustling around me, then Henry Reed was giving his valedictory address, "To Be or Not to Be." Hadn't he heard the whitefolks? We couldn't *be,* so the question was a waste of time. Henry's voice came out clear and strong. I feared to look at him. Hadn't he got the message? There was no "nobler in the mind" for Negroes because the world didn't think we had minds, and they let us know it. "Outrageous fortune"? Now, that was a joke. When the ceremony was over I had to tell Henry Reed some things. That is, if I still cared. Not "rub," Henry, "erase." "Ah, there's the erase." Us.

Henry had been a good student in elocution. His voice rose on tides of promise and fell on waves of warnings. The English teacher had helped him to create a sermon winging through Hamlet's soliloquy. To be a man, a doer, a builder, a leader, or to be a tool, an unfunny joke, a crusher of funky toadstools. I marveled that Henry could go through with the speech as if we had a choice.

I had been listening and silently rebutting each sentence with my eyes closed; then there was a hush, which in an audience warns that something unplanned is happening. I looked up and saw Henry Reed, the conservative, the proper, the A student, turn his back to the audience and turn to us (the proud graduating class of 1940) and sing, nearly speaking,

> Lift ev'ry voice and sing
> Till earth and heaven ring
> Ring with the harmonies of Liberty . . .

It was the poem written by James Weldon Johnson. It was the music composed by J. Rosamond Johnson. It was the Negro national anthem. Out of habit we were singing it.

Our mothers and fathers stood in the dark hall and joined

the hymn of encouragement. A kindergarten teacher led the small children onto the stage and the buttercups and daisies and bunny rabbits marked time and tried to follow:

> Stony the road we trod
> Bitter the chastening rod
> Felt in the days when hope, unborn, had died.
> Yet with a steady beat
> Have not our weary feet
> Come to the place for which our fathers sighed?

Every child I knew had learned that song with his ABC's and along with "Jesus Loves Me This I Know." But I personally had never heard it before. Never heard the words, despite the thousands of times I had sung them. Never thought they had anything to do with me.

On the other hand, the words of Patrick Henry had made such an impression on me that I had been able to stretch myself tall and trembling and say, "I know not what course others may take, but as for me, give me liberty or give me death."

And now I heard, really for the first time:

> We have come over a way that with tears
> has been watered,
> We have come, treading our path through
> the blood of the slaughtered.

While echoes of the song shivered in the air, Henry Reed bowed his head, said "Thank you," and returned to his place in the line. The tears that slipped down many faces were not wiped away in shame.

We were on top again. As always, again. We survived. The depths had been icy and dark, but now a bright sun spoke to our souls. I was no longer simply a member of the proud graduating class of 1940; I was a proud member of the wonderful, beautiful Negro race.

Oh, Black known and unknown poets, how often have your auctioned pains sustained us? Who will compute the lonely nights made less lonely by your songs, or by the empty pots made less tragic by your tales?

If we were a people much given to revealing secrets, we might raise monuments and sacrifice to the memories of our poets, but slavery cured us of that weakness. It may be enough, however, to have it said that we survive in exact relationship to the dedication of our poets (include preachers, musicians and blues singers).

James Farmer

(b. 1920)

from *Lay Bare the Heart*
"I'll Keep My Soul"

*James Farmer was born in Marshall, Texas. At the
age of three and a half he experienced the first instance
of racial discrimination—it was a hot summer day; he
wanted a Coke—that he remembers. That child fa-
thered the man who founded the Congress on Racial
Equality (CORE) in 1941 and who organized such civil
disobedience actions as the Freedom Rides and lunch-
counter sit-ins throughout the South. He served as
CORE's director for twenty-five years and became
so closely identified with the civil rights movement
in America that he aptly subtitled* Lay Bare the Heart
as An Autobiography of the Civil Rights Movement.

*In the following selection from that autobiography
Farmer recalls a month he spent inside Hinds County
Prison in Jackson, Mississippi, and a defining moment*

thirty-eight years earlier in the life of a little brown-eyed boy who wanted a Coke.

A caravan of police vans moved swiftly through the night with an escort of state and county police. Arriving at the county prison farm, we filed into the prison on order. Surrounded by guards, armed and ominous, we were herded together while the superintendent spoke to us.

Like an army sergeant spitting out orders, he told us that we were going to be put in our cells and the lights turned out for the night and there wasn't going to be any singing or any other noise. None at all! At six in the morning, we'd get breakfast. Then, one at a time, we'd be processed, and when asked questions we were going to answer "yes, sir" and "no, sir." There wasn't going to be any "yeah" or "naw." If anybody disobeyed this order, the guards standing by would correct his manners immediately. That was all.

As the cell gates slammed shut, I fervently hoped that attorney Jack Young remembered my request that he bail someone out quickly. Surreptitiously, we held a strategy conference, with each person's comments relayed from cell to cell. We readily agreed to forego singing for a day, and to reassess on the morrow. Then we tackled the issue at hand.

"I'd die before I'd say sir to these crackers," declared Six-Two. "I ain't gonna kiss *no* red-neck's ass."

"What's the big deal about saying sir?" asked Little Gandhi. "We say sir and ma'am to our professors and our parents and to a lot of people we don't even know, don't we?"

"Yeah," said someone else, "but these ain't our professors or our parents. These creeps want to see us dead."

"Right, but why you wanna take the bait and give them an excuse to kill us?"

"Man, they ain't going to kill nobody. They're just trying to scare us. If they killed any of us, Bobby Kennedy'd be down here the next day."

"Man, you know Bobby Kennedy ain't go'n bring his skinny ass down here. Or his brother, neither. They'd whip their butts, too."

"How they gonna whip their asses when they got the whole United States Army, Navy, and Marines to back 'em up?"

"They ain't never goin' to use all that to help *us.*"

"They might use it to help themselves, though."

"Well, if they don't come, I bet they'd send somebody. And that'd be the same thing."

Someone asked what I thought. Clearly, this was no time to pontificate; the pros and cons were both compelling, and the best response unclear to me. And broken heads were at stake.

I did not know what to do, but my gut reaction was to comply rather than be savaged over an issue of protocol instead of principle. But was this mere protocol when the method of addressing one another was the very essence of southern caste: the enforcement code of a racist society? Could we yield to this command and at the same time maintain dignity? Or would the next compromise, whatever it was, then come easier? Protocol could force one to bend the knee. Would there be a step-by-step process, eroding dignity and dragging us over the brink into the chasm of bowing and scraping, shuffling and scratching like many of the blacks down there? Who was strong enough or wise enough to draw the line where it could be moved no farther?

The fundamental issue was dignity. With that in mind, I tried, without confidence, to formulate an acceptable compromise.

"Let us keep our dignity at all costs. Why not say yes or no loudly. Then, after a brief pause, even more firmly, say sir. We will have complied with the letter of the command. But not its spirit. The *spirit* is the important thing."

Several riders said "Uh-huh." But Six-Two demurred: "Naw, I don't wanna compromise with no nigger-killin' racist bastards. Let's die like men insteada livin' like dogs."

Silence followed. No one else felt like venturing an opinion.

Clearly, there was no consensus. A unified policy was not available to us. Each was left to the counsel of his conscience and his God. I did ask, though, that each man processed reply loudly enough for us to hear, so we could prepare our response.

We slept fitfully and breakfast came early. Scrambled eggs, thick sliced country bacon, grits with a chunk of butter, hash brown potatoes, bread with a slab of butter, milk and coffee. And strawberry preserves.

"Maybe they're fattenin' us up for the kill," drawled Six-Two.

Two beefy guards lumbered down the corridor, stopped at one cell, and called out the name of one of its occupants. The Rider summoned walked out of the cell and disappeared down the corridor between the two guards.

None of us spoke a word, but all ears strained. We did not hear the question, but the answer came clear. "No," and then a louder "sir." The latter word was spat out with a vengeance. A long pause followed. Then the questioning continued.

After the interrogation, the Freedom Rider walked down the corridor accompanied by the guards, blackjacks in hand. "I did it, man," he whispered as he passed my cell. His meaning eluded the guards.

Next came the Reverend C. T. Vivian. This time, we heard the question: "Do you live in this state?" The answer was in a firm voice. And "sir" did not follow "no."

Almost instantly, came the sound of weapons against flesh. The thud of a slight body falling to the floor. Rapid voices, and the beating stopped. There was panic in the interrogation room. Moments later, male nurses were seen running through the corridor.

When C.T. was led back down the corridor, there were bandages over his right eye and his T-shirt was covered with blood. The huge guards, half carrying him, appeared frightened. There was a smile on C.T.'s face.

Those blackjacks—flat leather thongs stuffed with lead— were designed to beat into unconsciousness without leaving any telltale signs. But C.T.'s assailants had been overeager, striking with the edge of the weapon instead of its flush side. Blood had been shed.

After that, the processing was halted.

An hour later, Jack Young came with $500 bail-bond money for one Rider who had previously indicated a desire for release.

The timing was exquisite! The Freedom Rider bailed out had his press conference and called the FBI.

Two hours after the bail-out, the FBI arrived, and the lions of the county farm became mice, scurrying about. There was a hang-dog look about them as they kowtowed to their superiors.

That night, we were transported back to the Hinds County Jail in Jackson without incident.

Our return to the county jail cell block was like a homecoming. A half-dozen new occupants were there, having arrived during our absence. They had been informed of our transfer to the county farm by the trusties and the upstairs prisoners— those non-Freedom Riders who now sang Freedom Rider songs. The homecoming was celebrated with more singing, joined by the other three Rider groups and, occasionally, by the upstairs inmates.

Some in our group swaggered triumphantly, like conquering heroes. We had met the enemies at the dreaded county farm, and they were *ours*. We had survived it with a minimum of brutalization. We had forced them to retreat. Our tormentors were tormented. We had twisted the tail of the lion and lived to tell the story. Even the upstairs fellows were impressed.

The new Riders had come from all over. One, a tall, skinny kid in his senior year at Howard University, possessed an infectious smile and enormous charm. We instantly felt that we'd known him always. But he seemed so pliant and easygoing, so quiet and so shy, that I told myself he would never make it in this world. His name was Stokely Carmichael.

Our new cellmates brought us current on the outside world. The Freedom Ride, we learned, had captured the nation's imagination more than we'd ever dreamed. Front pages were still full of it. It was the most popular topic of conversation at meetings, cocktail parties, and in the streets. A common greeting among both whites and blacks had become, "Hi. Got your bus ticket?" Buses had become instruments of the struggle.

We also were told that several prominent persons had demonstrated their solidarity by flying into Jackson to have their encounter with Captain Ray. They jailed in, bailed out, and returned to their respective labors. Among them were Percy Sutton, who later became borough president of Manhattan; Mark Lane, then a rising New York politician; and the Reverend Wyatt Tee Walker, executive secretary of the Southern Christian Leadership Conference (SCLC), Dr. King's organization.

That night, once again, we slept little. There were too many fast-moving experiences to recount, too many mental notes to compare.

When breakfast came, we thought of the county farm, maybe a bit wistfully this time. The trusty who brought those tin plates of outrage also brought something else: information that, during the next night, we would be taking another ride. This time to the state penitentiary at Parchman.

We'd all heard of Parchman, of course, the most fabled state prison in the South. But it held no terrors for these victors in the Battle of the County Farm.

The ride, as usual, was a fast one and the drivers of the vans less than gentle. Sudden stops sent us tumbling to the front, and jack-rabbit starts returned us in a heap to the rear.

When we arrived, we were ordered out, under heavy guard, as dozens of red-necks stood by, staring. In a negative kind of way, we were celebrities and they had come to watch, some somber-faced and some grinning. It would be something to tell their children and grandchildren.

We were led into a large basement room and told to take all our clothes off, including shoes and socks. We stripped off our clothes, and with them a measure of dignity. The red-necks outside jostled for position at the barred windows, gawking. We were consumed by embarrassment. We stood for ages—uncomfortable, dehumanized. Our audience cackled with laughter and obscene comments. They had a fixation about genitals, a preoccupation with size.

"Holy Christ," said one, "look a' that lil' nigger there! He got one like a hoss." A touch of envy was in his voice.

"But look a' that one," said another. "He ain't hardly got nuthin'. And that one there—ya cain't hardly see it."

"His ain't no bigger'n Jeff's."

Jeff demurred: "You know ah got more'n that. Ask yo mama!"

The sound of brief scuffling ensued outside the window. And a few shouts. Then more guffaws.

An old stereotype had just been exploded. Could it be that a few sexual fears were also allayed?

Fleetingly, I recalled a conversation with Whitney Young, head of the National Urban League. He'd said, "Jim, I see in the papers that you've been running all over the country demolishing racial myths. Well, there's one myth I don't want you to mess with; leave that one alone." We both had laughed.

Deputy Tyson, who was in charge, obviously enjoyed his role as impresario of this scene. He twanged his orders repetitively in a penetrating voice, amazingly high-pitched for his ample size.

"Awright," he sang out, "y'all all a time wanna march someplace. Well, y'all gon' march right now, right t' yo cells. An' Ah'm gon' lead ya. Follow me. Ah'm Martinlutherking."

Naked, in single file, we trekked through corridors and up a short flight of stairs. That march of the naked Freedom Riders took an eternity; clothes were an invention, I think, to conceal man from his own perception of himself. Their absence stripped off all pretense, and shorn of the make-believe, who can strut and posture?

We were given time to wallow in our nakedness. Eventually, guards brought clothing—a pair of undershorts for each of us. Unerringly, they were the wrong size—little ones for the large men, big ones for the small. All of us, large and small, had to grip cloth at our navels to keep shorts from dropping to the floor.

Little Gandhi shouted, "If your cellmate is a different size, switch shorts." A great idea, but it didn't work; our jailers had planned too well. Small men were bunked with small men. My roommate was two inches taller and four inches broader than I.

"It's indecent," Six-Two exclaimed.

"Makes us feel like animals," moaned someone else.

Bible Student said, "What's this hang-up about clothes? Gandhi wrapped a rag around his balls and brought the whole British Empire to its knees!"

His profundity silenced all grumbling. I had underestimated Bible Student. Ill-fitting shorts were transformed miraculously into a symbol of our mission.

That obsession with clothes eliminated, we examined our cells. About six by seven in size, each had two steel bunks, with thin straw mattresses, a john, and a washbasin. Period.

This was death row, and it had been cleared out for us. We

were allowed no paper (except a roll of toilet paper), no pencils, no books. Neither were there goodies from a store. No cigarettes either, and some of us were chain smokers. The guards took pleasure in sauntering down the corridors, puffing deeply and blowing the smoke painstakingly into our cells.

Nicotine fits! Maybe, faced with necessity, we could quit. We'd all planned to do it before, but now our persecutors were our unwitting allies.

The food was worse than in the Hinds County Jail. I would not try a hunger strike; I was not convinced that was the appropriate tactic at this time. I would just stop eating, except for a taste of this or that. And a sip of the coffee, which was more like dishwater. Maybe I'd lose weight, if I could exercise, too. Without anything else to do in those tiny cells, at least exercise would kill time.

Hank Thomas, a lanky six-foot-four Howard University sophomore with the best voice in the whole place, became our impromptu song leader and director of calisthenics.

The singing went on at Parchman, and the group calisthenics, cell-to-cell, became a daily routine after breakfast. Each day, our numbers increased. We *were* filling up the jails.

Incoming white Freedom Riders were put in our cell block—at the far end, only partially segregated. This fact did not escape our attention. It provoked the anthem "We Shall Overcome," with emphasis on the "black and white together" stanza.

For Mississippi, that was not a surrender of principle. It was simply an acknowledgment that they were fast running out of cell space.

The white male Riders told us that the women were also in the same prison, in this maximum security unit, semisegregated. And their numbers were growing faster than that of the males. Each of them had been given a vaginal search by a female guard using the same rubber-gloved finger, without washing between searches.

We sighed. And ate the putrid meal served through the opening in the bars of each cell. Taste buds rebelled.

The quality of the repast drove Bible Student to prayer: "Let us all bow our heads. Father, forgive us for not offering thanks to Thee for the food we have just received. But we know that

Thou hast allowed us to eat that slop in order to test our faith. Thou hast made us descend into hell that we might better appreciate heaven when we get there. Forgive us if we spew it off our tongues, and give us strength to survive even this punishment dished out by this God-forsaken state. We ask it all in Freedom's name. Amen."

Throaty amens echoed around the cell block.

"It oughta be against the law to give anybody crap like that," moaned Six-Two. "They hadda go out of their way to make food that bad."

"That's right, man," came several responses.

"Whatta you guys expect?" countered Hank Thomas. "This ain't the Waldorf-Astoria."

But Six-Two was irrepressible. "I know it ain't," he said, "but just the same, I think we oughta protest. Let's go on strike. Let's refuse to eat and refuse to talk and refuse to recognize any orders they give us until the food gets better."

"Yeah," shouted several others. "Let's protest prison segregation, too. And the way these people *talk* to us. And let's demand a voice in making some of the decisions in this hellhole."

"Look, men," said Bob Singleton, A Freedom Rider from UCLA. "We didn't come here to improve the food or reform the prison system. We came to fill up the jails. Let's stick to one thing and take whatever this damn state can throw at us." He expressed my views precisely.

Hank Thomas boomed out, "Paul and Silas, bound in jail. Had nobody to go their bail. Keep your eyes on the prize. Hold on." Everyone joined in, including Six-Two.

Deputy Tyson rushed into the cell block, scooting around the corridor rapidly, shouting, "Now you boys goin' hav' to cut out that singin'. We ain't goin' have none of that here!"

That command, of course, was an invitation. The singing became louder. We went through our entire repertoire of Freedom Rider songs with Hank leading, until he called for me to start "Which Side Are You On?"

Tyson and his guards scurried about in confusion. The decision on how to stop our singing clearly had to be made higher up. There would be no repetition of the county farm, summoning the feds. They fairly ran out the door, expelled by the over-

whelming sound enveloping the cell block. Someone would
have to tell them what to do.

We sang until we were tired. Then sleep came easily in our
bare cells, whose only luxury was the thin mattress on each
steel bunk.

The next morning, we had an unannounced visitor who
walked slowly around the U-shaped corridor that wrapped the
rectangular cell block, looking into each cell. He paused in
front of my cell. He was a small-boned man with an enormous
potbelly and the sun-reddened, wrinkled neck of many middle-
aged white southerners. Neatly dressed in a pale blue-gray
seersucker suit, white shirt, and blue tie, he had an air of supreme self-assurance.

"What's your name?" he drawled, without rancor.

As I answered, I grasped in my fist the two ends of the
unbuttoned waistband of my undersized shorts, holding them
tight. He nodded and asked, "Are they treating you all right?"

"Well, there's been no physical brutality, if that's what you
mean," I answered.

Again he nodded and asked, "No complaints?"

"Oh, there are complaints, all right," I said. "The biggest
complaint is that we are *here*. We never should have been arrested for doing what the Supreme Court said we have a right
to do."

Our visitor was too sophisticated, too genteel, too different
from the men who had gawked through the barred windows of
the basement room to be shocked by that statement. His face
remained expressionless as he nodded again and walked
slowly out the door without looking back.

"Jim," shouted one of the white Riders at the far end of the
block. "Do you know who that was?"

I didn't know, so he yelled the answer, loud enough for all to
hear: "Ross Barnett."

We sang a good-bye serenade to the governor: "Ain't Gonna
Let Nobody Turn Me 'Round." Just in case Barnett was still
within earshot, Hank Thomas bellowed out my song, "Which
Side Are You On?" We all thundered the second stanza:

They say in Hinds County,
No neutrals have they met.

You're either for the Freedom Ride
Or you Tom for Ross Barnett.

Deputy Tyson came back in, walking slowly this time and
puffing on a gargantuan cigar. Blowing billows of smoke into
each cell, he spoke with tight-jawed deliberation: "Now y'all
gon' cut out that singin'! I ain't gon' tell y' no mo'. But if y' don'
cut it out, you'll wish you had! Now cut it out *right now!*"

He said it several more times as he walked around the
U-corridor and back again. I wondered if he now had a plan. I
could almost hear him pleading with the governor. "But,
Guv'nor, how we gon' stop their singin' if we cain't go up 'side
their heads?"

We stopped singing. Not because he ordered it, but because
we were hungry and it was chow time. Bad as the food was, it
was better than nothing.

Lunch came, delivered by black trusties, smoking cigarettes.
Six-Two asked a trusty in a loud whisper, "Hey, brother, how
'bout givin' me a cigarette?"

The trusty looked away, embarrassed, and walked to the
next cell. This was Parchman, not Hinds County.

On the way back, the trusty stopped at Six-Two's cell, looked
both ways, then handed him not one cigarette, but two. Six-
Two asked for a light. The trusty lit both.

Six-Two took a long drag on both his prize possessions, then
passed each around the partition to the next cell—one right
and one left.

When the butt reached me at the end of the row, little remained but the filter. I inhaled deeply, filling my lungs. There
was an immediate sensation of giddiness as nicotine-starved
cells soaked it up.

That night, I tossed on my thin-mattressed bunk, brooding
about what the prison response to the singing might be. Solitary confinement? That's the penal system's supreme reprisal.
They won't beat us. The feds from the FBI would be down
here. Yes, of course, it'll be solitary. How can I stand that? A
three-by-three hole with a hole in the floor—and not high
enough to stand up. I'll be screaming to get out. I'll go stark
raving mad. I can't even stand a small room if it's closed in, or a

small airplane where I can't stand up and stretch. I've been claustrophobic since I was seven, since daddy punished me by locking me in a dark closet. I screamed then and I'd scream now. And how will it be when they bring me back to my cell, cowering, tail between my legs. Oh, God, maybe I can bite my tongue and live through it—or die . . .

All thoughts were banished at last by the sweet embrace of sleep.

In the morning after the calisthenics ritual and breakfast, we sang some more, the songs summoning Deputy Tyson and his guards.

"I'm gon' tell you boys jus' one mo' time," he said. "If y' don' stop that singin' we gonna take away your mattresses. I asked ya nice an' ya wouldn' listen. So if there's any mo' singin' yo' mattresses gon' fly away." All the while, he was blowing smoke into each cell.

I thought, "Great. No solitary. At least not yet." But the singing stopped abruptly, and no one spoke for a long time.

Then Little Gandhi faced the malaise. "Look, men, we're all worrying about these thin, hard, stupid mattresses, because that's all we've got in this place. But these mattresses ain't anything but *things*. Things of the body. And we came down here for things of the *spirit*. Things like freedom and equality. And brotherhood. What's happening to us?"

"That's right," said Bible Student. "Satan put us in here for forty days and forty nights. To tempt us with the flesh. He's sayin' to us, 'If you'll just stop your singin' and bail outta there, I'll give you anything you want—soft, thick, cotton mattresses and down pillows and everything. Be good boys and I'll let you keep your mattresses. I'll let you have your lollipop.'"

The booming basso profundo of Hank Thomas thundered forth, "Guards! Guards! Guards!" Each time, the volume grew, and the bars almost rattled.

Tyson came through the door as if catapulted from a slingshot. He must have thought one of us was having a seizure.

"Come get my mattress," roared Hank. *"I'll keep my soul!"*

Instantly, song bounced off the walls and nearly split our own eardrums.

"We Shall Overcome." And this time, it was not slow like a funeral dirge, but quick and upbeat. Never before had I heard it sung with such powerful emphasis. Each beat was John Henry's sledgehammer. The prison walls were thick, so when we drew breath at the end of each line, we could scarcely hear the answering sound from the women's quarters of the maximum security unit.

Guards rushed around like ants, with black trusties obeying their every order, removing mattresses. One Rider lay on his mattress, hugging it, refusing to move. A heavily muscled black prisoner was brought in to remove him and pin him to the floor while the mattress was taken out.

When the mattresses were gone, it was like a heavy load lifted from our shoulders. We didn't have to sing for uplift. Our hearts sang.

After lunch, Deputy Tyson came into the corridor: "If you boys ain't gon' sing no mo', y' can have yo' mattresses back."

"Hey, Deputy Tyson," Little Gandhi called.

Tyson walked toward him and asked, "What you want, boy?"

"Since those mattresses are so valuable," Little Gandhi taunted, "why don't you auction them off and tell people that the Freedom Riders slept there. In that way, you can get back some of the money the Freedom Rides are costing you. And, we'll sing a little song at your auction, too." There was a smile on the small one's face.

"You shut yo' mouth, boy." Tyson walked out, a bit crestfallen.

"Why does he always call us boy?" asked Six-Two. "Next time he comes in here, I'm gonna tell him I'm a *man,* not a boy. And if he don't stop callin' me boy, I'm gonna call him Deputy Boy."

Bob Singleton from UCLA cautioned, "Now, wait a minute, you guys. Tyson doesn't mean anything derogatory by it. That's just the way they talk down here."

Little Gandhi asked, "Do you think so? Well, I'm going to ask him the next time he comes in here."

"Let's ask him now. I know how to get 'im here." It was Hank Thomas and he started singing.

Deputy Tyson took the cue. "This the las' time I'm gon' tell you boys. There ain't gon' be no mo' singin' in here."

"Quiet, you guys," yelled Little Gandhi. "I want to ask Deputy Tyson something."

The singing stopped as Tyson looked toward Little Gandhi's cell.

"Deputy Tyson," asked Little Gandhi in a most serious voice, "do you mean anything derogatory when you call us boy?"

"I don' know nuthin' 'bout no *'rogatory,"* replied Tyson. "All I know is if you boys don' stop that singin', y'all gon' be singin' in the rain."

Hank led off with "Which Side Are You On?" and made up a new stanza as he went along:

> Ole *big* man Deputy Tyson said,
> I *don'* wanna cause you pain,
> But *if* you don't stop that singin'
> > now
> You'll be singin' in the rain!

The words had barely left our throats when a fire hose was dragged in and we were washed down.

"Next time you're gonna do that," sputtered Six-Two, "let us know so we can have the soap ready."

That night, everything in the cells was wet, spirits included. My cellmate and I wrung out our shorts and hung them over the washbasin to dry. Lying on my wet bare bottom on the wet bare lower bunk, I was freezing. Cold in July. In Mississippi. They had opened windows and turned on powerful exhaust fans to draw the chilling draft over our goose-pimpled bodies. By morning, many of us had sniffles and didn't feel like singing much. Maybe the punishment fit the crime!

A few days later, we learned that the state's director of prisons was coming to inspect things at Parchman. When Tyson came by, blowing his smoke, I asked for an appointment with his big boss when he arrived.

"Ah don' know, Mr. Farmer," he said. "Ah'll check it out and let y' know."

The other men and I conferred, cell-to-cell, on an agenda, just in case I got the appointment. I would not raise the question of the food; we had gotten used to that. Furthermore, some of us on the portly side were losing weight; the fare did not tempt us to overindulge. Nor would I complain about our mattresses or the drenching or the exhaust fans. It was singularly important to us that we sing. And, for whatever reasons, it was equally important to the prison authorities that we not. So far, we seemed to be winning that contest of wills; at least we were not losing. In fact, I would not gripe about any prison conditions or regulations, per se. As Singleton had observed a few days ago, our objective was to fill up the jails, not reform them. One thing at a time. Prison reform was a different struggle. Some other day some other troops must fight that war. But this was *our* fight.

All that we'd ask would be the same privileges other prisoners had. One that stuck in our minds was the right to the sun, to the out-of-doors. We were sick of the dank, cold, concrete-and-steel cells. Prison pallor had crept into our faces and we wanted to fill our lungs with fresh air, to feel the sun on our backs. We even wanted to work; we could learn to chop cotton, or pick it, or whatever else other prisoners did. And we needed the exercise.

Tyson unlocked my cell gate and said, "Awright, Mr. Farmer, come on. He'll see ya now."

I walked behind him, waving with one hand to the men in the cells up the row behind me. With the other hand, I held my undersize unbuttoned shorts up, padding barefoot along the concrete floor.

The director of prisons was a stereotype of the cotton-belt plantation owner. His middle-aged face and neck were wrinkled by exposure to the sun. The white Palm Beach suit was wrinkled, too. Small eyes squinted through gold-rimmed spectacles and white hair peeped from under the Panama on his head.

He lounged in a huge, overstuffed chair, legs crossed, flicking ashes from the inevitable cigar into a floor-standing ash-tray.

I stood before him, holding my shorts up and trying to salvage what dignity I could. There was no other chair in the room, but I would not have been invited to sit anyway.

"Yes?" he drawled with rising inflection and, it seemed, without parting his lips.

I told him that we had just one request: to be allowed to go outside and work, along with the other prisoners.

"Naw, you all wouldn't las' two minutes out there. The other nigras'd kill you. If you want to get y'selves killed, it's all right with me. But y' ain't goin' to do it here."

I said that we would gladly take our chances with the other prisoners; that we would like sunlight and the exercise.

"Naw!" he shouted. "We ain't goin' to let y'all go no place." His face reddened perceptibly and lips quivered with hatred. "We didn' tell you all t' come down here, but y' came anyhow. Now, we want y' to stay in there an' *rot!* We've got to feed ya, but we can put so much salt in y' food that y' won't be able t' eat any of it. And that may be just what we're gonna do."

He twisted his body in the chair and looked away. A signal to me that the meeting was over.

I thanked him for his time. He made no reply. Deputy Tyson, waiting outside the door, led me back to my cell where I reported the failure of the mission. The next few meals were so loaded with salt as to be inedible.

We had learned to sleep on steel, to eat slop, to sing when we must, and to make a game of periodic floods. We also learned to count the days till bailout.

My fortieth day was just beyond the coming night. I lay down early to contemplate. Outside, as night began to fall, lightning knifed through heavy clouds and the skies opened up and dumped oceans on Parchman.

While the summer storm raged outside, my heart was at peace. Not one of the men and women who shared the Freedom Ride could ever be the same. Nothing would ever again be routine. No more humdrum. A Promethean spark somehow had been infused into the soul of each of us.

The younger ones had left a little of their youth in the prison cells. They had aged, matured. The older were surely younger now, more enthralled with freedom, imbued with its quest.

Freedom Ride imprisonment was almost over for me. But the state's ordeal would end only when I willed it. (I smiled at my own arrogance.) Nor could Mississippi soon recover its sleepy delta ways. Those who grew up in its closed society must now damn the light that filtered through the splintering door; but their children would be healthier, less myopic.

I myself, when a small child, had bumped my head on the closed door. The collision left a wound that never ceased re-opening. It would have been worse had I not been in a home with abundant bandages of love. And still worse, without the armor of my father's position in our proscribed community, sheltering me from the fiercest barbs from behind that door.

Tomorrow as a mature adult of forty-one I would face for the first time the world outside without dad. How different would it be? How would it be, leaving this place after forty days locked in our own closed society?

If I had been able to look ahead twelve hours, I'd have seen myself standing outside the door of the building, with my rumpled and dirty suit hanging on me like a tent (I had lost twenty-two pounds), awaiting the opening of the van door for the ride to Jack Young's home in Jackson. On the ground beside me would have been a large suitcase and a huge box containing forty copies of the *New York Times* and the two books from Roy Wilkins. If I could have looked ahead, I would have seen a van of white female Freedom Riders, including a pretty teenage redhead, pulling up to begin their Parchman stint. They would have recognized me, waved through the bars, and sung "We Shall Overcome." Two nondescript white men would have been standing by, staring at me murderously, chewing tobacco and spitting its juice precariously close to my feet. But my brain would not let the feet move. One would have said to the other in a voice I could hear, "He mus' be the big shit." The other would have responded, "Yeah. If Ah cud git mah hands on 'im he'd be a dead shit."

But this was tonight, not tomorrow. Tonight without the man who had been a Gibraltar in my life. My mind went back to the earliest days I could remember with dad.

Sleepless dreams. Sleep finally arrives, but dreams do not depart: a small boy holding onto his mother's finger as they trudge along an unpaved red dirt road on a hot midsummer day. The mother shops at the town square and they trudge homeward, the child still clinging to her finger. She removes a clean handkerchief from her purse and pats her son's face and then her own. The boy looks up at his mother and says, "Mommy, I want to get a Coke."

"You can't get a Coke here, Junior," the mother replies. "Wait till we get home. There's lots of Coke in the icebox."

"But, mommy," says the boy, "I don't want to wait. I want my Coke now. I have a nickel; daddy gave it to me yesterday."

"Junior, I told you you can't get a Coke now. There's lots of Coke in the icebox at home."

"Why can't I get a Coke now, when I have a nickel?"

"You just can't."

The child sees another boy enter a drugstore across the street. "Look, mommy," exclaims Junior, "I bet that boy's going to get a Coke. Come on, let's go see."

He pulls his mother by the finger across the street, and they look through the screen doors, closed to keep out the flies. Sure enough, the other kid is perched on a stool at the counter sipping a soft drink through a straw.

"See that, mommy," said the small boy. "We *can* get a Coke here. He got one. Let's go get ours."

"Son, I told you to wait till we get home. We *can't* get a Coke in there."

"Then why could he?"

"He's white."

"He's white? And me?" inquires the boy.

"You're colored."

I came awake; I knew the rest of the dream. In fact, I knew it all; it had recurred so many times through the years, and each time my chest filled up. Several years ago, I'd mentioned it to my mother and she remembered the incident just as clearly. The dream had been a reality.

We had walked home silently that day under the oppressive sun. I no longer held her finger; my hands were at my sides, and we kicked up red dust as we trudged along. She had thrown herself across the bed and wept. I didn't want the Coke anymore and had sat on the front porch steps with dry eyes, a little brown boy alone with his three-and-a-half-year-old thoughts. Thoughts of the present and of the future. I don't recall the thoughts, only the thinking.

My father had come out and sat beside me in silence.

Would the man have been in a cell in Parchman in 1961, if the child had not been denied his soft drink in Holly Springs thirty-eight years before?

James Baldwin

(1924–1987)

---

from *Notes of a Native Son*
Autobiographical Notes

James Baldwin stands among America's foremost writers. He was born in New York City. After 1941, on and off for more than fifteen years, he lived in Europe. In 1987 he died in Paris. Wherever he had traveled, slept, ate, laughed, observed, studied, celebrated, argued, or explored in those five decades, Baldwin had also done what he'd had to do. He had worked; he had written award-winning novels like Another Country *and essays like* The Fire Next Time *in his own distinctive, eloquent American voice.*

Baldwin defined himself by his work. In his work he realized his personal dream to be a writer, and as a black writer he continually rediscovered and redefined his experience as an African American. "Autobiographical Notes" provides a glimpse into the birth of Baldwin's personal dream and the emergence of his black consciousness.

I was born in Harlem thirty-one years ago. I began plotting novels at about the time I learned to read. The story of my childhood is the usual bleak fantasy, and we can dismiss it with the restrained observation that I certainly would not consider living it again. In those days my mother was given to the exasperating and mysterious habit of having babies. As they were born, I took them over with one hand and held a book with the other. The children probably suffered, though they have since been kind enough to deny it, and in this way I read *Uncle Tom's Cabin* and *A Tale of Two Cities* over and over and over again; in this way, in fact, I read just about everything I could get my hands on—except the Bible, probably because it was the only book I was encouraged to read. I must also confess that I wrote —a great deal—and my first professional triumph, in any case, the first effort of mine to be seen in print, occurred at the age of twelve or thereabouts, when a short story I had written about the Spanish revolution won some sort of prize in an extremely short-lived church newspaper. I remember the story was censored by the lady editor, though I don't remember why, and I was outraged.

Also wrote plays, and songs, for one of which I received a letter of congratulations from Mayor La Guardia, and poetry, about which the less said, the better. My mother was delighted by all these goings-on, but my father wasn't; he wanted me to be a preacher. When I was fourteen I became a preacher, and when I was seventeen I stopped. Very shortly thereafter I left home. For God knows how long I struggled with the world of commerce and industry—I guess they would say they struggled with *me*—and when I was about twenty-one I had enough done of a novel to get a Saxton Fellowship. When I was twenty-two the fellowship was over, the novel turned out to be unsalable, and I started waiting on tables in a Village restaurant and writing book reviews—mostly, as it turned out, about the Negro problem, concerning which the color of my skin made me automatically an expert. Did another book, in company with photographer Theodore Pelatowski, about the store-front churches in Harlem. This book met exactly the same fate as my first—fellowship, but no sale. (It was a Rosenwald Fellowship.) By the time I was twenty-four I had decided to stop reviewing books about the Negro problem—which, by this time, was only slightly less horrible in print than it was in life— and I packed my bags and went to France, where I finished, God knows how, *Go Tell It on the Mountain.*

Any writer, I suppose, feels that the world into which he was born is nothing less than a conspiracy against the cultivation of his talent—which attitude certainly has a great deal to support it. On the other hand, it is only because the world looks on his talent with such a frightening indifference that the artist is compelled to make his talent important. So that any writer, looking back over even so short a span of time as I am here forced to assess, finds that the things which hurt him and the things which helped him cannot be divorced from each other; he could be helped in a certain way only because he was hurt in a certain way; and his help is simply to be enabled to move from one conundrum to the next—one is tempted to say that he moves from one disaster to the next. When one begins looking for influences one finds them by the score. I haven't thought much about my own, not enough anyway; I hazard that the King James Bible, the rhetoric of the store-front church, something ironic and violent and perpetually understated in Negro speech—and something of Dickens' love for bravura— have something to do with me today; but I wouldn't stake my life on it. Likewise, innumerable people have helped me in many ways; but finally, I suppose, the most difficult (and most rewarding) thing in my life has been the fact that I was born a Negro and was forced, therefore, to effect some kind of truce with this reality. (Truce, by the way, is the best one can hope for.)

One of the difficulties about being a Negro writer (and this is not special pleading, since I don't mean to suggest that he has it worse than anybody else) is that the Negro problem is written about so widely. The bookshelves groan under the weight of information, and everyone therefore considers himself informed. And this information, furthermore, operates usually

(generally, popularly) to reinforce traditional attitudes. Of traditional attitudes there are only two—For or Against—and I, personally, find it difficult to say which attitude has caused me the
most pain. I am speaking as a writer; from a social point of view
I am perfectly aware that the change from ill-will to good-will,
however motivated, however imperfect, however expressed, is
better than no change at all.

But it is part of the business of the writer—as I see it —to
examine attitudes, to go beneath the surface, to tap the source.
From this point of view the Negro problem is nearly inaccessi-
ble. It is not only written about so widely; it is written about so
badly. It is quite possible to say that the price a Negro pays for
becoming articulate is to find himself, at length, with nothing
to be articulate about. ("You taught me language," says Caliban
to Prospero, "and my profit on't is I know how to curse.")
Consider: the tremendous social activity that this problem gen-
erates imposes on whites and Negroes alike the necessity of
looking forward, of working to bring about a better day. This is
fine, it keeps the waters troubled; it is all, indeed, that has
made possible the Negro's progress. Nevertheless, social affairs are not generally speaking the writer's prime concern,
whether they ought to be or not; it is absolutely necessary that
he establish between himself and these affairs a distance which
will allow, at least, for clarity, so that before he can look forward in any meaningful sense, he must first be allowed to take
a long look back. In the context of the Negro problem neither
whites nor blacks, for excellent reasons of their own, have the
faintest desire to look back; but I think that the past is all that
makes the present coherent, and further, that the past will
remain horrible for exactly as long as we refuse to assess it
honestly.

I know, in any case, that the most crucial time in my own
development came when I was forced to recognize that I was a
kind of bastard of the West; when I followed the line of my past
I did not find myself in Europe but in Africa. And this meant
that in some subtle way, in a really profound way, I brought to
Shakespeare, Bach, Rembrandt, to the stones of Paris, to the
cathedral at Chartres, and to the Empire State Building, a special attitude. These were not really my creations, they did not
contain my history; I might search in them in vain forever for

any reflection of myself. I was an interloper; this was not my heritage. At the same time I had no other heritage which I could possibly hope to use—I had certainly been unfitted for the jungle or the tribe. I would have to appropriate these white centuries, I would have to make them mine—I would have to accept my special attitude, my special place in this scheme— otherwise I would have no place in *any* scheme. What was the most difficult was the fact that I was forced to admit something I had always hidden from myself, which the American Negro has had to hide from himself as the price of his public progress; that I hated and feared white people. This did not mean that I loved black people; on the contrary, I despised them, possibly because they failed to produce Rembrandt. In effect, I hated and feared the world. And this meant, not only that I thus gave the world an altogether murderous power over me, but also that in such a self-destroying limbo I could never hope to write.

One writes out of one thing only—one's own experience. Everything depends on how relentlessly one forces from this experience the last drop, sweet or bitter, it can possibly give. This is the only real concern of the artist, to recreate out of the disorder of life that order which is art. The difficulty then, for me, of being a Negro writer was the fact that I was, in effect, prohibited from examining my own experience too closely by the tremendous demands and the very real dangers of my social situation.

I don't think the dilemma outlined above is uncommon. I do think, since writers work in the disastrously explicit medium of language, that it goes a little way towards explaining why, out of the enormous resources of Negro speech and life, and despite the example of Negro music; prose written by Negroes has been generally speaking so pallid and so harsh. I have not written about being a Negro at such length because I expect that to be my only subject, but only because it was the gate I had to unlock before I could hope to write about anything else. I don't think that the Negro problem in America can be even discussed coherently without bearing in mind its context; its context being the history, traditions, customs, the moral assumptions and preoccupations of the country; in short, the general social fabric. Appearances to the contrary, no one in

America escapes its effects and everyone in America bears some responsibility for it. I believe this the more firmly because it is the overwhelming tendency to speak of this problem as though it were a thing apart. But in the work of Faulkner, in the general attitude and certain specific passages in Robert Penn Warren, and, most significantly, in the advent of Ralph Ellison, one sees the beginnings—at least—of a more genuinely penetrating search. Mr. Ellison, by the way, is the first Negro novelist I have ever read to utilize in language, and brilliantly, some of the ambiguity and irony of Negro life.

About my interests: I don't know if I have any, unless the morbid desire to own a sixteen-millimeter camera and make experimental movies can be so classified. Otherwise, I love to eat and drink—it's my melancholy conviction that I've scarcely ever had enough to eat (this is because it's *impossible* to eat enough if you're worried about the next meal)—and I love to argue with people who do not disagree with me too profoundly, and I love to laugh. I do *not* like bohemia, or bohemians, I do not like people whose principal aim is pleasure, and I do not like people who are *earnest* about anything. I don't like people who like me because I'm a Negro; neither do I like people who find in the same accident grounds for contempt. I love America more than any other country in the world, and, exactly for this reason, I insist on the right to criticize her perpetually. I think all theories are suspect, that the finest principles may have to be modified, or may even be pulverized by the demands of life, and that one must find, therefore, one's own moral center and move through the world hoping that this center will guide one aright. I consider that I have many responsibilities, but none greater than this: to last, as Hemingway says, and get my work done.

I want to be an honest man and a good writer.

bell hooks

---

from *Talking Back*

A graduate of the University of California at Santa Cruz and more recently a professor at Oberlin College, bell hooks began truly to find her personal voice and publicly to define herself when she started openly defying authority by "talking back." Nor has bell hooks stopped talking back. Continually asserting herself as an independent questioning, thinking person, as an individual woman with needs, opinions, desires, and dreams, she has become one of America's foremost black feminist theorists and activists.

In the excerpt that follows hooks recalls how she found, and liberated, her personal voice as she calls upon all women of color to make themselves heard not merely by speaking up but also by talking back.

In the world of the southern black community I grew up in, "back talk" and "talking back" meant speaking as an equal to an authority figure. It meant daring to disagree and sometimes it just meant having an opinion. In the "old school," children were meant to be seen and not heard. My great-grandparents, grandparents, and parents were all from the old school. To make yourself heard if you were a child was to invite punishment, the back-hand lick, the slap across the face that would catch you unaware, or the feel of switches stinging your arms and legs.

To speak then when one was not spoken to was a courageous act—an act of risk and daring. And yet it was hard not to speak in warm rooms where heated discussions began at the crack of dawn, women's voices filling the air, giving orders, making threats, fussing. Black men may have excelled in the art of poetic preaching in the male-dominated church, but in the church of the home, where the everyday rules of how to live and how to act were established, it was black women who preached. There, black women spoke in a language so rich, so poetic, that it felt to me like being shut off from life, smothered to death if one were not allowed to participate.

It was in that world of woman talk (the men were often silent, often absent) that was born in me the craving to speak, to have a voice, and not just any voice but one that could be identified as belonging to me. To make my voice, I had to speak, to hear myself talk—and talk I did—darting in and out of grown folks' conversations and dialogues, answering questions that were not directed at me, endlessly asking questions, making speeches. Needless to say, the punishments for these acts of speech seemed endless. They were intended to silence me—the child—and more particularly the girl child. Had I been a boy, they might have encouraged me to speak believing that I might someday be called to preach. There was no "calling" for talking girls, no legitimized rewarded speech. The punishments I received for "talking back" were intended to suppress all possibility that I would create my own speech. That speech was to be suppressed so that the "right speech of womanhood" would emerge.

Within feminist circles, silence is often seen as the sexist "right speech of womanhood"—the sign of woman's submission to patriarchal authority. This emphasis on woman's silence may be an accurate remembering of what has taken place in the households of women from WASP backgrounds in the United States, but in black communities (and diverse ethnic communities), women have not been silent. Their voices can be heard. Certainly for black women, our struggle has not been to emerge from silence into speech but to change the nature and direction of our speech, to make a speech that compels listeners, one that is heard.

Our speech, "the right speech of womanhood," was often the soliloquy, the talking into thin air, the talking to ears that do not hear you—the talk that is simply not listened to. Unlike the black male preacher whose speech was to be heard, who was to be listened to, whose words were to be remembered, the voices of black women—giving orders, making threats, fussing —could be tuned out, could become a kind of background music, audible but not acknowledged as significant speech. Dialogue—the sharing of speech and recognition—took place not between mother and child or mother and male authority figure but among black women. I can remember watching fascinated as our mother talked with her mother, sisters, and women friends. The intimacy and intensity of their speech—the satisfaction they received from talking to one another, the pleasure, the joy. It was in this world of woman speech, loud talk, angry words, women with tongues quick and sharp, tender sweet tongues, touching our world with their words, that I made speech my birthright—and the right to voice, to authorship, a privilege I would not be denied. It was in that world and because of it that I came to dream of writing, to write.

Writing was a way to capture speech, to hold onto it, keep it close. And so I wrote down bits and pieces of conversations, confessing in cheap diaries that soon fell apart from too much handling, expressing the intensity of my sorrow, the anguish of speech—for I was always saying the wrong thing, asking the

wrong questions. I could not confine my speech to the necessary corners and concerns of life. I hid these writings under
my bed, in pillow stuffings, among faded underwear. When my
sisters found and read them, they ridiculed and mocked me—
poking fun. I felt violated, ashamed, as if the secret parts of my
self had been exposed, brought into the open, and hung like
newly clean laundry, out in the air for everyone to see. The
fear of exposure, the fear that one's deepest emotions and in-
nermost thoughts will be dismissed as mere nonsense, felt by
so many young girls keeping diaries, holding and hiding
speech, seems to me now one of the barriers that women have
always needed and still need to destroy so that we are no
longer pushed into secrecy or silence.

Despite my feelings of violation, of exposure, I continued to
speak and write, choosing my hiding places well, learning to
destroy work when no safe place could be found. I was never
taught absolute silence, I was taught that it was important to
speak but to talk a talk that was in itself a silence. Taught to
speak and yet beware of the betrayal of too much heard
speech, I experienced intense confusion and deep anxiety in
my efforts to speak and write. Reciting poems at Sunday afternoon church service might be rewarded. Writing a poem
(when one's time could be "better" spent sweeping, ironing,
learning to cook) was luxurious activity, indulged in at the expense of others. Questioning authority, raising issues that were
not deemed appropriate subjects brought pain, punishments—
like telling mama I wanted to die before her because I could
not live without her—that was crazy talk, crazy speech, the
kind that would lead you to end up in a mental institution.
"Little girl," I would be told, "if you don't stop all this crazy talk
and crazy acting you are going to end up right out there at
Western State."

Madness, not just physical abuse, was the punishment for
too much talk if you were female. Yet even as this fear of madness haunted me, hanging over my writing like a monstrous
shadow, I could not stop the words, making thought, writing
speech. For this terrible madness which I feared, which I was
sure was the destiny of daring women born to intense speech
(after all, the authorities emphasized this point daily), was not
as threatening as imposed silence, as suppressed speech.

Safety and sanity were to be sacrificed if I was to experience defiant speech. Though I risked them both, deep-seated fears and anxieties characterized my childhood days. I would speak but I would not ride a bike, play hardball, or hold the gray kitten. Writing about the ways we are traumatized in our growing-up years, psychoanalyst Alice Miller makes the point in *For Your Own Good* that it is not clear why childhood wounds become for some folk an opportunity to grow, to move forward rather than backward in the process of self-realization. Certainly, when I reflect on the trials of my growing-up years, the many punishments, I can see now that in resistance I learned to be vigilant in the nourishment of my spirit, to be tough, to courageously protect that spirit from forces that would break it.

While punishing me, my parents often spoke about the necessity of breaking my spirit. Now when I ponder the silences, the voices that are not heard, the voices of those wounded and/or oppressed individuals who do not speak or write, I contemplate the acts of persecution, torture—the terrorism that breaks spirits, that makes creativity impossible. I write these words to bear witness to the primacy of resistance struggle in any situation of domination (even within family life); to the strength and power that emerges from sustained resistance and the profound conviction that these forces can be healing, can protect us from dehumanization and despair.

These early trials, wherein I learned to stand my ground, to keep my spirit intact, came vividly to mind after I published *Ain't I A Woman* and the book was sharply and harshly criticized. While I had expected a climate of critical dialogue, I was not expecting a critical avalanche that had the power in its intensity to crush the spirit, to push one into silence. Since that time, I have heard stories about black women, about women of color, who write and publish (even when the work is quite successful) having nervous breakdowns, being made mad because they cannot bear the harsh responses of family, friends, and unknown critics, or becoming silent, unproductive. Surely, the absence of a humane critical response has tremendous impact on the writer from any oppressed, colonized group who endeavors to speak. For us, true speaking is not solely an expression of creative power; it is an act of resistance, a political gesture that challenges politics of domination that would render us nameless and voiceless. As such, it is a courageous act—as such, it represents a threat. To those who wield oppressive power, that which is threatening must necessarily be wiped out, annihilated, silenced.

Recently, efforts by black women writers to call attention to our work serve to highlight both our presence and absence. Whenever I peruse women's bookstores, I am struck not by the rapidly growing body of feminist writing by black women, but by the paucity of available published material. Those of us who write and are published remain few in number. The context of silence is varied and multi-dimensional. Most obvious are the ways racism, sexism, and class exploitation act to suppress and silence. Less obvious are the inner struggles, the efforts made to gain the necessary confidence to write, to re-write, to fully develop craft and skill—and the extent to which such efforts fail.

Although I have wanted writing to be my life-work since childhood, it has been difficult for me to claim "writer" as part of that which identifies and shapes my everyday reality. Even after publishing books, I would often speak of wanting to be a writer as though these works did not exist. And though I would be told, "you are a writer," I was not yet ready to fully affirm this truth. Part of myself was still held captive by domineering forces of history, of familial life that had charted a map of silence, of right speech. I had not completely let go of the fear of saying the wrong thing, of being punished. Somewhere in the deep recesses of my mind, I believed I could avoid both responsibility and punishment if I did not declare myself a writer.

One of the many reasons I chose to write using the pseudonym bell hooks, a family name (mother to Sarah Oldham, grandmother to Rosa Bell Oldham, great-grandmother to me), was to construct a writer-identity that would challenge and subdue all impulses leading me away from speech into silence. I was a young girl buying bubble gum at the corner store when I first really heard the full name bell hooks. I had just "talked back" to a grown person. Even now I can recall the surprised look, the mocking tones that informed me I must be kin to bell hooks—a sharp-tongued woman, a woman who spoke her mind, a woman who was not afraid to talk back. I claimed this legacy of defiance, of will, of courage, affirming my link to female ancestors who were bold and daring in their speech. Unlike my bold and daring mother and grandmother, who were not supportive of talking back, even though they were assertive and powerful in their speech, bell hooks as I discovered, claimed, and invented her was my ally, my support.

That initial act of talking back outside the home was empowering. It was the first of many acts of defiant speech that would make it possible for me to emerge as an independent thinker and writer. In retrospect, "talking back" became for me a rite of initiation, testing my courage, strengthening my commitment, preparing me for the days ahead—the days when writing, rejection notices, periods of silence, publication, ongoing development seem impossible but necessary.

Moving from silence into speech is for the oppressed, the colonized, the exploited, and those who stand and struggle side by side a gesture of defiance that heals, that makes new life and new growth possible. It is that act of speech, of "talking back," that is no mere gesture of empty words, that is the expression of our movement from object to subject—the liberated voice.

II

The World Remade

Vision is dynamic. . . .
It alters what it reflects:
an individual's history, a particular time and place,
an ideology, cultural identity,
the collective experience of a people. . . .
It redefines and reshapes the larger world.

Langston Hughes

(1902–1967)

Question and Answer

Many have asked the questions Langston Hughes asks in the poem that follows. Some few—among them the writers included in the second part of this book— have dared to act upon the answer.

"Question and Answer" first appeared in the volume of poetry that Hughes titled The Panther and the Lash.

Durban, Birmingham,
Cape Town, Atlanta,
Johannesburg, Watts,
The earth around
Struggling, fighting,
Dying—for what?

A world to gain.

Groping, hoping,
Waiting—for what?

A world to gain.

Dreams kicked asunder,
Why not go under?

There's a world to gain.

But suppose I don't want it,
Why take it?

To remake it.

David Walker

(1785–1830)

---

from *An Appeal to the Coloured
Citizens of the World*
Our Wretchedness in Consequence
of the Preachers of the Religion
of Jesus Christ

*The son of a free mother and slave father, David
Walker left his native North Carolina for Boston,
where he operated a secondhand clothing store and set
up a shelter for the homeless. In 1829 Walker published* An Appeal to the Coloured Citizens of the
World, *an incendiary abolitionist tract that created a
furor in the South. A bounty was placed on Walker's
head, and in 1830, shortly after the third edition of the*
Appeal *had appeared, Walker was found dead in the
doorway of his old clothes store.*

In this excerpt from Article III of the Appeal *Walker
gives voice to his vision of freedom as he calls for "one
continual cry . . . to overthrow the system of slavery,
in every part of this country."*

Religion, my brethren, is a substance of deep consideration among all nations of the earth. The Pagans have a kind, as well as the Mahometans, the Jews and the Christians. But pure and undefiled religion, such as was preached by Jesus Christ and his apostles, is hard to be found in all the earth. God, through his instrument, Moses, handed a dispensation of his Divine will, to the children of Israel after they had left Egypt for the land of Canaan or of Promise, who through hypocrisy, oppression and unbelief, departed from the faith.—He then, by his apostles, handed a dispensation of his, together with the will of Jesus Christ, to the Europeans in Europe, who, in open violation of which, have made *merchandise* of us, and it does appear as though they take this very dispensation to aid them in their *infernal* depredations upon us. Indeed, the way in which religion was and is conducted by the Europeans and their descendants, one might believe it was a plan fabricated by themselves and the *devils* to oppress us. But hark! My master has taught me better than to believe it—he has taught me that his gospel as it was preached by himself and his apostles remains the same, notwithstanding Europe has tried to mingle blood and oppression with it.

It is well known to the Christian world, that Bartholomew Las Casas, that very very notoriously avaricious Catholic priest or preacher, and adventurer with Columbus in his second voyage, proposed to his countrymen, the Spaniards in Hispaniola to import the Africans from the Portuguese settlement in Africa, to dig up gold and silver, and work their plantations for them, to effect which, he made a voyage thence to Spain, and opened the subject to his master, Ferdinand then in declining health, who listened to the plan: but who died soon after, and left it in the hand of his successor, Charles V.* This wretch,

* See Butler's History of the United States, vol. 1, page 24.—See also, page 25. [The citation is to Frederick Butler, *A Complete History of the United States of America, Embracing the Whole Period from the Discovery of North America, down to the Year 1820.* 3 vols., Hartford, 1821. Ed.]

("Las Casas, the Preacher,") succeeded so well in his plans of oppression, that in 1503, the first blacks had been imported into the new world. Elated with this success, and stimulated by sordid avarice only, he importuned Charles V. in 1511, to grant permission to a Flemish merchant, to import 4000 blacks at one time.* Thus we see, through the instrumentality of a pretended preacher of the gospel of Jesus Christ our common master, our wretchedness first commenced in America—where it has been continued from 1503, to this day, 1829. A period of three hundred and twenty-six years. But two hundred and nine, from 1620 [1619]—when twenty of our fathers were brought into Jamestown, Virginia, by a Dutch man of war, and sold off like brutes to the highest bidders; and there is not a doubt in my mind, but that tyrants are in hope to perpetuate our miseries under them and their children until the final consumation of all things. —But if they do not get dreadfully deceived, it will be because God has forgotten them.

The Pagans, Jews and Mahometans try to make proselytes to their religions, and whatever human beings adopt their religions they extend to them their protection. But Christian Americans, not only hinder their fellow creatures, the Africans, but thousands of them *will absolutely beat a coloured person nearly to death, if they catch him on his knees, supplicating the throne of grace.* This barbarous cruelty was by all the heathen nations of antiquity, and is by the Pagans, Jews and Mahometans of the present day, left entirely to Christian Americans to inflict on the Africans and their descendants, that their cup which is nearly full may be completed. I have known tyrants or usurpers of human liberty in different parts of this country to take their fellow creatures, the coloured people, and

* It is not unworthy of remark, that the Portuguese and Spaniards, were among, if not the very first Nations upon Earth, about three hundred and fifty or sixty years ago—But see what those *Christians* have come to now in consequence of afflicting our fathers and us, who have never molested, or disturbed them or any other of the white *Christians,* but have they received one quarter of what the Lord will yet bring upon them, for the murders they have inflicted upon us? —They have had, and in some degree have now, sweet times on our blood and groans, the time however, of bitterness have sometime since commenced with them.—There is a God the Maker and preserver of all things, who will as sure as the world exists, give all his creatures their just recompense of reward in this and in the world to come,—we may fool or deceive, and keep each other in the most profound ignorance, beat murder and keep each other out of what is our lawful rights, or the rights of man, yet it is impossible for us to deceive or escape the Lord Almighty.

beat them until they would scarcely leave life in them; what for? Why they say "The black devils had the audacity to be found *making prayers and supplications to the God who made them! ! ! !*" Yes, I have known small collections of coloured people to have convened together, for no other purpose than to worship God Almighty, in spirit and in truth, to the best of their knowledge; when tyrants, calling themselves *patrols,* would also convene and wait almost in breathless silence for the poor coloured people to commence singing and praying to the Lord our God, as soon as they had commenced, the wretches would burst in upon them and drag them out and commence beating them as they would rattle-snakes—many of whom, they would beat so unmercifully, that they would hardly be able to crawl for weeks and sometimes for months. Yet the American ministers send out missionaries to convert the heathen, while they keep us and our children sunk at their feet in the most abject ignorance and wretchedness that ever a people was afflicted with since the world began. Will the Lord suffer this people to proceed much longer? Will he not stop them in their career? Does he regard the heathens abroad, more than the heathens among the Americans? Surely the Americans must believe that God is partial, notwithstanding his Apostle Peter, declared before Cornelius and others that he has no respect to persons, but in every nation he that feareth God and worketh righteousness is accepted with him.—"The word," said he, "which God sent unto the children of Israel, preaching peace, by Jesus Christ, (he is Lord of all."*) Have not the Americans the Bible in their hands? Do they believe it? Surely they do not. See how they treat us in open violation of the Bible! ! They no doubt will be greatly offended with me, but if God does not awaken them, it will be, because they are superior to other men, as they have represented themselves to be. Our divine Lord and Master said, "all things whatsoever ye would that men should do unto you, do ye even so unto them." But an American minister, with the Bible in his hand, holds us and our children in the most abject slavery and wretchedness. Now I ask them, would they like for us to hold them and their children in abject slavery and wretchedness? No, says one, that never can be done—you are

* See Acts of the Apostles, chap. x. v.–25–27. [The citation should be to Acts 10:36. Ed.]

too abject and ignorant to do it—you are not men—you were made to be slaves to us, to dig up gold and silver for us and our children. Know this, my dear sirs, that although you treat us and our children now, as you do your domestic beast—yet the final result of all future events are known but to God Almighty alone, who rules in the armies of heaven and among the inhabitants of the earth, and who dethrones one earthly king and sits up another, as it seemeth good in his holy sight. We may attribute these vicissitudes to what we please, but the God of armies and of justice rules in heaven and in earth, and the whole American people shall see and know it yet, to their satisfaction. I have known pretended preachers of the gospel of my Master, who not only held us as their natural inheritance, but treated us with as much rigor as any Infidel or Deist in the world—just as though they were intent only on taking our blood and groans to glorify the Lord Jesus Christ. The wicked and ungodly, seeing their preachers treat us with so much cruelty, they say: our preachers, who must be right, if any body are, treat them like brutes, and why cannot we?—They think it is no harm to keep them in slavery and put the whip to them, and why cannot we do the same! —They being preachers of the gospel of Jesus Christ, if it were any harm, they would surely preach against their oppression and do their utmost to erase it from the country; not only in one or two cities, but one continual cry would be raised in all parts of this confederacy, and would cease only with the complete overthrow of the system of slavery, in every part of the country.

Jane Johnson

(b. 1830?)

The Rescue of Jane Johnson

In July 1855, at Bloodgood's Hotel in Philadelphia, Jane Johnson, a slave woman en route to New York with her master, Colonel John H. Wheeler of North Carolina, enlisted the aid of hotel porters to help her win freedom for herself and her two young daughters. The porters contacted the Vigilance Committee, which in turn mobilized one of its white members to intercept Johnson and her children the following day at the Philadelphia harbor. After informing Johnson that the laws of Pennsylvania granted all slaves their freedom, the white abolitionist led her and her two daughters away from the harbor—to the protestations of the outraged Colonel Wheeler. Unusually for that time, Jane Johnson testified on her own behalf in court and legally won her freedom. That testimony, which follows, evidences how the politically activist Vigilance Committee and the legal process enabled Jane Johnson to make of her personal dream a reality.

AFFIDAVIT AND TESTIMONY OF JANE JOHNSON STATE OF NEW YORK, CITY AND COUNTY OF NEW YORK.

Jane Johnson being sworn, makes oath and says—

My name is Jane—Jane Johnson: I was the slave of Mr. Wheeler of Washington; he bought me and my two children, about two years ago, from Mr. Cornelius Crew, of Richmond, Va.; my youngest child is between six and seven years old, the other between ten and eleven; I have one other child only, and he is in Richmond; I have not seen him for about two years; never expect to see him again; Mr. Wheeler brought me and my two children to Philadelphia, on the way to Nicaragua, to wait on his wife; I didn't want to go without my two children, and he consented to take them; we came to Philadelphia by the cars; stopped at Mr. Sully's, Mr. Wheeler's father-in-law, a few moments; then went to the steamboat for New York at 2 o'clock, but were too late; we went into Bloodgood's Hotel; Mr. Wheeler went to dinner; Mr. Wheeler had told me in Washington to have nothing to say to colored persons, and if any of them spoke to me, to say I was a free woman traveling with a minister; we staid at Bloodgood's till 5 o'clock; Mr. Wheeler kept his eye on me all the time except when he was at dinner; he left his dinner to come and see if I was safe, and then went back again; while he was at dinner, I saw a colored woman and told her I was a slave woman, that my master had told me not to speak to colored people, and that if any of them spoke to me to say that I was free; but I am not free; but I want to be free; she said: 'poor thing, I pity you;' after that I saw a colored man and said the same thing to him, he said he would telegraph to New York, and two men would meet me at 9 o'clock and take me with them; after that we went on board the boat, Mr. Wheeler sat beside me on the deck; I saw a colored gentleman come on board, he beckoned to me; I nodded my head, and could not go; Mr. Wheeler was beside me and I was afraid; a white gentleman then came and said to Mr. Wheeler, 'I want to speak to your servant, and tell her of her rights;' Mr. Wheeler rose and said, 'If you have anything to say, say it to me—she knows her rights;' the white gentleman asked me if I wanted to be free; I said 'I do, but I belong to this gentleman and I can't have it;' he replied, 'Yes, you can, come with us, you are as free as your master, if you want your freedom come now; if you go back to Washington you may never get it;' I rose to go, Mr. Wheeler spoke, and said, 'I will give you your freedom,' but he had never promised it before, and I knew he would never give it to me; the white gentleman held out his hand and I went toward him; I was ready for the word before it was given me; I took the children by the hands, who both cried, for they were frightened, but both stopped when they got on shore; a colored man carried the little one, I led the other by the hand. We walked down the street till we got to a hack; nobody forced me away; nobody pulled me, and nobody led me; I went away of my own free will; I always wished to be free and meant to be free when I came North; I hardly expected it in Philadelphia, but I thought I should get free in New York; I have been comfortable and happy since I left Mr. Wheeler, and so are the children; I don't want to go back; I could have gone in Philadelphia if I had wanted to; I could go now; but I had rather die than go back. I wish to make this statement before a magistrate, because I understand that Mr. Williamson is in prison on my account, and I hope the truth may be of benefit to him.

her

Jane X Johnson

mark

James Madison Bell

(1826–1902)

The Day and the War

Born in Gallipolis, Ohio, James Madison Bell was a plasterer by trade, but he is better known as a poet and abolitionist. His politics took him as a delegate to the 1868 Republican Convention that nominated Ulysses S. Grant for the eighteenth presidency of the United States. His poem "The Day and the War," a lament on the tragedy in America's past and a celebration of its future promise, was delivered on January 1, 1864, the first anniversary of the Emancipation Proclamation. Bell dedicated the poem to John Brown, who led a small band of abolitionists in his raid at Harpers Ferry in 1859.

Twelve score of years were long to wait
A fitting day to celebrate:
'Twere long upon one's native soil
A feeless drudge in pain to toil.
But Time that fashions and destroys,
And breeds our sorrows, breeds our joys,
Hence we at length have come with cheer,
To greet the dawning of the year—
The bless'd return of that glad day,
When, through Oppression's gloom, a ray
Of joy and hope and freedom burst,
Dispelling that insatiate thirst,
Which anxious years of toil and strife
Had mingled with the bondman's life.

A fitting day for such a deed,
But far more fit, when it shall lead
To the final abolition
Of the last slave's sad condition;
Then, when the New Year ushers in,
A grand rejoicing shall begin;
Then shall Freedom's clarion tone
Arouse no special class alone,
But all the land its blast shall hear,
And hail with joy the jubilant year;
And maid and matron, youth and age,
Shall meet upon one common stage,
And Proclamation Day shall be
A National Day of Jubilee.

No longer 'neath the weight of years—
No longer merged in hopeless fears—
Is now that good time, long delayed,
When right, not might, shall all pervade.
Drive hence despair—no longer doubt,
Since friends within and foes without
Their might and main conjointly blend
To reach the same great, glorious end—
The sweeping from this favored land
The last foul chain and slavish brand.

No longer need the bondman fear,
For lo! the good time 's almost here,
And doubtless some beneath our voice
Shall live to hail it and rejoice;
For almost now the radiant sheen
Of freedom's glad hosts may be seen;
The ear can almost catch the sound,
The eye can almost see them bound,
As thirty million voices rise
In grateful paeans to the skies.

But of the present we would sing,
    And of a land all bathed in blood—
A land where plumes the eagle's wing,
    Whose flaming banner, stars bestud—
A land where Heaven, with bounteous hand,
    Rich gifts hath strewn for mortal weal,
Till vale and plain and mountain grand
    Have each a treasure to reveal:
A land with every varying clime,
    From torrid heat to frigid cold—
With natural scenery more sublime
    Than all the world beside unfold,
Where vine-clad France may find a peer,
    And Venice an Italian sky,
With streams whereon the gondolier
    His feather'd oar with joy may ply.
O, heaven-blest and favored land,
    Why are thy fruitful fields laid waste?
Why with thy fratricidal hand
    Hast thou thy beauty half defaced?
Why do the gods disdain thy prayer?
    And why in thy deep bitterness
Comes forth no heaven-clothed arm to share
    A part, and help in the distress?

Hast thou gone forth to reap at noon
And gather where thou hadst not strewn
Hast thou kept back the hireling's fee,
And mocked him in his poverty?

Hast thou, because thy God hath made
Thy brother of a different shade,
Bound fast the iron on his limb,
And made a feeless drudge of him?
Hast thou, to fill thy purse with gold,
The offsprings of his nature sold?
And in thy brutal lust, beguiled
His daughter and his couch defiled?

   For all this wrong and sad abuse,
Hast thou no offering of excuse?
No plea to urge in thy defense
'Gainst helpless, outraged innocence?
Then fearful is thy doom indeed,
If guilty thou canst only plead.
Thy sin is dark, and from the law
No dint of pity canst thou draw.
If thou are charged, 'twill hear thy suit;
If guilty, swift to execute,
Eye for an eye and tooth for tooth;
Yet, Oh forbid it, God of truth:
Let not thine arm in anger fall,
But hear a guilty nation's call;
And stay the vial of wrath at hand,
Pour not its contents on the land;
Should they the last dregs in the cup
Of bitterness be called to sup,
And all the contents of the vial
Of thy just wrath be poured the while,
With all the tortures in reserve,
'Twould scarce be more than they deserve,
For they have sinned 'gainst thee and man.
But wilt thou not, by thy own plan,
Bring them past this sea of blood,
Ere they are buried 'neath its flood?

   America! I thee conjure,
By all that's holy, just and pure,
To cleanse thy hands from Slavery's stain,
And banish from thy soil the chain.

Thou canst not thrive, while with the sweat
Of unpaid toil thy lands are wet,
Nor canst thou hope for peace or joy
Till thou Oppression doth destroy.

Already in the tented field
Are thy proud hosts that will not yield—
Already are they sweeping forth,
Like mighty whirlwinds from the North,
And from the East and West afar
With earthquake tread they press to war,
Until, from where Atlantic raves,
And wildly beats his rock-bound shore,
To where the calm Pacific laves
A land of fruits and shining oar,
The thundering voice of Mars is heard,
And echoing vales repeat each word,
And mountains tremble to their base!
For lo! in arms a mighty race,
Of mighty genius, mighty strength,
Have ta'en the field as foes at length,—
A nation, whom but yesterday
The bands of union joined in one,
Now clad in war's dread panoply,
Their marshaling hosts to battle run.
But not as blind ambition's slaves
Rush wildly on those breathing waves:
Nor as the dread sirocco's breath,
All indiscriminate in death—
But they (as freemen should and must,
When ruthless, ruffian hands assail
Their rightful cause of sacred trust,
And 'gainst that cause would fain prevail),
Have seized the rifle, sword and spear,
And charged upon the foeman near.

And Europe's clans all interest grew,
When North and South their sabres drew,
For they had long with jealous fear
Marked this vast Republic here,

And watched its almost magic growth,
Compared with their dull rounds of sloth;
Hence, when the bomb on Sumter fell,
They felt a half-unconscious swell
Of exultation flame the heart,
And only hoped, that bomb might part
The web and woof which bound in one
Their greatest rival 'neath the sun.
For where's the monarch that could rest
Secure beneath his royal crest,
And see a land like this of ours—
Radiant with eternal flowers,
With hills and vales of solid gold,
That centuries yet will scarce unfold,
And holding out a welcome hand
To all the subjects of his land,
And they responding to the call
Like the sear'd foliage of the fall—
And feel no inward joy or pride
In aught that promised to divide,
And e'en to tatter'd fragments rend,
The land where all those virtues blend?
For scarce a wave that sweeps the sea,
However small or great it be,
Nor scarce a sail that drinks the spray,
But bears some despot's slave away.

Hence to the North their word of mouth,
While heart and soul's been with the South—
Been with the South from first to last,
And will be till the war is past,
Despite non-intervention's cry,—
Which, by-the-way, a blacker lie
Ne'er came from Pandemonium's cell
Nor from the foulest niche in hell,
Than 'twere for Europe to affirm
    That she has wholly neutral kept,
The while this dark and fearful storm
    Of civil war has o'er us swept;
Not intervene, and still erect

Rebel warships by the score,
And give them succor, and protect
 Upon her coast as many more?
Not intervene! Whence the supply
 Of war munitions by the ton,
That sweep our blocking squadrons by,
 And into Southern harbors run?
Not intervene, and 'neath her dock
 Shelter a well-known privateer—
And to prevent her capture, mock
 With self-raised queries till she's clear?
Not intervene! and yet propose
 To recognize the South when she
Discards the source of half her woes,
 And sets her long bound captives free?
If this non-intervention is,
 Then O may Jeff deliver us:
For better had we bow as his,
 Than fall where nations reason thus.

All this was done, but wonder not
The half-healed wound is ne'er forgot;
It may assume perfection's state
And e'en the heart with joy elate;
While crouched beneath a gauze-like crest,
Its germ and root and fibres rest;
Where slightest scratch or bruise or sprain
May wake them into life again.

Thus Britain wounded years before,
Remembers still the painful sore,
And were the time more opportune,
Columbia's sun she'd veil at noon.
She's envious of her growing wealth,
Her fruitful fields, her joy, her health,
Her mighty rivers grand and free,
Creation's highways to the sea:
And fain would sway her sceptred hand,
And bring them all 'neath her command;

For kindred spirits there are none,
Twixt a Republic and a throne.

Then wonder not that Europe's choice,
Her strength of purse, her strength of voice,
Have favored every foul excess
Through which this nation might grow less.
And that this wasting war proceed,
And to the utter ruin lead
Of this Republic, they have prayed,
And praying lent the South their aid;
And hence the war is raging still,
And the nation's good or ill
Hangs on the issue of the fight—
The triumph of the wrong or right.

Many have been the grounds of strife
Where man has sacrificed his life,
And many causeless wars have been
Since Michael fought and conquered sin;
Yet many battles have been fought,
And many lands that blood have bought,
Through wars that have been justified,
Where struggling thousands fought and died—
Fought and died, and were proud that they
On the shrine of truth had a life to lay;
Fought and died, nor trembling came
They to the life-devouring flame,
But, like Winkleride of yore,
Their sheathless breasts they bravely bore.

For he who battles for the right,
When in the thickest of the fight,
Doth feel a God-approving glow,
Which bids defiance to the foe;
And though he falls beside his shield,
He sleeps a victor on the field.
And Freedom is that sacred cause,
　　Where he that doth his lancet poise,

Shall, living, reap the world's applause,
 Or, dying, win unclouded joys.

 But now the query to be solved
Is, shall the Union be dissolved?
Shall this fair land, our fathers gave
Ungrudgingly their lives to save
From kingly rule and tyranny,
Be rent in twain by Slavery?
And shall the line of Plymouth stock—
Whose sires trod that hoary rock,
Which rendered sacred e'en the soil
Whereon they after deign'd to toil—
Allow this refuge of black lies,
Quintessence of all villainies,
To rear thereon his demon throne,
Or claim one footprint as his own?

What, though the dark and foulsome raid
Of South Carolina should pervade
The whole entire South, and they,
Like hungry wolves in quest of prey,
Rush down upon the Union fold,
Rivaling e'en the Gauls of old?
Shall we, because of that dark raid,
See Freedom's shrine in ruins laid,
And her long-spread banner furl'd,
To grow the butt of all the world:
And passive keep, the while this horde,
From mountain height and valley pour'd,
Ride rampant over field and plain,
Dread carnage strewing in their train,
Until they plant their standard, where
Old Bunker rears his head in air?

 To gain this zenith of their pride,
Through human gore waste-deep they'd ride.
Waist-deep! aye, more—they love the sin,
And some would brave it to the chin,
Could they upon old Bunker's mound

Dole out their man flesh by the pound!
Nor would they with their souls demur,
E'en though the venal purchaser
Should in his fiendish lust demand
The fairest daughters of the land;
Nor would they scruple as to hue,
But eyes of jet and eyes of blue,
And fair-brow'd maids with flowing hair,
Such as Anglo-Saxons wear,
Would grace as oft their auction-blocks
As those less fair with fleecy locks.

But never! never! never, no!
No, never while the North winds blow,
Shall vile oppression desecrate
One foot of earth in that old State!
Not while the gallant Fifty-fourth,
In all the spirit of the North,
Stand pledged Secession to defy,
Or in the cause of Freedom die;
Not while a single hand remains
To grasp the sword or touch the spring,
Shall that foul dagon god of chains
Thither his courts and altars bring.

To this audacious end they've bent
Their ever-craven, vulturous eye,
Till now their fiendish, dark intent,
Stands out before the noonday sky;
And all equip'd for death and war,
With rifle, bomb and cimeter,
They boldly stand on Richmond's height,
And claim secession as a right.
But, whether right or wrong, still they
Have sworn no longer to obey
Edict sent or mandate given,
From any court this side of Heaven,
Except that court in concert be
With chains and endless slavery.

At length the war assumes a phase,
　Though long apparent, oft denied:
We speak it in the nation's praise—
　The land they never can divide.
Therefore this fact should none surprise—
If Slavery lives, the Union dies;
And if the Union's e'er restored,
'Twill be when Freedom is secured;
And liberty, man's rightful due,
Is not proscribed by grade nor hue.
Hence he that would avert the doom,
And rescue from sepulchral gloom
His freedom, must, with sword in hand,
March 'gainst the slavery of this land.

　Then gird thy loins, for lo! thy course,
O brother! long oppress'd by force,
With stalwart arm and ebon brow,
Was never half so plain as now:
Nor half so ominously bright
With Hope's refulgent beams of light—
For with each deafening cannon's roar,
Thy hated chains grow less secure:
And, like the fumes of war, shall they
Dissolve ere long, and pass away.
Meanwhile, from thraldom's gloomy slough
Millions shall come forth such as thou,
And Fame a laurel wreath shall twine
For many a brow of Afric line.

　But prate thou not of liberty,
While still in shackled slavery
The most remote of all thy kin
Bow down beneath its damning sin!
Nor make thy boast of English birth,
Nor French descent, nor Celtic worth;
This leave for English, French or Dane,
Whose kindred wear no galling chain.
But thou, O man of Afric hue,
This vaunting spirit pray subdue,

And bide thy time to boast till he,
Thy last chained brother, shall be free.

Not only free from lash and yoke,
But free from all that should provoke
The just, indignant wrath of those
Who now his budding rights oppose;
Not only free to shoulder arms,
When foeman thick as locusts swarm,
Securely wrapped in coats of mail,
Seem almost certain to prevail;
Not only free to pay a tax
To each scrip-monger, who exacts
His hard-earned dollar as a rule,
For purposes of State or school:
While they the children of his loins,
Through some base act which hate enjoins,
Are not allowed within the door
Where Wisdom sits to bless the poor!
Not only free to tell the truth
Where Justice, mocked at, sits forsooth!
But free from all that should impair
The rights of freemen anywhere!

Till then, thou shouldst not, must not boast,
But rather at thy lowly post,
With zeal and fortitude combined,
Discharge the duties there assigned.
Should struggling Freedom call for thee,
Come forth with proud alacrity;
Gird on dread war's habiliments,
And nobly stand in her defense,
And thereby thou shalt win a place
For thee and for thy injured race,
Above the vulgar taunt and jeer,
That grates so harshly on thy ear.

———————

Though Tennyson, the poet king,
  Has sung of Balaklava's charge,

Until his thund'ring cannons ring
  From England's center to her marge,
The pleasing duty still remains
To sing a people from their chains—
To sing what none have yet assay'd,
The wonders of the Black Brigade.
The war had raged some twenty moons,
Ere they in columns or platoons,
To win them censure or applause,
Were marshal'd in the Union cause—
Prejudged of slavish cowardice,
While many a taunt and foul device
Came weekly forth with Harper's sheet,
To feed that base, infernal cheat.

  But how they would themselves demean,
Has since most gloriously been seen.
'Twas seen at Milliken's dread bend!
Where e'en the Furies seemed to lend
To dark Secession all their aid,
To crush the Union Black Brigade.
The war waxed hot, and bullets flew
  Like San Francisco's summer sand,
But they were there to dare and do,
  E'en to the last, to save the land.
And when the leaders of their corps
  Grew wild with fear, and quit the field,
The dark remembrance of their scars
  Before them rose, they could not yield:
And, sounding o'er the battle din,
  They heard their standard-bearer cry—
"Rally! and prove that ye are men!
  Rally! and let us do or die!
For war, nor death, shall boast a shade
  To daunt the Union Black Brigade!"

And thus he played the hero's part,
  Till on the ramparts of the foe
A score of bullets pierced his heart,
  He sank within the trench below.

His comrades saw, and fired with rage,
Each sought his man, him to engage
In single combat. Ah! 'twas then
The Black Brigade proved they were men!
For ne'er did Swiss! or Russ! or knight!
　Against such fearful odds arrayed,
With more persistent valor fight,
　Than did the Union Black Brigade!

As five to one, so stood their foes,
When that defiant shout arose,
And 'long their closing columns ran,
Commanding each to choose his man!
And ere the sound had died away,
Full many a ranting rebel lay
Gasping piteously for breath—
Struggling with the pangs of death,
From bayonet thrust or shining blade,
Plunged to the hilt by the Black Brigade.
　And thus they fought, and won a name—
None brighter on the scroll of Fame;
For out of one full corps of men,
But one remained unwounded, when
The dreadful fray had fully past—
All killed or wounded but the last!

　And though they fell, as has been seen,
Each slept his lifeless foes between,
And marked the course and paved the way
To ushering in a better day.
Let Balaklava's cannons roar,
　And Tennyson his hosts parade,
But ne'er was seen and never more
　The equals of the Black Brigade!

　Then nerve thy heart, gird on thy sword,
For dark Oppression's ruthless horde
And thy tried friends are in the field—
Say which shall triumph, which shall yield?
Shall they that heed not man nor God—
Vile monsters of the *gory rod*—

Dark forgers of the *rack* and *chain:*
Shall *they* prevail—and Thraldom's reign,
With all his dark unnumber'd ills,
Become eternal as the hills?
No! by the blood of freemen slain,
On hot-contested field and main,
And by the mingled sweat and tears,
Extorted through these many years
From Afric's patient sons of toil—
Weak victims of a braggart's spoil—
This bastard plant, the Upas tree,
Shall not supplant our liberty!
But in the right, our sword of power
We'll firmly grasp in this dread hour,
And in the life-tide's crimson flow
Of those that wrong us, write our No!
No! by all that's great and good;
No! by a common brotherhood,
The wrong no longer shall prevail,
Its myriad horrors to entail!

Better in youth pass off life's stage,
Battling 'gainst a tyrant's rage,
Than live to three-score years and ten,
Disown'd of God, despised of men;
Better that cities, hamlets, towns,
And every hut where life abounds,
In conflagration's ruins lie,
Than men as things should live and die;
Better the whetted knife be brought,
And quick as lightning speeds a thought,
Hurl life all wreaking from its throne,
Than live their manhood to disown,
Sooner than bear a hell of pain,
And wear a festering, galling chain,
To hoary age e'en from their birth,
And die the meanest thing on earth.

There is no deed they should not do,
Could they thereby obtain the clue,

The motive power and the might
To set their outraged people right!
Then grasp the sword, discard the sheath,
And strike for Liberty or Death!
But what is death? 'Tis, after all,
The merest transit from this ball
To some bright state or gloomy sphere,
Remote, perhaps—perhaps quite near.
And what is life? Hath it a charm,
While fetters gall the neck and arm,
And from no species of contempt,
However base, to be exempt?
'Tis true a noble bard hath said
That to the regions of the dead
"What dreams *may* come, *now* give us pause."
But who can so thwart Nature's laws
As to evade that dread unknown,
Through aid or effort of his own?

But is there aught to haunt a dream,
That man should so unwelcome deem,
As to regard it worse than stripes—
Worse than slavery's mildest types?
No, no! there's nothing, rest assured,
In life or death to be endured—
There are no tortures to excel
The fires of a Southern hell!
The lash, the yoke, the gag, the chain,
May each produce a world of pain;
But what are these, though all combined,
To gross sterility of mind?

To chain and scourge this mortal frame,
It were a sin and burning shame;
But who can estimate the doom
Of those that quench and shroud in gloom
The only lamp which God hath given,
To light the soul in earth or heaven?
While this external will expand,
In proud defiance of the brand,

The mind, that germ of tender growth—
That plant of far transcendent worth,
Will neither bud nor bloom nor bear,
Where thraldom's breath infects the air.
Then onward roll, thou dreadful War,
   If thou, and thou alone, canst bring
The boon of Freedom from afar;
   Roll darkly on then, while we sing:
We would not have thee slack thy speed,
   Nor change the tenor of thy way,
Till each infernal law and creed
   That fosters wrong, is swept away!
If needs be, lay proud cities waste!
   And slay thy thousands at a meal!
But in thy wake let Freedom haste,
   With oil to soothe and balm to heal.

———————

AND here permit me to diverge
From real to fancy's flow'ry marge,
And sing of what I seem'd to see
While there, enshrined in reverie.
The past, and what is yet to be
Reveal'd in blank futurity,
Swept like a phantom through my brain,
Of which some shadows still remain:
And to those shadows let me call
The eye and silent ear of all.

One evening, wrapp'd in pensive mood,
   On fancy's wing I soar'd afar,
Till, seeing and unseen, I stood
   Amid the hidden springs of War:
And there, upon a canvas vast,
I saw this cruel war sweep past—
Its former battles fought again,
With all the unfought in their train.
Upon the sea and on the shore
Each battle scene, was marked with gore;

And bleaching there, on sea and plain,
Lay mangled bodies of the slain.
Of some were nothing save their trunk,
Whose life the thirsty earth had drunk:
With legs and arms all torn away
By some dread shell's destructive play;
And massive trees ball-riven stood,
All draped with powder, drenched with blood,
While clotted hair and flesh still clung
Their sear'd and shattered boughs among.
And 'neath the deep and angry waves,
Thousands had found their liquid graves:
And sleeping there 'mid shells and rocks,
Were many braves with fleecy locks.
Of such were many of the slain,
On every battle-field and plain.

But wild to pierce futurity,
Its deep veiled ultimatum see,
And learn the final of this war—
The waning of our evil star—
I turned the tardy canvas from,
And sped me on, when lo! a bomb,
Deeper in tone than aught I'd heard—
So deep the very earth was stirr'd,
As though the gods, in wrath or sport,
Had touch'd some pillar of their court;
Of Peace it was the harbinger—
The long-prayed, welcome messenger.

But eager still, I onward sped,
Unknowing why, or whither led,
Till in my path an angel rose,
My further progress to oppose.
His form was tall and passing fair—
His raiment like the driven snow,
And trod he on the ambient air
As mortals walk the earth below.
His voice, though soft, seemed to expand,
And e'en in compass to increase,

Till every nook of our fair land
Rang with the joyous song of PEACE!
Peace! and the loud-mouth'd cannon's roar
In silence slept, to wake no more!
Peace! and the soldier quits the field,
And doffs his corslet, sword and shield,
And in the burden of his lay,
The din of battle died away:
And lilies bloom'd and olives spread
In rich profusion o'er the dead.

The dark Rebellion had been crushed,
And every wailing sound was hushed;
And there was not a slavish chain
In all Columbia's fair domain.
And then and there I saw unfold,
All fresh and bright from Freedom's mould,
A real Republic—such a one
As should have passed from sire to son;
A real Republic—free! uncurs'd!
The sole intention of the first—
In which the bright Damascus blade
Became the farmer's plowing spade:
And with the spear he pois'd of yore
His golden harvest did secure.

And far away as the eye could span,
In its vast sweep from strand to strand,
I saw no South, North, East nor West,
But one broad land, all free and blest;
And there was not a jarring sound
In all the vastitude profound—
No wail, no sob, no sigh, no tear,
To dim the eye or mar the ear.
And violets bloomed the banks along,
And the lark poured forth his matin song,
And the lowly cot and massive dome
Had each the air of a joyous home;
And temples rear'd their spires on high,
Pointing away to the clear blue sky;

And myriad souls had gathered there,
Whose grateful hearts went up in prayer
To the God of love, whose gracious hand
Had clothed in peace their bleeding land.

With one allusion, we have done
The task so joyously begun:
It is to speak, in measured lays,
Of him the Nation loves to praise.

When that inspired instrument,
The subject of this great event,
Forth from the Halls of Congress came,
With even justice as its aim,
'Twas deem'd by some a fiendish rod,
But otherwise adjudged of God,
Who, turning earthward from His throne,
Beheld great Lincoln all alone,
With earth-bent brow, in pensive mood,
Pondering o'er some unsubdued
And knotty problem, half dissolved,
And half in mystery yet involved.

The interest of a continent,
All broken up by discontent—
His own dear land, land of his love,
The fairest 'neath the realms above—
Weighed down his form and rack'd his brain,
And filled his patriot heart with pain.
But when his mind conceived the thought
   To WRITE FOUR MILLION CAPTIVES FREE!
An angel to his conscience brought
   Approving smiles of Deity;
And ere he had with flesh conferr'd,
   He gave the bright conception birth,
And distant nations saw and heard,
   And bless'd his mission on the earth.

And we today reiterate,
With warmth of heart and depth of soul,

God bless Americ's Magistrate!
Long may he live to guide, control;
Long may that arching brow and high—
That spiritual and piercing eye:
That tall, majestic, manly form—
Live, our rainbow 'midst the storm;
And when the roar of battle's pass'd;
When vain Secession's breath'd his last;
When peace and order are restored,
And Freedom sits at every board;
And when the Nation shall convene
In mass, as ne'er before was seen,
And render eulogistic meeds
To worthy heroes' noble deeds,
A lengthened train shall claim their boast,
But Lincoln's name shall lead the host!
His name shall grow a household word,
Where'er the human voice is heard;
And tribes and peoples yet unborn,
Shall hail and bless his natal morn.

Frederick Douglass

(1817–1895)

Reconstruction

Abolitionist, journalist, diplomat, statesman, Frederick Douglass never knew his white father. His mother was a slave, and he was born in Tuckahoe, Maryland. After Douglass escaped to freedom in 1828 he continued his self-education with the reading and writing skills he had learned from the wife of his mother's slavemaster. From 1847 to 1860 he edited his own newspaper, the North Star, *and during the Civil War he served as an advisor to President Lincoln. In 1889 he was appointed the United States Minister to Haiti.*

"Reconstruction" was first published in The Atlantic Monthly *in 1866. In it Douglass puts forth his vision of a post-Civil War America as a nation which empowers all its men and women, regardless of race or color, by extending to them the franchise and all other of their constitutional rights as U.S. citizens.*

. . . Whether the tremendous war so heroically fought and so victoriously ended shall pass into history, a miserable failure, barren of permanent results,—a scandalous and shocking waste of blood and treasure,—a strife for empire, as Earl Russell characterized it, of no value to liberty or civilization,—an attempt to re-establish a Union by force, which must be the merest mockery of a Union, —an effort to bring under Federal authority States into which no loyal man from the North may safely enter, and to bring men into the national councils who deliberate with daggers and vote with revolvers, and who do not even conceal their deadly hate of the country that conquered them; or whether, on the other hand, we shall, as the rightful reward of victory over treason, have a solid nation, entirely delivered from all contradictions and social antagonisms, based upon loyalty, liberty, and equality, must be determined one way or the other by the present session of Congress. The last session really did nothing which can be considered final as to these questions. The Civil Rights Bill and the Freedmen's Bureau Bill and the proposed constitutional amendments, with the amendment already adopted and recognized as the law of the land, do not reach the difficulty, and cannot, unless the whole structure of the government is changed from a government by States to something like a despotic central government, with power to control even the municipal regulations of States, and to make them conform to its own despotic will. While there remains such an idea as the right of each State to control its own local affairs,—an idea, by the way, more deeply rooted in the minds of men of all sections of the country than perhaps any one other political idea,—no general assertion of human rights can be of any practical value. To change the character of the government at this point is neither possible nor desirable. All that is necessary to be done is to make the government consistent with itself and render the rights of the States compatible with the sacred rights of human nature.

The arm of the Federal government is long, but it is far too short to protect the rights of individuals in the interior of distant States. They must have the power to protect themselves, or they will go unprotected, in spite of all the laws the Federal government can put upon the national statute-book.

Slavery, like all other great systems of wrong, founded in the depths of human selfishness, and existing for ages, has not neglected its own conservation. It has steadily exerted an influence upon all around it favorable to its own continuance. And to-day it is so strong that it could exist, not only without law, but even against law. Custom, manners, morals, religion, are all on its side everywhere in the South; and when you add the ignorance and servility of the ex-slave to the intelligence and accustomed authority of the master, you have the conditions, not out of which slavery will again grow, but under which it is impossible for the Federal government to wholly destroy it, unless the Federal government be armed with despotic power, to blot out State authority, and to station a Federal officer at every cross-road. This, of course, cannot be done, and ought not even if it could. The true way and the easiest way is to make our government entirely consistent with itself, and give to every loyal citizen the elective franchise, —a right and power which will be ever present, and will form a wall of fire for his protection.

One of the invaluable compensations of the late Rebellion is the highly instructive disclosure it made of the true source of danger to republican government. Whatever may be tolerated in monarchical and despotic governments, no republic is safe that tolerates a privileged class, or denies to any of its citizens equal rights and equal means to maintain them. What was theory before the war has been made fact by the war . . .

It is asked, said Henry Clay, on a memorable occasion, Will slavery never come to an end? That question, said he, was asked fifty years ago, and it has been answered by fifty years of unprecedented prosperity. In spite of the eloquence of the earnest abolitionists, —poured out against slavery during thirty years,—even they must confess, that, in all the probabilities of the case, that system of barbarism would have continued its horrors far beyond the limits of the nineteenth century but for the Rebellion, and perhaps only have disappeared at last in a fiery conflict, even more fierce and bloody than that which has now been suppressed.

It is no disparagement to truth, that it can only prevail where reason prevails. War begins where reason ends. The thing worse than rebellion is the thing that causes rebellion. What that thing is, we have been taught to our cost. It remains now to be seen whether we have the needed courage to have that cause entirely removed from the Republic. At any rate, to this grand work of national regeneration and entire purification Congress must now address itself, with full purpose that the work shall this time be thoroughly done. The deadly upas, root and branch, leaf and fibre, body and sap, must be utterly destroyed. The country is evidently not in a condition to listen patiently to pleas for postponement, however plausible, nor will it permit the responsibility to be shifted to other shoulders. Authority and power are here commensurate with the duty imposed. There are no cloud-flung shadows to obscure the way. Truth shines with brighter light and intenser heat at every moment, and a country torn and rent and bleeding implores relief from its distress and agony.

If time was at first needed, Congress has now had time. All the requisite materials from which to form an intelligent judgment are now before it. Whether its members look at the origin, the progress, the termination of the war, or at the mockery of a peace now existing, they will find only one unbroken chain of argument in favor of a radical policy of reconstruction. . . . Radicalism, so far from being odious, is now the popular passport to power. The men most bitterly charged with it go to Congress with the largest majorities, while the timid and doubtful are sent by lean majorities, or else left at home. The strange controversy between the President and Congress, at one time so threatening, is disposed of by the people. The high reconstructive powers which he so confidently, ostentatiously, and haughtily claimed, have been disallowed, denounced, and utterly repudiated; while those claimed by Congress have been confirmed.

Without attempting to settle here the metaphysical and somewhat theological question (about which so much has already been said and written), whether once in the Union means always in the Union,—agreeably to the formula, Once in grace always in grace,—it is obvious to common sense that the rebellious States stand to-day, in point of law, precisely where they stood when, exhausted, beaten, conquered, they fell powerless at the feet of Federal authority. Their State governments were overthrown, and the lives and property of the leaders of the Rebellion were forfeited. In reconstructing the institutions of these shattered and overthrown States, Congress should begin with a clean slate, and make clean work of it. Let there be no hesitation. It would be a cowardly deference to a defeated and treacherous President, if any account were made of the illegitimate, one-sided, sham governments hurried into existence for a malign purpose in the absence of Congress. These pretended governments, which were never submitted to the people, and from participation in which four millions of the loyal people were excluded by Presidential order, should now be treated according to their true character, as shams and impositions, and supplanted by true and legitimate governments, in the formation of which loyal men, black and white, shall participate.

It is not, however, within the scope of this paper to point out the precise steps to be taken, and the means to be employed. The people are less concerned about these than the grand end to be attained. They demand such a reconstruction as shall put an end to the present anarchical state of things in the late rebellious States,—where frightful murders and wholesale massacres are perpetrated in the very presence of Federal soldiers. This horrible business they require shall cease. They want a reconstruction such as will protect loyal men, black and white, in their persons and property; such a one as will cause Northern industry, Northern capital, and Northern civilization to flow into the South, and make a man from New England as much at home in Carolina as elsewhere in the Republic. No Chinese wall can now be tolerated. The South must be opened to the light of law and liberty, and this session of Congress is relied upon to accomplish this important work.

The plain, common-sense way of doing this work, as intimated at the beginning, is simply to establish in the South one law, one government, one administration of justice, one condition to exercise of the elective franchise, for men of all races and colors alike. This great measure is sought as earnestly by loyal white men as by loyal blacks, and is needed alike by both. Let sound political prescience but take the place of an unreasoning prejudice, and this will be done.

Men denounce the negro for his prominence in this discussion; but it is no fault of his that in peace as in war, that in conquering Rebel armies as in reconstructing the rebellious States, the right of the negro is the true solution of our national troubles. The stern logic of events which goes directly to the point, disdaining all concern for the color or features of men, has determined the interests of the country as identical with and inseparable from those of the negro.

The policy that emancipated and armed the negro—now seen to have been wise and proper by the dullest—was not certainly more sternly demanded than is now the policy of enfranchisement. If with the negro was success in war, and without him failure, so in peace it will be found that the nation must fall or flourish with the negro.

Fortunately, the Constitution of the United States knows no distinction between citizens on account of color. Neither does it know any difference between a citizen of a State and a citizen of the United States. Citizenship evidently includes all the rights of citizens, whether State or national. If the Constitution knows none, it is clearly no part of the duty of a Republican Congress now to institute one. The mistake of the last session was the attempt to do this very thing by a renunciation of its power to secure political rights to any class of citizens, with the obvious purpose to allow the rebellious States to disfranchise, if they should see fit, their colored citizens. This unfortunate blunder must now be retrieved, and the emasculated citizenship given to the negro supplanted by that contemplated in the Constitution of the United States, which declares that the citizens of each State shall enjoy all the rights and immunities of citizens of the several States,—so that a legal voter in any State shall be a legal voter in all the States.

Booker T. Washington

(1856?–1915)

An Address Delivered at the Opening of the Cotton States Exposition in Atlanta, Georgia, September, 1895

"Cast down your buckets where you are," Booker T. Washington exhorts African Americans in this address as he encourages them not to flee the South but to take full advantage of its educational opportunities and their own personal resources in order to improve their lot and rise up in the ranks of American society. While the address clearly attempts to appease white Southerners in its decrial of political protest and violent demonstration, it at the same time calls upon whites to acknowledge fully the contribution of black Americans to the building of the nation.

Mr. President and Gentlemen of the Board of Directors and Citizens: One-third of the population of the South is of the Negro race. No enterprise seeking the material, civil, or moral welfare of this section can disregard this element of our population and reach the highest success. I but convey to you, Mr. President and Directors, the sentiment of the masses of my race when I say that in no way have the value and manhood of the American Negro been more fittingly and generously recognized than by the managers of this magnificent Exposition at every stage of its progress. It is a recognition that will do more to cement the friendship of the two races than any occurrence since the dawn of freedom.

Not only this, but the opportunity here afforded will awaken among us a new era of industrial progress. Ignorant and inexperienced, it is not strange that in the first years of our new life we began at the top instead of at the bottom; that a seat in Congress or the State Legislature was more sought than real estate or industrial skill; that the political convention or stump speaking had more attractions than starting a dairy farm or truck garden.

A ship lost at sea for many days suddenly sighted a friendly vessel. From the mast of the unfortunate vessel was seen a signal, "Water, water; we die of thirst!" The answer from the friendly vessel at once came back: "Cast down your bucket where you are." A second time the signal, "Water, water; send us water!" ran up from the distressed vessel, and was answered: "Cast down your bucket where you are." The captain of the distressed vessel, at last heeding the injunction, cast down his bucket, and it came up full of fresh, sparkling water from the mouth of the Amazon River. To those of my race who depend upon bettering their condition in a foreign land, or who underestimate the importance of cultivating friendly relations with the Southern white man, who is his next door neighbor, I would say: "Cast down your bucket where you are"—cast it down in making friends in every manly way of the people of all races by whom we are surrounded.

Cast it down in agriculture, mechanics, in commerce, in domestic service, and in the professions. And in this connection it is well to bear in mind that whatever other sins the South may be called to bear, when it comes to business, pure and simple, it is in the South that the Negro is given a man's chance in the commercial world, and in nothing is this Exposition more eloquent than in emphasizing this chance. Our greatest danger is, that in the great leap from slavery to freedom we may overlook the fact that the masses of us are to live by the productions of our hands, and fail to keep in mind that we shall prosper in proportion as we learn to dignify and glorify common labor, and put brains and skill into the common occupations of life; shall prosper in proportion as we learn to draw the line between the superficial and the substantial, the ornamental gewgaws of life and the useful. No race can prosper till it learns that there is as much dignity in tilling a field as in writing a poem. It is at the bottom of life we must begin, and not at the top. Nor should we permit our grievances to overshadow our opportunities.

To those of the white race who look to the incoming of those of foreign birth and strange tongue and habits for the prosperity of the South, were I permitted I would repeat what I say to my own race, "Cast down your bucket where you are." Cast it down among the 8,000,000 Negroes whose habits you know, whose fidelity and love you have tested in days when to have proved treacherous meant the ruin of your firesides. Cast down your bucket among these people who have, without strikes and labor wars, tilled your fields, cleared your forests, builded your railroads and cities, and brought forth treasures from the bowels of the earth, and helped make possible this magnificent representation of the progress of the South. Casting down your bucket among my people, helping and encouraging them as you are doing on these grounds, and, with education of head, hand and heart, you will find that they will buy your surplus land, make blossom the waste places in your fields, and run your factories. While doing this, you can be sure in the future, as in the past, that you and your families will be surrounded by the most patient, faithful, law-abiding, and unresentful people that the world has seen. As we have proved our loyalty to you in the past, in nursing your children, watching by the sick bed of your mothers and fathers, and often following them with tear-dimmed eyes to their graves, so in the future, in our humble way, we shall stand by you with a devotion that no foreigner can approach, ready to lay down our lives, if need be, in defense of yours, interlacing our industrial, commercial, civil, and religious life with yours in a way that shall make the interests of both races one. In all things that are purely social we can be as separate as the fingers, yet one as the hand in all things essential to mutual progress.

There is no defense or security for any of us except in the highest intelligence and development of all. If anywhere there are efforts tending to curtail the fullest growth of the Negro, let these efforts be turned into stimulating, encouraging, and making him the most useful and intelligent citizen. Effort or means so invested will pay a thousand per cent interest. These efforts will be twice blessed—blessing him that gives and him that takes.

There is no escape through law of man or God from the inevitable:

> The laws of changeless justice bind
>   Oppressor with oppressed;
> And close as sin and suffering joined
>   We march to fate abreast.

Nearly sixteen millions of hands will aid you in pulling the load upwards or they will pull against you the load downwards. We shall constitute one-third and more of the ignorance and crime of the South, or one-third its intelligence and progress; we shall contribute one-third to the business and industrial prosperity of the South, or we shall prove a veritable body of death, stagnating, depressing, retarding every effort to advance the body politic.

Gentlemen of the Exposition, as we present to you our humble effort at an exhibition of our progress, you must not expect overmuch. Starting thirty years ago with ownership here and

there in a few quilts and pumpkins and chickens (gathered
from miscellaneous sources), remember the path that has led
from these to the invention and production of agricultural im-
plements, buggies, steam engines, newspapers, books, statu-
ary, carving, paintings, the management of drug stores and
banks has not been trodden without contact with thorns and
thistles. While we take pride in what we exhibit as a result of
our independent efforts, we do not for a moment forget that
our part in this exhibition would fall far short of your expectations but for the constant help that has come to our educational
life, not only from the Southern States, but especially from
Northern philanthropists, who have made their gifts a constant
stream of blessing and encouragement.

The wisest among my race understand that the agitation of
questions of social equality is the extremest folly, and that progress in the enjoyment of all the privileges that will come to us
must be the result of severe and constant struggle rather than
of artificial forcing. No race that has anything to contribute to
the markets of the world is long in any degree ostracized. It is
important and right that all privileges of the law be ours, but it
is vastly more important that we be prepared for the exercise
of those privileges. The opportunity to earn a dollar in a factory
just now is worth infinitely more than the opportunity to spend
a dollar in an opera house.

In conclusion, may I repeat that nothing in thirty years has
given us more hope and encouragement, and drawn us so near
to you of the white race, as this opportunity offered by the
Exposition; and here bending, as it were, over the altar that
represents the results of the struggles of your race and mine,
both starting practically empty-handed three decades ago, I
pledge that, in your effort to work out the great and intricate
problem which God has laid at the doors of the South, you
shall have at all times the patient, sympathetic help of my race;
only let this be constantly in mind that, while from representa-
tions in these buildings of the products of field, of forest, of
mine, of factory, letters, and art, much good will come, yet far
above and beyond material benefits will be the higher good,
that let us pray God will come, in a blotting out of sectional
differences and racial animosities and suspicions, in a determi-

nation to administer absolute justice, in a willing obedience among all classes to the mandates of law. This, coupled with our material prosperity, will bring into our beloved South a new heaven and a new earth.

W. E. B. Du Bois

(1868–1963)

---

from *The Souls of Black Folk*
Of the Sons of Master and Man

A native of Great Barrington, Massachusetts, W. E. B. Du Bois attended Fisk University before earning his Ph.D. at Harvard with a dissertation on the African slave trade. At a time when Social Darwinists were attempting to justify racism on scientific grounds (In The Negro: A Beast *Charles Carroll, for one, set out to prove in 1900 that blacks were a lower class of animal), Du Bois argued that the struggle for equality was essentially ideological. To change society it was necessary first to change minds, he said, and in his groundbreaking* The Souls of Black Folk *(1903), he revolutionized America's habits of thought regarding race. The following excerpt from that work defines a vision vastly different from that of Du Bois's contemporary Booker T. Washington: a vision for black equality that requires political mobilization, economic indepen-*

dence, psychological restoration, and Afrocentric education.

Later in life Du Bois was a moving force behind Ghanaian President Nkrumah's pan-African congress, and when he renounced his American citizenship he settled in Ghana, where he died at the age of ninety-five.

The world-old phenomenon of the contact of diverse races of men is to have new exemplification during the new century. Indeed, the characteristic of our age is the contact of European civilization with the world's undeveloped peoples. Whatever we may say of the results of such contact in the past, it certainly forms a chapter in human action not pleasant to look back upon. War, murder, slavery, extermination, and debauchery,— this has again and again been the result of carrying civilization and the blessed gospel to the isles of the sea and the heathen without the law. Nor does it altogether satisfy the conscience of the modern world to be told complacently that all this has been right and proper, the fated triumph of strength over weakness, of righteousness over evil, of superiors over inferiors. It would certainly be soothing if one could readily believe all this; and yet there are too many ugly facts for everything to be thus easily explained away. We feel and know that there are many delicate differences in race psychology, numberless changes that our crude social measurements are not yet able to follow minutely, which explain much of history and social development. At the same time, too, we know that these considerations have never adequately explained or excused the triumph of brute force and cunning over weakness and innocence.

It is, then, the strife of all honorable men of the twentieth century to see that in the future competition of races the survival of the fittest shall mean the triumph of the good, the beautiful, and the true; that we may be able to preserve for future civilization all that is really fine and noble and strong, and not continue to put a premium on greed and impudence and cruelty. To bring this hope to fruition, we are compelled daily to turn more and more to a conscientious study of the phenomena of race-contact, —to a study frank and fair, and not falsified and colored by our wishes or our fears. And we have in the South as fine a field for such a study as the world affords, —a field, to be sure, which the average American scientist deems somewhat beneath his dignity, and which the average man who is not a scientist knows all about, but nevertheless a line of study which by reason of the enormous race complications with which God seems about to punish this nation must increasingly claim our sober attention, study, and thought, we must ask, what are the actual relations of whites and blacks in the South? and we must be answered, not by apology or fault-finding, but by a plain, unvarnished tale.

In the civilized life of to-day the contact of men and their relations to each other fall in a few main lines of action and communication: there is, first, the physical proximity of home and dwelling-places, the way in which neighborhoods group themselves, and the contiguity of neighborhoods. Secondly, and in our age chiefest, there are the economic relations, —the methods by which individuals coöperate for earning a living, for the mutual satisfaction of wants, for the production of wealth. Next, there are the political relations, the coöperation in social control, in group government, in laying and paying the burden of taxation. In the fourth place there are the less tangible but highly important forms of intellectual contact and commerce, the interchange of ideas through conversation and conference, through periodicals and libraries; and, above all, the gradual formation for each community of that curious *tertium quid* which we call public opinion. Closely allied with this come the various forms of social contact in everyday life, in travel, in theatres, in house gatherings, in marrying and giving in marriage. Finally, there are the varying forms of religious enterprise, of moral teaching and benevolent endeavor. These are the principle ways in which men living in the same communities are brought into contact with each other. It is my present task, therefore, to indicate, from my point of view, how the black race in the South meet and mingle with the whites in these matters of everyday life.

First, as to physical dwelling. It is usually possible to draw in nearly every Southern community a physical color-line on the map, on the one side of which whites dwell and on the other Negroes. The winding and intricacy of the geographical color-line varies, of course, in different communities. I know some towns where a straight line drawn through the middle of the main street separates nine-tenths of the whites from nine-tenths of the blacks. In other towns the older settlement of whites has been encircled by a broad band of blacks; in still other cases little settlements or nuclei of blacks have sprung up amid surrounding whites. Usually in cities each street has its distinctive color, and only now and then do the colors meet in close proximity. Even in the country something of this segregation is manifest in the smaller areas, and of course in the larger phenomena of the Black Belt.

All this segregation by color is largely independent of that natural clustering by social grades common to all communities. A Negro slum may be in dangerous proximity to a white residence quarter, while it is quite common to find a white slum planted in the heart of a respectable Negro district. One thing, however, seldom occurs: the best of the whites and the best of the Negroes almost never live in anything like close proximity. It thus happens that in nearly every Southern town and city, both whites and blacks see commonly the worst of each other. This is a vast change from the situation in the past, when, through the close contact of master and house-servant in the patriarchal big house, one found the best of both races in close contact and sympathy, while at the same time the squalor and dull round of toil among the field-hands was removed from the sight and hearing of the family. One can easily see how a person who saw slavery thus from his father's parlors, and sees freedom on the streets of a great city, fails to grasp or comprehend the whole of the new picture. On the other hand, the settled belief of the mass of the Negroes that the Southern white people do not have the black man's best interests at heart has been intensified in later years by this continual daily contact of the better class of blacks with the worst representatives of the white race.

Coming now to the economic relations of the races, we are on ground made familiar by study, much discussion, and no

little philanthropic effort. And yet with all this there are many
essential elements in the coöperation of Negroes and whites
for work and wealth that are too readily overlooked or not
thoroughly understood. The average American can easily con-
ceive of a rich land awaiting development and filled with black
laborers. To him the Southern problem is simply that of making efficient workingmen out of this material, by giving them
the requisite technical skill and the help of invested capital.
The problem, however, is by no means as simple as this, from
the obvious fact that these workingmen have been trained for
centuries as slaves. They exhibit, therefore, all the advantages
and defects of such training; they are willing and good-natured,
but not self-reliant, provident, or careful. If now the economic
development of the South is to be pushed to the verge of exploitation, as seems probable, then we have a mass of workingmen thrown into relentless competition with the workingmen of the world, but handicapped by a training the very
opposite to that of the modern self-reliant democratic laborer.
What the black laborer needs is careful personal guidance,
group leadership of men with hearts in their bosoms, to train
them to foresight, carefulness, and honesty. Nor does it require any fine-spun theories of racial differences to prove the
necessity of such group training after the brains of the race
have been knocked out by two hundred and fifty years of assid-
uous education in submission, carelessness, and stealing. After
Emancipation, it was the plain duty of some one to assume this
group leadership and training of the Negro laborer. I will not
stop here to inquire whose duty it was—whether that of the
white ex-master who had profited by unpaid toil, or the Northern philanthropist whose persistence brought on the crisis, or
the National Government whose edict freed the bondmen; I
will not stop to ask whose duty it was, but I insist it was the
duty of some one to see that these workingmen were not left
alone and unguided, without capital, without land, without skill,
without economic organization, without even the bald protection of law, order, and decency,—left in a great land, not to
settle down to slow and careful internal development, but des-
tined to be thrown almost immediately into relentless and
sharp competition with the best of modern workingmen under
an economic system where every participant is fighting for

himself, and too often utterly regardless of the rights or welfare of his neighbor.

For we must never forget that the economic system of the South to-day which has succeeded the old regime is not the same system as that of the old industrial North, of England, or of France, with their trade-unions, their restrictive laws, their written and unwritten commercial customs, and their long experience. It is, rather, a copy of that England of the early nineteenth century, before the factory acts,—the England that wrung pity from thinkers and fired the wrath of Carlyle. The rod of empire that passed from the hands of Southern gentlemen in 1865, partly by force, partly by their own petulance, has never returned to them. Rather it has passed to those men who have come to take charge of the industrial exploitation of the New South,—the sons of poor whites fired with a new thirst for wealth and power, thrifty and avaricious Yankees, and unscrupulous immigrants. Into the hands of these men the Southern laborers, white and black, have fallen; and this to their sorrow. For the laborers as such, there is in these new captains of industry neither love nor hate, neither sympathy nor romance; it is a cold question of dollars and dividends. Under such a system all labor is bound to suffer. Even the white laborers are not yet intelligent, thrifty, and well trained enough to maintain themselves against the powerful inroads of organized capital. The results among them, even, are long hours of toil, low wages, child labor, and lack of protection against usury and cheating. But among the black laborers all this is aggravated, first, by a race prejudice which varies from a doubt and distrust among the best element of whites to a frenzied hatred among the worst; and, secondly, it is aggravated, as I have said before, by the wretched economic heritage of the freedmen from slavery. With this training it is difficult for the freedman to learn to grasp the opportunities already opened to him, and the new opportunities are seldom given him, but go by favor to the whites.

Left by the best elements of the South with little protection or oversight, he has been made in law and custom the victim of the worst and most unscrupulous men in each community. The crop-lien system which is depopulating the fields of the South is not simply the result of shiftlessness on the part of Negroes,

but is also the result of cunningly devised laws as to mort-
gages, liens, and misdemeanors, which can be made by con-
scienceless men to entrap and snare the unwary until escape is
impossible, further toil a farce, and protest a crime. I have
seen, in the Black Belt of Georgia, an ignorant, honest Negro
buy and pay for a farm in installments three separate times,
and then in the face of law and decency the enterprising American who sold it to him pocketed the money and deed and left
the black man landless, to labor on his own land at thirty cents
a day. I have seen a black farmer fall in debt to a white storekeeper, and that storekeeper go to his farm and strip it of every
single marketable article,—mules, ploughs, stored crops, tools,
furniture, bedding, clocks, looking-glass,—and all this without
a sheriff or officer, in the face of the law for homestead exemp-
tions, and without rendering to a single responsible person any
account or reckoning. And such proceedings can happen, and
will happen, in any community where a class of ignorant toilers
are placed by custom and race-prejudice beyond the pale of
sympathy and race-brotherhood. So long as the best elements
of a community do not feel in duty bound to protect and train
and care for the weaker members of their group, they leave
them to be preyed upon by these swindlers and rascals.

This unfortunate economic situation does not mean the hin-
drance of all advance in the black South, or the absence of a
class of black landlords and mechanics who, in spite of disadvantages, are accumulating property and making good citizens.
But it does mean that this class is not nearly so large as a fairer
economic system might easily make it, that those who survive
in the competition are handicapped so as to accomplish much
less than they deserve to, and that, above all, the *personnel* of
the successful class is left to chance and accident, and not to
any intelligent culling or reasonable methods of selection. As a
remedy for this, there is but one possible procedure. We must
accept some of the race prejudice in the South as a fact, —
deplorable in its intensity, unfortunate in results, and dangerous for the future, but nevertheless a hard fact which only time
can efface. We cannot hope, then, in this generation, or for
several generations, that the mass of the whites, can be
brought to assume that close sympathetic and self-sacrificing
leadership of the blacks which their present situation so elo-

quently demands. Such leadership, such social teaching and
example, must come from the blacks themselves. For some
time men doubted as to whether the Negro could develop such
leaders; but to-day no one seriously disputes the capability of
individual Negroes to assimilate the culture and common sense
of modern civilization, and to pass it on, to some extent at least,
to their fellows. If this is true, then here is the path out of the
economic situation, and here is the imperative demand for
trained Negro leaders of character and intelligence,—men of
skill, men of light and leading, college-bred men, black captains
of industry, and missionaries of culture; men who thoroughly
comprehend and know modern civilization, and can take hold
of Negro communities and raise and train them by force of
precept and example, deep sympathy, and the inspiration of
common blood and ideals. But if such men are to be effective
they must have some power,—they must be backed by the best
public opinion of these communities, and able to wield for their
objects and aims such weapons as the experience of the world
has taught are indispensable to human progress.

Of such weapons the greatest, perhaps, in the modern world
is the power of the ballot; and this brings me to a consideration
of the third form of contact between whites and blacks in the
South,—political activity.

In the attitude of the American mind toward Negro suffrage
can be traced with unusual accuracy the prevalent conceptions
of government. In the fifties we were near enough the echoes
of the French Revolution to believe pretty thoroughly in universal suffrage. We argued, as we thought then rather logically,
that no social class was so good, so true, and so disinterested
as to be trusted wholly with the political destiny of its neighbors; that in every state the best arbiters of their own welfare
are the persons directly affected; consequently that it is only by
arming every hand with a ballot,—with the right to have a
voice in the policy of the state,—that the greatest good to the
greatest number could be attained. To be sure, there were objections to these arguments, but we thought we had answered
them tersely and convincingly; if some one complained of the
ignorance of voters, we answered, "Educate them." If another
complained of their venality, we replied, "Disfranchise them or
put them in jail." And, finally, to the men who feared dema-

gogues and the natural perversity of some human beings we
insisted that time and bitter experience would teach the most
hardheaded. It was at this time that the question of Negro
suffrage in the South was raised. Here was a defenceless people suddenly made free. How were they to be protected from
those who did not believe in their freedom and were determined to thwart it? Not by force, said the North; not by government guardianship, said the South; then by the ballot, the sole
and legitimate defence of a free people, said the Common
Sense of the Nation. No one thought, at the time, that the ex-
slaves could use the ballot intelligently or very effectively; but
they did think that the possession of so great power by a great
class in the nation would compel their fellows to educate this
class to its intelligent use.

Meantime, new thoughts came to the nation: the inevitable
period of moral retrogression and political trickery that ever
follows in the wake of war overtook us. So flagrant became the
political scandals that reputable men began to leave politics
alone, and politics consequently became disreputable. Men began to pride themselves on having nothing to do with their own
government, and to agree tacitly with those who regarded public office as a private perquisite. In this state of mind it became
easy to wink at the suppression of the Negro vote in the South,
and to advise self-respecting Negroes to leave politics entirely
alone. The decent and reputable citizens of the North who neglected their own civic duties grew hilarious over the exaggerated importance with which the Negro regarded the franchise.
Thus it easily happened that more and more the better class of
Negroes followed the advice from abroad and the pressure
from home, and took no further interest in politics, leaving to
the careless and the venal of their race the exercise of their
rights as voters. The black vote that still remained was not
trained and educated, but further debauched by open and un-
blushing bribery, or force and fraud; until the Negro voter was
thoroughly inoculated with the idea that politics was a method
of private gain by disreputable means.

And finally, now, to-day, when we are awakening to the fact
that the perpetuity of republican institutions on this continent
depends on the purification of the ballot, the civic training of
voters, and the raising of voting to the plane of a solemn duty

which a patriotic citizen neglects to his peril and to the peril of his children's children,—in this day, when we are striving for a renaissance of civic virtue, what are we going to say to the black voter of the South? Are we going to tell him still that politics is a disreputable and useless form of human activity? Are we going to induce the best class of Negroes to take less and less interest in government, and to give up their right to take such an interest, without a protest? I am not saying a word against all legitimate efforts to purge the ballot of ignorance, pauperism, and crime. But few have pretended that the present movement for disfranchisement in the South is for such a purpose; it has been plainly and frankly declared in nearly every case that the object of the disfranchising laws is the elimination of the black man from politics.

Now, is this a minor matter which has no influence on the main question of the industrial and intellectual development of the Negro? Can we establish a mass of black laborers and artisans and landholders in the South who, by law and public opinion, have absolutely no voice in shaping the laws under which they live and work? Can the modern organization of industry, assuming as it does free democratic government and the power and ability of the laboring classes to compel respect for their welfare,—can this system be carried out in the South when half its laboring force is voiceless in the public councils and powerless in its own defence? To-day the black man of the South has almost nothing to say as to how much he shall be taxed, or how those taxes shall be expended; as to who shall execute the laws, and how they shall do it; as to who shall make the laws, and how they shall be made. It is pitiable that frantic efforts must be made at critical times to get law-makers in some States even to listen to the respectful presentation of the black man's side of a current controversy. Daily the Negro is coming more and more to look upon law and justice, not as protecting safeguards, but as sources of humiliation and oppression. The laws are made by men who have little interest in him; they are executed by men who have absolutely no motive for treating the black people with courtesy or consideration; and, finally, the accused law-breaker is tried, not by his peers, but too often by men who would rather punish ten innocent Negroes than let one guilty one escape.

I should be the last one to deny the patent weaknesses and shortcomings of the Negro people; I should be the last to withhold sympathy from the white South in its efforts to solve its intricate social problems. I freely acknowledged that it is possible, and sometimes best, that a partially undeveloped people should be ruled by the best of their stronger and better neighbors for their own good, until such time as they can start and fight the world's battles alone. I have already pointed out how sorely in need of such economic and spiritual guidance the emancipated Negro was, and I am quite willing to admit that if the representatives of the best white Southern public opinion were the ruling and guiding powers in the South to-day the conditions indicated would be fairly well fulfilled. But the point I have insisted upon and now emphasize again, is that the best opinion of the South to-day is not the ruling opinion. That to leave the Negro helpless and without a ballot to-day is to leave him, not to the guidance of the best, but rather to the exploitation and debauchment of the worst; that this is no truer of the South than of the North,—of the North than of Europe: in any land, in any country under modern free competition, to lay any class of weak and despised people, be they white, black, or blue, at the political mercy of their stronger, richer, and more resourceful fellows, is a temptation which human nature seldom has withstood and seldom will withstand.

Moreover, the political status of the Negro in the South is closely connected with the question of Negro crime. There can be no doubt that crime among Negroes has sensibly increased in the last thirty years, and that there has appeared in the slums of great cities a distinct criminal class among the blacks. In explaining this unfortunate development, we must note two things: (1) that the inevitable result of Emancipation was to increase crime and criminals, and (2) that the police system of the South was primarily designed to control slaves. As to the first point, we must not forget that under a strict slave system there can scarcely be such a thing as crime. But when these variously constituted human particles are suddenly thrown broadcast on the sea of life, some swim, some sink, and some hang suspended, to be forced up or down by the chance currents of a busy hurrying world. So great an economic and social revolution as swept the South in '63 meant a weeding out among the Negroes of the incompetents and vicious, the beginning of a differentiation of social grades. Now a rising group of people are not lifted bodily from the ground like an inert solid mass, but rather stretch upward like a living plant with its roots still clinging in the mould. The appearance, therefore, of the Negro criminal was a phenomenon to be awaited; and while it causes anxiety, it should not occasion surprise.

Here again the hope for the future depended peculiarly on careful and delicate dealing with these criminals. Their offences at first were those of laziness, carelessness, and impulse, rather than of malignity or ungoverned viciousness. Such misdemeanors needed discriminating treatment, firm but reformatory, with no hint of injustice, and full proof of guilt. For such dealing with criminals, white or black, the South had no machinery, no adequate jails or reformatories; its police system was arranged to deal with blacks alone, and tacitly assumed that every white man was *ipso facto* a member of that police. Thus grew up a double system of justice, which erred on the white side by undue leniency and the practical immunity of red-handed criminals, and erred on the black side by undue severity, injustice, and lack of discrimination. For, as I have said, the police system of the South was originally designed to keep track of all Negroes, not simply of criminals; and when the Negroes were freed and the whole South was convinced of the impossibility of free Negro labor, the first and almost universal device was to use the courts as a means of reënslaving the blacks. It was not then a question of crime, but rather one of color, that settled a man's conviction on almost any charge. Thus Negroes came to look upon courts as instruments of injustice and oppression, and upon those convicted in them as martyrs and victims.

When, now, the real Negro criminal appeared, and instead of petty stealing and vagrancy we began to have highway robbery, burglary, murder, and rape, there was a curious effect on both sides the color-line: the Negroes refused to believe the evidence of white witnesses or the fairness of white juries, so that the greatest deterrent to crime, the public opinion of one's own social caste, was lost, and the criminal was looked upon as crucified rather than hanged. On the other hand, the whites, used to being careless as to the guilt or innocence of accused

Negroes, were swept in moments of passion beyond law, reason, and decency. Such a situation is bound to increase crime,
and has increased it. To natural viciousness and vagrancy are
being daily added motives of revolt and revenge which stir up
all the latent savagery of both races and make peaceful attention to economic development often impossible.

But the chief problem in any community cursed with crime
is not the punishment of the criminals, but the preventing of
the young from being trained to crime. And here again the
peculiar conditions of the South have prevented proper precau-
tions. I have seen twelve-year-old boys working in chains on
the public streets of Atlanta, directly in front of the schools, in
company with old and hardened criminals; and this indiscriminate mingling of men and women and children makes the
chain-gangs perfect schools of crime and debauchery. The
struggle for reformatories, which has gone on in Virginia,
Georgia, and other States, is the one encouraging sign of the
awakening of some communities to the suicidal results of this
policy.

It is the public schools, however, which can be made, outside
the homes, the greatest means of training decent self-respecting citizens. We have been so hotly engaged recently in dis-
cussing trade-schools and the higher education that the pitiable plight of the public-school system in the South has almost
dropped from view. Of every five dollars spent for public education in the State of Georgia, the white schools get four dollars and the Negro one dollar; and even then the white public-
school system, save in the cities, is bad and cries for reform. If
this is true of the whites, what of the blacks? I am becoming
more and more convinced, as I look upon the system of common-school training in the South, that the national government
must soon step in and aid popular education in some way. Today it has been only by the most strenuous efforts on the part
of the thinking men of the South that the Negro's share of the
school fund has not been cut down to a pittance in some half-
dozen States; and that movement not only is not dead, but in
many communities is gaining strength. What in the name of
reason does this nation expect of a people, poorly trained and
hard pressed in severe economic competition, without political
rights, and with ludicrously inadequate common-school facili-

ties? What can it expect but crime and listlessness, offset here and there by the dogged struggles of the fortunate and more determined who are themselves buoyed by the hope that in due time the country will come to its senses?

I have thus far sought to make clear the physical, economic, and political relations of the Negroes and whites in the South, as I have conceived them, including, for the reasons set forth, crime and education. But after all that has been said on these more tangible matters of human contact, there still remains a part essential to a proper description of the South which it is difficult to describe or fix in terms easily understood by strangers. It is, in fine, the atmosphere of the land, the thought and feeling, the thousand and one little actions which go to make up life. In any community or nation it is these little things which are most elusive to the grasp and yet most essential to any clear conception of the group life taken as a whole. What is thus true of all communities is peculiarly true of the South, where, outside of written history and outside of printed law, there has been going on for a generation as deep a storm and stress of human souls, as intense a ferment of feeling, as intricate a writhing of spirit, as ever a people experienced. Within and without the sombre veil of color vast social forces have been at work,—efforts for human betterment, movements toward disintegration and despair, tragedies and comedies in social and economic life, and a swaying and lifting and sinking of human hearts which have made this land a land of mingled sorrow and joy, of change and excitement and unrest.

The centre of this spiritual turmoil has ever been the millions of black freedmen and their sons, whose destiny is so fatefully bound up with that of the nation. And yet the casual observer visiting the South sees at first little of this. He notes the growing frequency of dark faces as he rides along,—but otherwise the days slip lazily on, the sun shines, and this little world seems as happy and contented as other worlds he has visited. Indeed, on the question of questions—the Negro problem—he hears so little that there almost seems to be a conspiracy of silence; the morning papers seldom mention it, and then usually in a far-fetched academic way, and indeed almost every one seems to forget and ignore the darker half of the land, until the astonished visitor is inclined to ask if after all there *is* any problem here. But if he lingers long enough there comes the awakening: perhaps in a sudden whirl of passion which leaves him gasping at its bitter intensity; more likely in a gradually dawning sense of things he had not at first noticed. Slowly but surely his eyes begin to catch the shadows of the color-line: here he meets crowds of Negroes and whites; then he is suddenly aware that he cannot discover a single dark face; or again at the close of a day's wandering he may find himself in some strange assembly, where all faces are tinged brown or black, and where he has the vague, uncomfortable feeling of the stranger. He realizes at last that silently, resistlessly, the world about flows by him in two great streams: they ripple on in the same sunshine, they approach and mingle their waters in seeming carelessness,—then they divide and flow wide apart. It is done quietly; no mistakes are made, or if one occurs, the swift arm of the law and of public opinion swings down for a moment, as when the other day a black man and a white woman were arrested for talking together on Whitehall Street in Atlanta.

Now if one notices carefully one will see that between these two worlds, despite much physical contact and daily intermingling, there is almost no community of intellectual life or point of transference where the thoughts and feelings of one race can come into direct contact and sympathy with the thoughts and feelings of the other. Before and directly after the war, when all the best of the Negroes were domestic servants in the best of the white families, there were bonds of intimacy, affection, and sometimes blood relationship, between the races. They lived in the same home, shared in the family life, often attended the same church, and talked and conversed with each other. But the increasing civilization of the Negro since then has naturally meant the development of higher classes: there are increasing numbers of ministers, teachers, physicians, merchants, mechanics, and independent farmers, who by nature and training are the aristocracy and leaders of the blacks. Between them, however, and the best element of the whites, there is little or no intellectual commerce. They go to separate churches, they live in separate sections, they are strictly separated in all public gatherings, they travel separately, and they are beginning to read different papers and books. To most libraries, lectures, concerts, and museums, Negroes are either not admitted at all, or on terms peculiarly galling to the pride of the very classes who might otherwise be attracted. The daily paper chronicles the doings of the black world from afar with no great regard for accuracy; and so on, throughout the category of means for intellectual communication, —schools, conferences, efforts for social betterment, and the like,—it is usually true that the very representatives of the two races, who for mutual benefit and the welfare of the land ought to be in complete understanding and sympathy, are so far strangers that one side thinks all whites are narrow and prejudiced, and the other thinks educated Negroes dangerous and insolent. Moreover, in a land where the tyranny of public opinion and the intolerance of criticism is for obvious historical reasons so strong as in the South, such a situation is extremely difficult to correct. The white man, as well as the Negro, is bound and barred by the color-line, and many a scheme of friendliness and philanthropy, of broad-minded sympathy and generous fellowship between the two has dropped still-born because some busybody has forced the color-question to the front and brought the tremendous force of unwritten law against the innovators.

It is hardly necessary for me to add very much in regard to the social contact between the races. Nothing has come to replace that finer sympathy and love between some masters and house servants which the radical and more uncompromising drawing of the color-line in recent years has caused almost completely to disappear. In a world where it means so much to take a man by the hand and sit beside him, to look frankly into his eyes and feel his heart beating with red blood; in a world where a social cigar or a cup of tea together means more than legislative halls and magazine articles and speeches,—one can imagine the consequences of the almost utter absence of such social amenities between estranged races, whose separation extends even to parks and streetcars.

Here there can be none of that social going down to the people,—the opening of heart and hand of the best to the worst, in generous acknowledgment of a common humanity and a common destiny. On the other hand, in matters of simple almsgiving, where there can be no question of social contact, and in the succor of the aged and sick, the South, as if stirred by a feeling of its unfortunate limitations, is generous to a fault. The black beggar is never turned away without a good deal more than a crust, and a call for help for the unfortunate meets quick response. I remember, one cold winter, in Atlanta, when I refrained from contributing to a public relief fund lest Negroes should be discriminated against, I afterward inquired of a friend: "Were any black people receiving aid?" "Why," said he, "they were *all* black."

And yet this does not touch the kernel of the problem. Human advancement is not a mere question of almsgiving, but rather of sympathy and coöperation among classes who would scorn charity. And here is a land where, in the higher walks of life, in all the higher striving for the good and noble and true, the color-line comes to separate natural friends and co-workers; while at the bottom of the social group, in the saloon, the gambling-hell, and the brothel, that same line wavers and disappears.

I have sought to paint an average picture of real relations between the sons of master and man in the South. I have not glossed over matters for policy's sake, for I fear we have already gone too far in that sort of thing. On the other hand, I have sincerely sought to let no unfair exaggerations creep in. I do not doubt that in some Southern communities conditions are better than those I have indicated; while I am no less certain that in other communities they are far worse.

Nor does the paradox and danger of this situation fail to interest and perplex the best conscience of the South. Deeply religious and intensely democratic as are the mass of the whites, they feel acutely the false position in which the Negro problems place them. Such an essentially honest-hearted and generous people cannot cite the caste-levelling precepts of Christianity, or believe in equality of opportunity for all men, without coming to feel more and more with each generation that the present drawing of the color-line is a flat contradiction to their beliefs and professions. But just as often as they come to this point, the present social condition of the Negro stands as a menace and a portent before even the most open-minded: if there were nothing to charge against the Negro but his blackness or other physical peculiarities, they argue, the problem would be comparatively simple; but what can we say to his ignorance, shiftlessness, poverty, and crime? can a self-respecting group hold anything but the least possible fellowship with such persons and survive? and shall we let a mawkish sentiment sweep away the culture of our fathers or the hope of our children? The argument so put is of great strength, but it is not a whit stronger than the argument of thinking Negroes: granted, they reply, that the condition of our masses is bad; there is certainly on the one hand adequate historical cause for this, and unmistakable evidence that no small number have, in spite of tremendous disadvantages, risen to the level of American civilization. And when, by proscription and prejudice, these same Negroes are classed with and treated like the lowest of their people, simply *because* they are Negroes, such a policy not only discourages thrift and intelligence among black men, but puts a direct premium on the very things you complain of, —inefficiency and crime. Draw lines of crime, of incompetency, of vice, as tightly and uncompromisingly as you will, for these things must be proscribed; but a color-line not only does not accomplish this purpose, but thwarts it.

In the face of two such arguments, the future of the South depends on the ability of the representatives of these opposing views to see and appreciate and sympathize with each other's position,—for the Negro to realize more deeply than he does at present the need of uplifting the masses of his people, for the white people to realize more vividly than they have yet done the deadening and disastrous effect of a color-prejudice that classes Phillis Wheatley and Sam Hose in the same despised class.

It is not enough for the Negroes to declare that color-prejudice is the sole cause of their social condition, nor for the white South to reply that their social condition is the main cause of prejudice. They both act as reciprocal cause and effect, and a change in neither alone will bring the desired effect. Both must change, or neither can improve to any great extent. The Negro cannot stand the present reactionary tendencies and unreasoning drawing of the color-line indefinitely without discouragement and retrogression. And the condition of the Negro is ever the excuse for further discrimination. Only by a union of intelli-

gence and sympathy across the color-line in this critical period
of the Republic shall justice and right triumph,
            "That mind and soul according well,
            May make one music as before,
                    But vaster."

Ida B. Wells-Barnett

(1862–1931)

from *Crusade for Justice*
Illinois Lynchings

Ida B. Wells-Barnett was born in Holly Springs,
Mississippi, to recently freed slave parents. Taught to
read early on by her father, a carpenter, she went on to
become a writer, teacher, and activist, perhaps best
known for a campaign against lynching that eventu-
ally took her to Europe.

In the following excerpt from her autobiography
Wells-Barnett recounts her visit, in the aftermath of a
lynching, to Cairo, Illinois, where she enlisted the aid
of a local lawyer to effect change and to pursue her
personal dream of justice first in the courts and finally
in the office of the governor.

Directly after the Springfield riot, at the next session of the legislature, a law was enacted which provided that any sheriff who permitted a prisoner to be taken from him and lynched should be removed from office. This bill was offered by Edward D. Green, who had been sent to Springfield to represent our race. Illinois had had not only a number of lynchings, but also a three days' riot at Springfield.

In due course of time the daily press announced that a lynching had taken place in Cairo, Illinois. The body of a white woman had been found in an alley in the residential district and, following the usual custom, the police immediately looked for a Negro. Finding a shiftless, penniless colored man known as "Frog" James, who seemed unable to give a good account of himself, according to police, this man was locked up in the police station and according to the newspapers a crowd began to gather around the station and the sheriff was sent for.

Mr. Frank Davis, the sheriff, after a brief conversation with the prisoner, took him to the railroad station, got on the train, and took him up into the woods accompanied by a single deputy. They remained there overnight. Next morning, when a mob had grown to great proportions, they too went up into the country and had no trouble in locating the sheriff and his prisoner. He was placed on a train and brought back to town, accompanied by the sheriff. The newspapers announced that as the train came to a standstill, some of the mob put a rope around "Frog's" neck and dragged him out of the train and to the most prominent corner of the town, where the rope was thrown over an electric light arch and the body hauled up above the heads of the crowd.

Five hundred bullets were fired into it, some of which cut the rope, and the body dropped to the ground. Members of the mob seized hold of the rope and dragged the body up Washington Street, followed by men, women, and children, some of the women pushing baby carriages. The body was taken near to the place where the corpse of the white girl had been found. Here they cut off his head, stuck it on a fence post, built a fire around the body and burned it to a crisp.

When the news of this horrible thing appeared in the papers, immediately a meeting was called and a telegram sent to Governor Deneen demanding that the sheriff of Alexander County be dispossessed. The newspapers had already quoted the governor as saying that he did not think it mandatory on him to displace the sheriff. But when our telegram reached him calling attention to the law, he immediately ousted him by telegram.

This same law provided that after the expiration of a short time, the sheriff would have the right to appear before the governor and show cause why he ought to be reinstated. We had a telegram from Governor Deneen informing us that on the following Wednesday the sheriff would appear before him demanding reinstatement. Mr. Barnett spent some time urging representative men of our race to appear before the governor and fight the sheriff's reinstatement.

Colonel Frank Dennison and Robert Taylor had been down in that county hunting at the time of this occurrence, and they were reported as saying they had seen signals being wig-wagged between the mob which was hunting "Frog" James and the sheriff who had him in charge. Colonel Dennison was asked to appear. He refused, saying that the whole episode was going to be a whitewash and he wasn't going to have anything to do with it. When he and others were reminded that it was their duty to fight the effort to reinstate the sheriff, they still refused.

This information was given us at the dinner table by Mr. Barnett, and he wound up his recital of his fruitless efforts that Saturday afternoon to get someone to appear by saying, "And so it would seem that you will have to go to Cairo and get the facts with which to confront the sheriff next Wednesday morning. And your train leaves at eight o'clock." I objected very strongly because I had already been accused by some of our men of jumping in ahead of them and doing work without giving them a chance.

It was not very convenient for me to be leaving home at that time, and for once I was quite willing to let them attend to the

job. Mr. Barnett replied that I knew it was important that somebody gather the evidence as well as he did, but if I was not
willing to go, there was nothing more to be said. He picked up
the evening paper and I picked up my baby and took her upstairs to bed. As usual I not only sang her to sleep but put
myself to sleep lying there beside her.

I was awakened by my oldest child, who said, "Mother, Pa
says it is time to go." "Go where?" I said. He said, "To take the
train to Cairo." I said, "I told your father downstairs that I was
not going. I don't see why I should have to go and do the work
that the others refuse." My boy was only ten years old. He and
the other children had been present at the dinner table when
their father told the story. He stood by the bedside a little
while and then said, "Mother if you don't go nobody else will."

I looked at my child standing there by the bed reminding me
of my duty, and I thought of that passage of Scripture which
tells of the wisdom from the mouths of babes and sucklings. I
thought if my child wanted me to go that I ought not to fall by
the wayside, and I said, "Tell daddy it is too late to catch the
train now, that I'll go in the morning. It is better for me to
arrive in Cairo after nightfall anyway."

Next morning all four of my children accompanied my husband and me to the station and saw me start on the journey.
They were intensely interested and for the first time were willing to see me leave home.

I reached Cairo after nightfall, and was driven to the home of
the leading A.M.E. minister, just before he went into church
for his evening service. I told him why I was there and asked if
he could give me any help in getting the sentiment of the
colored people and investigating facts. He said that they all
believed that "Frog" James had committed that murder. I
asked him if he had anything upon which to base that belief.
"Well," he said, "he was a worthless sort of fellow, just about
the kind of a man who would do a trick like that. Anyhow, all of
the colored people believe that and many of us have written
letters already to the governor asking the reinstatement of the
sheriff."

I sprang to my feet and asked him if he realized what he had
done in condoning the horrible lynching of a fellowman who
was a member of his race. Did he not know that if they con-

doned the lynching of one man, the time might come when they would have to condone that of other men higher up, providing they were black?

I asked him if he could direct me to the home of some other colored persons; that I had been sent to see all of them, and it wouldn't be fair for me to accept reports from one man alone. He gave me the names of one or two others, and I withdrew. I had expected to stop at his home, but after he told me that I had no desire to do so. One of the men named was Will Taylor, a druggist, whom I had known in Chicago, and I asked to be directed to his place. The minister's wife went with me because it was dark.

Mr. Taylor greeted me very cordially and I told him what my mission was. He also secured me a stopping place with persons by the name of Lewis, whom I afterward found were teachers in the colored high schools, both the man and his wife. They welcomed me very cordially and listened to my story. I told them why I was there; they gave me a bed. The next morning Mrs. Lewis came and informed me that she had already telephoned Dr. Taylor that she was sorry she could not continue to keep me. I found afterward that after they heard the story they felt that discretion was the better part of valor.

Mr. Taylor and I spent the day talking with colored citizens and ended with a meeting that night. I was driven to the place where the body of the murdered girl had been found, where the Negro had been burned, and saw about twenty-five representative colored people of the town that day. Many of those whom I found knew nothing whatever of the action that had been taken by the citizens of Chicago.

The meeting was largely attended and in my statement to them I said I had come down to be their mouthpiece; that I correctly understood how hard it would be for those who lived there to take an active part in the movement to oust the sheriff; that we were willing to take the lead in the matter but they must give me the facts; that it would be endangering the lives of other colored people in Illinois if we did not take a stand against the all too frequent lynchings which were taking place.

I went on to say that I came because I knew that they knew of my work against lynching for fifteen years past and felt that they would talk more freely to me and trust me more fully than they would someone of whom they knew nothing. I wanted them to tell me if Mr. Frank Davis had used his great power to protect the victim of the mob; if he had at any time placed him behind bars of the county jail as the law required; and if he had sworn in any deputies to help protect his prisoner as he was obliged by law to do until such time as he could be tried by due process of law. Although the meeting lasted for two hours, and although most of those present and speaking were friends of Frank Davis, some of whom had been deputy sheriffs in his office, not one of them could honestly say that Frank Davis had put his prisoner in the county jail or had done anything to protect him. I therefore offered a resolution to that effect which was almost unanimously adopted. There was one single objection by the ubiquitous "Uncle Tom" Negro who seems always present. I begged the people, if they could do nothing to help the movement to punish Frank Davis for such glaring negligence of his duty, that they would do nothing to hinder us.

Next morning before taking the train I learned of a Baptist ministers' meeting that was being held there and decided to attend for the purpose of having them pass the same resolution. I was told that it would do no good to make the effort and that it would delay me until midnight getting into Springfield. But I went, got an opportunity to speak, offered the resolution, told of the men who had sent letters to the governor, showed how that would confuse his mind as to the attitude of the colored people on the subject, and stated clearly that all such action would mean that we would have other lynchings in Illinois whenever it suited the mob anywhere.

I asked the adoption of the resolution passed the night before. There was discussion pro and con, and finally the moderator arose and said, "Brethren, they say an honest confession is good for the soul. I, too, am one of those men who have written to the governor asking Frank Davis's reinstatement. I knew he was a friend of ours; that the man who had taken his place has turned out all Negro deputies and put in Democrats, and I was told that when the mob placed the rope around "Frog" James's neck the sheriff tried to prevent them and was knocked down for his pains. But now that the sister has shown us plainly the construction that would be placed upon that letter, I want her when she appears before the governor tomorrow to tell him that I take that letter back and hereby sign my name to this resolution." By this time the old man was shedding tears. Needless to say the resolution went through without any further objections.

Mr. Barnett had told me that he would prepare a brief based upon what had been gleaned from the daily press, which would be in the post office at Springfield when I got there Wednesday morning; that if I found any facts contrary to those mentioned I could easily make the correction. There had been no precedent for this procedure, but he assumed that the attorney general would be present to represent the people.

When I entered the room at ten o'clock that morning I looked around for some of my own race, thinking that perhaps they would journey to Springfield for the hearing, even though they had been unwilling to go to Cairo to get the facts. Not a Negro face was in evidence! On the other side of the room there was Frank Davis, and with him one of the biggest lawyers in southern Illinois, so I was afterward told, who was also a state senator.

There was the parish priest, the state's attorney of Alexander County, the United States land commissioner, and about half a dozen other representative white men who had journeyed from Cairo to give aid and comfort to Frank Davis in his fight for reinstatement.

The governor said that they had no precedent and that he would now hear the plea to be made by the sheriff; whereupon this big lawyer proceeded to present his petition for reinstatement and backed it up with letters and telegrams from Democrats and Republicans, bankers, lawyers, doctors, editors of both daily papers, and heads of women's clubs and of men's organizations. The whole of the white population of Cairo was evidently behind Frank Davis and his demand for reinstatement.

In addition to this there were read these letters from Negro ministers and colored politicians. Special emphasis was laid upon them. Just before reading one of them the state senator said, "Your Excellency, I have known the writer of this letter since I was a boy. He has such a standing for truth and veracity in the community that if he were to tell me that black was white

I would believe him, and he, too, has written to ask that Frank Davis be reinstated."

And then he presented the names of nearly five hundred Negro men that had been signed to petitions circulated in three Negro barbershops. I had heard about these petitions while I was in Cairo and I went to the barbershops and saw them myself. Of course, there were only a few signers present when I was there, but to the few who happened to be standing around I gave the most blistering talk that I could lay my tongue to.

When the gentlemen had finished, Governor Deneen said, "I understand Mrs. Barnett is here to represent the colored people of Illinois." Not until that moment did I realize that the burden depended upon me. It so happened that Attorney A. M. Williams, a Negro lawyer of Springfield, having heard that I was in town, came over to the Capitol to invite me to his home for dinner. Finding me by myself, he immediately camped by my side and remained with me all through the ordeal. I was indeed thankful for this help, since never before had I been confronted with a situation that called for legal knowledge.

I began by reading the brief which Mr. Barnett prepared in due legal form. I then launched out to tell of my investigation in Cairo. Before I had gotten very far the clock struck twelve, and Springfield being a country town, everything stopped so people could go home to dinner, which was served in the middle of the day. I did not go with Mr. Williams to his home but urged him to do so.

I went to his office and stayed there, getting the balance of my address in shape. At two o'clock he came for me and we went back to the Capitol. I resumed the statement of facts I had found—of the meeting held Monday night and of the resolution passed there which stated Frank Davis had not put his prisoner in the county jail or sworn in deputies to protect him although he knew there was talk of mob violence.

I was interrupted at this point by Mr. Davis's lawyer. "Who wrote that resolution?" he asked. "Don't answer him," said Mr. Williams, "he is only trying to confuse you." "Isn't it a fact," said Mr. Davis's counsel, "that you wrote that resolution?" "Yes," I said, "I wrote the resolution and presented it, but the audience adopted and passed it. It was done in the same way as the petition which you have presented here. Those petitions were signed by men, but they were typewritten and worded by somebody who was interested enough in Mr. Davis to place them where the men could reach them. But that is not all, Governor; I have here the signature of that leading Baptist minister who has been so highly praised to you. I went to his meeting yesterday and when I told him what a mistake it was to seem to condone the outrage on a human being by writing a letter asking for the reinstatement of a man who permitted it to be done, he rose and admitted he had sent the letter which has been read in your hearing, but having realized his mistake he wanted me to tell you that he endorsed the resolutions which I have here, and here is his name signed to them."

And then I wound up by saying, "Governor, the state of Illinois has had too many terrible lynchings within her borders within the last few years. If this man is sent back it will be an encouragement to those who resort to mob violence and will do so at any time, well knowing they will not be called to account for so doing. All the colored friends in Cairo are friends of Mr. Davis and they seem to feel that because his successor, a Democrat, has turned out all the Republican deputies, they owe their duty to the party to ask the return of a Republican sheriff. But not one of these, Mr. Davis's friends, would say that for one moment he had his prisoner in the county jail where the law demands that he should be placed or that he swore in a single deputy to help protect his life until he could be tried by law. It looked like encouragement to the mob to have the chief law officer in the county take that man up in the woods and keep him until the mob got big enough to come after him. I repeat, Governor, that if this man is reinstated, it will simply mean an increase of lynchings in the state of Illinois and an encouragement to mob violence."

When I had finished it was late in the afternoon, and the governor said that as he wanted to leave town next day he would suggest that both sides get together and agree upon a statement of fact. He asked that we return that evening about eight o'clock. The big lawyer was very unwilling to do this. He and his party expected to go through the form of presenting that petition and taking the afternoon train back to Cairo, arriving there in time for dinner.

Instead we had to have a night session which would necessitate their remaining over until the next day. He angrily tossed the petition across the table like a bone to a dog and insisted that there was nothing else to be considered. But the governor held firm, and I was quite willing to go home and get something to eat. I was quite surprised when the session adjourned that every one of those white men came over and shook my hand and congratulated me on what they called the wonderful speech I had made. Mr. Frank Davis himself shook hands with me and said, "I bear you no grudge for what you have done, Mrs. Barnett." The state's attorney of Alexander County wanted to know if I was not a lawyer. The United States land commissioner, a little old man, said, "Whether you are a lawyer or not you made the best speech of the day." It was he who told me that the state senator who had represented Mr. Davis, whose name I have forgotten, was the biggest lawyer in southern Illinois.

When we returned to the night session, there was all the difference in the world in the attitude of those white men. The state's attorney and the big lawyer had already drawn up what they called an agreed statement of fact and were waiting for my ratification of the same. When I picked up the pen and began to draw a line through some of the phrases which described the occurrence in Cairo, the state's attorney asked what I was doing.

I told him that although I was not a lawyer, I did know a statement of fact when I saw one, and that in the description of the things which had taken place on the day of "Frog" James's arrest, he had said that "the sheriff, fearing an outbreak by the mob, had taken 'Frog' to the railroad station." I had drawn a line through the words which said, "fearing an outbreak by the mob," because that was his opinion rather than a fact. His face grew red, but he let it ride.

By the time we had finished it was ten o'clock. The governor had been waiting in the room across the hall while we argued back and forth over this agreed statement of fact. He then suggested that it was too late to go on, and asked that we return next morning. This we did and when I walked up the Capitol steps next morning every one of those white men with whom I had been in battle the day before swept off his hat at my approach. The big lawyer said, "Mrs. Barnett, we have decided that if you are willing we won't make another argument over this matter but will submit it all for the governor's action." I replied that whatever my lawyer advised, that I would do, and turned to Mr. Williams, who was still with me.

After scanning the papers he, too, agreed to their suggestion. We went into the governor's office and submitted the case without further argument, bade each other adieu and left for our homes. Mr. Williams said as we went down the steps, "Oh, the governor's going to send him back. I don't see how he can help it with such terrific pressure being brought to bear to have him to do so. But, by george, if I had time to dig up the law I would have furnished him so much of it that he wouldn't dare do so." I said, "We have done the best we could under the circumstances, and angels could do no more."

The following Tuesday morning Governor Deneen issued one of the finest state papers that emanated from him during his whole eight years in the Capitol. The summary of his proclamation was that Frank Davis could not be reinstated because he had not properly protected the prisoner within his keeping and that lynch law could have no place in Illinois.

That was in 1909, and from that day until the present there has been no lynching in the state. Every sheriff, whenever there seem to be any signs of the kind, immediately telegraphs the governor for troops. And to Governor Deneen belongs the credit.*

---

* The *Chicago Defender,* 1 January 1910, carried the following account of the manner in which Mrs. Barnett followed up the Cairo investigation: "The Bethel Literary and History Club held its first meeting under the leadership of newly elected officers last Sunday. Mrs. Ida B. Wells-Barnett gave a report of her investigation of the recent Cairo, Illinois, lynching which was commendable in every detail. If we only had a few men with the backbone of Mrs. Barnett, lynching would soon come to a halt in America. A collection of $13.25 was taken and turned over to the citizens committee to apply on money spent by Mrs. Barnett in making her investigation."

Mary McLeod Bethune

(1875–1955)

A College on a Garbage Dump

Born into a family of seventeen children in Maysville, South Carolina, educator Mary McLeod Bethune dedicated her considerable talents, a rich genius, and boundless energy to improving opportunity for the black youth of America. To that end she founded the school that eventually became Bethune-Cookman College and served as its president from 1904 to 1942. She was also a special advisor on minority affairs to President Franklin D. Roosevelt, who in 1936 appointed her to the directorship of the Division of Negro Affairs of the National Youth Administration. During World War II she worked as a special assistant to the Secretary of State and was appointed by President Truman to the twelve-member Committee for National Defense. Among her numerous awards are eleven university honorary degrees and the Springarn Medal of the NAACP.

*In the article that follows, from the June 1941 issue
of* Who, The Magazine About People, *Bethune recounts
how she began to make her vision of a better future for
young black Americans come true.*

I was born in Maysville, South Carolina, a country town in the
midst of rice and cotton fields. My mother, father, and older
brothers and sisters had been slaves until the Emancipation
Proclamation. . . . After Mother was freed she continued in
the McIntosh employ until she had earned enough to buy five
acres of her own from her former master. Then my parents
built our cabin, cutting and burning the logs with their own
hands. I was the last of seventeen children, ten girls and seven
boys. When I was born, the first free child in their own home,
my mother exulted, "Thank God, Mary came under our own
vine and fig tree."

Mother was of royal African blood, of a tribe ruled by ma-
triarchs. . . . Throughout all her bitter years of slavery she
had managed to preserve a queenlike dignity. She supervised
all the business of the family. Over the course of years, by the
combined work and thrift of the family, and Mother's foresight,
Father was able to enlarge our home site to thirty-five acres.

Most of my brothers and sisters had married and left home
when I was growing up—there were only seven or eight children still around. Mother worked in the fields at Father's side,
cutting rice and cotton, and chopping fodder. Each of us children had tasks to perform, according to our aptitudes. Some
milked the cows, others helped with the washing, ironing,
cooking, and house-cleaning. I was my father's champion cotton picker. When I was only nine, I could pick 250 pounds of
cotton a day. . . .

[In those days] it was almost impossible for a Negro child,
especially in the South, to get education. There were hundreds
of square miles, sometimes entire states, without a single Negro school, and colored children were not allowed in public

schools with white children. Mr. Lincoln had told our race we were free, but mentally we were still enslaved.

A knock on our door changed my life over-night. There stood a young woman, a colored missionary sent by the Northern Presbyterian Church to start a school near by. She asked my parents to send me. Every morning I picked up a little pail of milk and bread, and walked five miles to school; every afternoon, five miles home. But I walked always on winged feet.

The whole world opened to me when I learned to read. As soon as I understood something, I rushed back and taught it to the others at home. My teacher had a box of Bibles and texts, and she gave me one of each for my very own. That same day the teacher opened the Bible to John 3:16, and read: "For God so loved the world, that He gave His only begotten Son, that whosoever believeth in Him should not perish, but have everlasting life."

With these words the scales fell from my eyes and the light came flooding in. My sense of inferiority, my fear of handicaps, dropped away. "Whosoever," it said. No Jew nor Gentile, no Catholic nor Protestant, no black nor white; just "whosoever." It meant that I, a humble Negro girl, had just as much chance as anybody in the sight and love of God. These words stored up a battery of faith and confidence and determination in my heart, which has not failed me to this day. . . .

By the time I was fifteen I had taken every subject taught at our little school and could go no farther. Dissatisfied, because this taste of learning had aroused my appetite, I was forced to stay at home. Father's mule died—a major calamity—and he had to mortgage the farm to buy another. In those days, when a Negro mortgaged his property they never let him get out of debt.

I used to kneel in the cotton fields and pray that the door of opportunity should be opened to me once more, so that I might give to others whatever I might attain.

My prayers were answered. A white dressmaker, way off in Denver, Colorado, had become interested in the work of our little neighborhood school and had offered to pay for the higher education of some worthy girl. My teacher selected me, and I was sent to Scotia Seminary in Concord, North Carolina. There I studied English, Latin, higher mathematics, and science, and after classes I worked in the Scotia laundry and kitchen to earn as much extra money as I could. . . .

When I was graduated, I offered myself eagerly for missionary service in Africa, but the church authorities felt I was not sufficiently mature. Instead, they gave me another scholarship, and I spent two years at the Moody Bible School, in Chicago. Again I offered myself for missionary service, and again I was refused. Cruelly disappointed, I got a position at Haines Institute, in Augusta, Georgia, presided over by dynamic Lucy C. Laney, a pioneer Negro educator. From her I got a new vision: my life work lay not in Africa but in my own country. And with the first money I earned I began to save in order to pay off Father's mortgage, which had hung over his head for ten years!

During my early teaching days I met my future husband. He too was then a teacher, but to him teaching was only a job. Following our marriage, he entered upon a business career. When our baby son was born, I gave up my work temporarily, so that I could be all mother for one precious year. After that I got restless again to be back at my beloved work, for having a child made me more than ever determined to build better lives for my people. . . .

In 1904 I heard . . . [that] Henry Flagler was building the Florida East Coast Railroad, and hundreds of Negroes had gathered in Florida for construction work. . . .

I [went to] Daytona Beach, a beautiful little village, shaded by great oaks and giant pines. . . . I found a shabby four-room cottage, for which the owner wanted a rental of eleven dollars a month. My total capital was a dollar and a half, but I talked him into trusting me until the end of the month for the rest. This was in September. A friend let me stay at her home, and I plunged into the job of creating something from nothing. I spoke at churches, and the ministers let me take up collections. I buttonholed every woman who would listen to me. . . .

On October 3, 1904, I opened the doors of my school, with an enrollment of five little girls, aged from eight to twelve, whose parents paid me fifty cents' weekly tuition. My own child was the only boy in the school. Though I hadn't a penny left, I considered cash money as the smallest part of my resources. I had faith in a living God, faith in myself, and a desire to serve. . . .

We burned logs and used the charred splinters as pencils, and mashed elderberries for ink. I begged strangers for a broom, a lamp, a bit of cretonne to put around the packing case which served as my desk. I haunted the city dump and the trash piles behind hotels, retrieving discarded linen and kitchenware, cracked dishes, broken chairs, pieces of old lumber. Everything was scoured and mended. This was part of the training to salvage, to reconstruct, to make bricks without straw. As parents began gradually to leave their children overnight, I had to provide sleeping accommodations. I took corn sacks for mattresses. Then I picked Spanish moss from trees, dried and cured it, and used it as a substitute for mattress hair.

The school expanded fast. In less than two years I had 250 pupils. In desperation I hired a large hall next to my original little cottage, and used it as a combined dormitory and classroom. I concentrated more and more on girls, as I felt that they especially were hampered by lack of educational opportunities. . . .

I had many volunteer workers and a few regular teachers, who were paid from fifteen to twenty-five dollars a month and board. I was supposed to keep the balance of the funds for my own pocket, but there was never any balance—only a yawning hole. I wore old clothes sent me by mission boards, recut and redesigned for me in our dress-making classes. At last I saw that our only solution was to stop renting space, and to buy and build our own college.

Near by was a field, popularly called Hell's Hole, which was used as a dumping ground. I approached the owner, determined to buy it. The price was $250. In a daze, he finally agreed to take five dollars down, and the balance in two years. I promised to be back in a few days with the initial payment. He never knew it, but I didn't have five dollars. I raised this sum selling ice cream and sweet-potato pies to the workmen on construction jobs, and I took the owner his money in small change wrapped in my handkerchief.

That's how the Bethune-Cookman college campus started.

We at once discovered the need of an artesian well. The estimate was two hundred dollars. Here again we started with an insignificant payment, the balance remaining on trust. But what use was a plot without a building? I hung onto contractors' coat-tails, begging for loads of sand and second-hand bricks. I went to all the carpenters, mechanics, and plasterers in town, pleading with them to contribute a few hours' work in the evening in exchange for sandwiches and tuition for their children and themselves.

Slowly the building rose from its foundations. The name over the entrance still reads Faith Hall.

I had learned already that one of my most important jobs was to be a good beggar! I rang doorbells and tackled cold prospects without a lead. I wrote articles for whoever would print them, distributed leaflets, rode interminable miles of dusty roads on my old bicycle; invaded churches, clubs, lodges, chambers of commerce. . . .

Strongly interracial in my ideas, I looked forward to an advisory board of trustees composed of both white and colored people. I did my best missionary work among the prominent winter visitors to Florida. I would pick out names of "newly arrived guests," from the newspapers, and write letters asking whether I could call.

One of these letters went to James N. Gamble, of Procter & Gamble. He invited me to call at noon the next day. . . .

Mr. Gamble himself opened the door, and when I gave my name he looked at me in astonishment. "Are you the woman trying to build a school here? Why, I thought you were a white woman."

I laughed. "Well, you see how white I am." Then I told my story. "I'd like you to visit my school and, if it pleases you, to stand behind what I have in my mind," I finished.

He consented. . . . The next day . . . he made a careful tour of inspection, agreed to be a trustee, and gave me a check for $150—although I hadn't mentioned money. For many years he was one of our most generous friends.

Another experience with an unexpected ending was my first meeting with J. S. Peabody, of Columbia City, Indiana. After I had made an eloquent appeal for funds he gave me exactly twenty-five cents. I swallowed hard, thanked him smilingly, and later entered the contribution in my account book.

Two years later he reappeared. "Do you remember me?" he

asked. "I'm one of your contributors." I greeted him cordially. He went on: "I wonder if you recall how much I gave you when I was here last?"

Not wishing to embarrass him, I told a white lie: "I'll have to look it up in my account book." Then after finding the entry, I said, "Oh, yes, Mr. Peabody, you gave us twenty-five cents."

Instead of being insulted, he was delighted that we kept account of such minute gifts. He immediately handed me a check for a hundred dollars and made arrangements to furnish the building. When he died, a few years later, he left the school $10,000. . . .

One evening I arranged a meeting at an exclusive hotel, expecting to talk to a large audience of wealthy people. But so many social functions were taking place that same night that I was greeted by an audience of exactly six. I was sick at heart—but I threw all my enthusiasm into my talk. At the end a gentleman dropped a twenty-dollar bill in the hat.

The next day he unexpectedly appeared at the school. He said his name was Thomas H. White, but it meant nothing to me. He looked around, asked where the shabby but immaculate straw matting on the floor came from. I said, "The city dump." He saw a large box of corn meal, and inquired what else there was to eat. I replied, "That's all we have at the moment." Then he walked about the grounds and saw an unfinished building, on which construction work had been temporarily abandoned for lack of funds. That was nothing new—there were always unfinished buildings cluttering up the landscape of our school. But I think the crowning touch was when he saw our dressmaking class working with a broken-down Singer sewing machine.

He turned to me, saying, "I believe you are on the right track. This is the most promising thing I've seen in Florida." He pressed a check in my hand, and left. The check was for $250. The following day he returned again, with a new sewing machine. Only then did I learn that Mr. White was the Singer people's principal competitor.

Mr. White brought plasterers, carpenters, and materials to finish our new building. Week after week he appeared, with blankets for the children, shoes and a coat for me, everything we had dreamed of getting. When I thanked him, with tears in my eyes, for his generosity, he waved me aside.

"I've never invested a dollar that has brought greater returns than the dollars I have given you," he told me. And when this great soul died, he left a trust of $67,000, the interest to be paid us "as long as there is a school."

Do you wonder I have faith?

I never stop to plan. I take things step by step. For thirty-five years we have never had to close our doors for lack of food or fuel, although often we had to live from day to day. . . .

As the school expanded, whenever I saw a need for some training or service we did not supply, I schemed to add it to our curriculum. Sometimes that took years. When I came to Florida, there were no hospitals where a Negro could go. A student became critically ill with appendicitis, so I went to a local hospital and begged a white physician to take her in and operate. My pleas were so desperate he finally agreed. A few days after the operation, I visited my pupil.

When I appeared at the front door of the hospital, the nurse ordered me around to the back way. I thrust her aside—and found my little girl segregated in a corner of the porch behind the kitchen. Even my toes clenched with rage.

That decided me. I called on three of my faithful friends, asking them to buy a little cottage behind our school as a hospital. They agreed, and we started with two beds.

From this humble start grew a fully equipped twenty-bed hospital—our college infirmary and a refuge for the needy throughout the state. It was staffed by white and black physicians and by our own student nurses. We ran this hospital for twenty years as part of our contribution to community life; but a short time ago, to ease our financial burden, the city took it over.

Gradually, as educational facilities expanded and there were other places where small children could go, we put the emphasis on high-school and junior-college training. In 1922, Cookman College, a men's school, the first in the state for the higher education of Negroes, amalgamated with us. The combined coeducational college, now run under the auspices of the Methodist Episcopal Church, is called Bethune-Cookman College. We have fourteen modern buildings, a beautiful campus of thirty-two acres, an enrollment in regular and summer sessions of 600 students, a faculty and staff of thirty-two, and 1,800 graduates. The college property, now valued at more than $800,000, is entirely unencumbered.

When I walk through the campus, with its stately palms and well-kept lawns, and think back to the dump-heap foundation, I rub my eyes and pinch myself. And I remember my childish visions in the cotton fields.

But values cannot be calculated in ledger figures and property. More than all else the college has fulfilled my ideals of distinctive training and service. Extending far beyond the immediate sphere of its graduates and students, it has already enriched the lives of 100,000 Negroes.

In 1934, President Franklin D. Roosevelt appointed me director of the division of Negro affairs of the National Youth Administration. My main task now is to supervise the training provided for 600,000 Negro children, and I have to run the college by remote control. Every few weeks, however, I snatch a day or so and return to my beloved home.

This is a strenuous program. The doctor shakes his head and says, "Mrs. Bethune, slow down a little. Relax! Take it just a little easier." I promise to reform, but in an hour the promise is forgotten.

For I am my mother's daughter, and the drums of Africa still beat in my heart. They will not let me rest while there is a single Negro boy or girl without a chance to prove his worth.

Martin Luther King, Jr.

(1929–1968)

I Have a Dream

Martin Luther King, Jr., was born in Atlanta, Georgia. He graduated from Morehouse College with a bachelor of arts degree at the age of eighteen; he received his Ph.D. in theology seven years later from Boston University. In December 1955 King had been the pastor of Dexter Avenue Baptist Church in Montgomery, Alabama, for more than a year when Rosa Parks made national headlines by refusing to surrender her seat to a white man on a segregated bus. Her protest led to the Montgomery bus boycott, the first of the many organized acts of civil disobedience that fueled the civil rights movement, as well as to the foundation of the Southern Christian Leadership Conference under King's direction. Under his charismatic leadership the SCLC and the movement flourished until King's assassination on the balcony of the Lorraine Motel in Memphis on April 4, 1968.

"I Have a Dream" is King's most famous speech. It was delivered on August 28, 1963, to more than two hundred thousand people at the March on Washington.

I am happy to join with you today in what will go down in history as the greatest demonstration for freedom in the history of our nation.

Fivescore years ago, a great American, in whose symbolic shadow we stand today, signed the Emancipation Proclamation. This momentous decree came as a great beacon light of hope to millions of Negro slaves who had been seared in the flames of withering injustice. It came as a joyous daybreak to end the long night of their captivity.

But one hundred years later, the Negro still is not free; one hundred years later, the life of the Negro is still sadly crippled by the manacles of segregation and the chains of discrimination; one hundred years later, the Negro lives on a lonely island of poverty in the midst of a vast ocean of material prosperity; one hundred years later, the Negro is still languished in the corners of American society and finds himself in exile in his own land.

So we've come here today to dramatize a shameful condition. In a sense we've come to our nation's capital to cash a check. When the architects of our republic wrote the magnificent words of the Constitution and the Declaration of Independence, they were signing a promissory note to which every American was to fall heir. This note was the promise that all men, yes, black men as well as white men, would be guaranteed the unalienable rights of life, liberty, and the pursuit of happiness.

It is obvious today that America has defaulted on this promissory note in so far as her citizens of color are concerned. Instead of honoring this sacred obligation, America has given the Negro people a bad check; a check which has come back marked "insufficient funds." We refuse to believe that there are insufficient funds in the great vaults of opportunity of this nation. And so we've come to cash this check, a check that will give us upon demand the riches of freedom and the security of justice.

We have also come to this hallowed spot to remind America of the fierce urgency of now. This is no time to engage in the luxury of cooling off or to take the tranquilizing drug of gradualism. Now is the time to make real the promises of democracy; now is the time to rise from the dark and desolate valley of segregation to the sunlit path of racial justice; now is the time to lift our nation from the quicksands of racial injustice to the solid rock of brotherhood; now is the time to make justice a reality for all God's children. It would be fatal for the nation to overlook the urgency of the moment. This sweltering summer of the Negro's legitimate discontent will not pass until there is an invigorating autumn of freedom and equality.

Nineteen sixty-three is not an end, but a beginning. And those who hope that the Negro needed to blow off steam and will now be content, will have a rude awakening if the nation returns to business as usual.

There will be neither rest nor tranquility in America until the Negro is granted his citizenship rights. The whirlwinds of revolt will continue to shake the foundations of our nation until the bright day of justice emerges.

But there is something that I must say to my people who stand on the warm threshold which leads into the palace of justice. In the process of gaining our rightful place we must not be guilty of wrongful deeds.

Let us not seek to satisfy our thirst for freedom by drinking from the cup of bitterness and hatred. We must forever conduct our struggle on the high plane of dignity and discipline. We must not allow our creative protest to degenerate into physical violence. Again and again we must rise to the majestic heights of meeting physical force with soul force.

The marvelous new militancy which has engulfed the Negro community must not lead us to a distrust of all white people, for many of our white brothers, as evidenced by their presence here today, have come to realize that their destiny is tied up with our destiny and they have come to realize that their freedom is inextricably bound to our freedom. This offense we share mounted to storm the battlements of injustice must be carried forth by a biracial army. We cannot walk alone.

And as we walk, we must make the pledge that we shall always march ahead. We cannot turn back. There are those who are asking the devotees of civil rights, "When will you be satisfied?" We can never be satisfied as long as the Negro is the victim of the unspeakable horrors of police brutality.

We can never be satisfied as long as our bodies, heavy with fatigue of travel, cannot gain lodging in the motels of the highways and the hotels of the cities. We cannot be satisfied as long as the Negro's basic mobility is from a smaller ghetto to a larger one.

We can never be satisfied as long as our children are stripped of their selfhood and robbed of their dignity by signs stating "for whites only." We cannot be satisfied as long as a Negro in Mississippi cannot vote and a Negro in New York believes he has nothing for which to vote. No, we are not satisfied, and we will not be satisfied until justice rolls down like waters and righteousness like a mighty stream.

I am not unmindful that some of you have come here out of excessive trials and tribulation. Some of you have come fresh from narrow jail cells. Some of you have come from areas where your quest for freedom left you battered by the storms of persecution and staggered by the winds of police brutality. You have been the veterans of creative suffering. Continue to work with the faith that unearned suffering is redemptive.

Go back to Mississippi; go back to Alabama; go back to South Carolina; go back to Georgia; go back to Louisiana; go back to the slums and ghettos of the northern cities, knowing that somehow this situation can, and will be changed. Let us not wallow in the valley of despair.

So I say to you, my friends, that even though we must face the difficulties of today and tomorrow, I still have a dream. It is a dream deeply rooted in the American dream that one day this nation will rise up and live out the true meaning of its creed— we hold these truths to be self-evident, that all men are created equal.

I have a dream that one day on the red hills of Georgia, sons of former slaves and sons of former slave-owners will be able to sit down together at the table of brotherhood.

I have a dream that one day, even the state of Mississippi, a state sweltering with the heat of injustice, sweltering with the heat of oppression, will be transformed into an oasis of freedom and justice.

I have a dream my four little children will one day live in a nation where they will not be judged by the color of their skin but by content of their character. I have a dream today!

I have a dream that one day, down in Alabama, with its vicious racists, with its governor having his lips dripping with the words of interposition and nullification, that one day, right there in Alabama, little black boys and black girls will be able to join hands with little white boys and white girls as sisters and brothers. I have a dream today!

I have a dream that one day every valley shall be exalted, every hill and mountain shall be made low, the rough places shall be made plain, and the crooked places shall be made straight and the glory of the Lord will be revealed and all flesh shall see it together.

This is our hope. This is the faith that I go back to the South with.

With this faith we will be able to hear out of the mountain of despair a stone of hope. With this faith we will be able to transform the jangling discords of our nation into a beautiful symphony of brotherhood.

With this faith we will be able to work together, to pray together, to struggle together, to go to jail together, to stand up for freedom together, knowing that we will be free one day. This will be the day when all of God's children will be able to sing with new meaning—"my country 'tis of thee; sweet land of liberty; of thee I sing; land where my fathers died, land of the pilgrim's pride; from every mountain side, let freedom ring" — and if America is to be a great nation, this must become true.

So let freedom ring from the prodigious hilltops of New Hampshire.

Let freedom ring from the mighty mountains of New York.

Let freedom ring from the heightening Alleghenies of Pennsylvania.

Let freedom ring from the snow-capped Rockies of Colorado.

Let freedom ring from the curvaceous slopes of California.

But not only that.

Let freedom ring from Stone Mountain of Georgia.

Let freedom ring from Lookout Mountain of Tennessee.

Let freedom ring from every hill and molehill of Mississippi, from every mountainside, let freedom ring.

And when we allow freedom to ring, when we let it ring from every village and hamlet, from every state and city, we will be able to speed up that day when all of God's children—black men and white men, Jews and Gentiles, Catholics and Protestants—will be able to join hands and to sing in the words of the old Negro spiritual, "Free at last, free at last; thank God Almighty, we are free at last."

III

A Different Image

*African Americans needed a dream—and a history—of their own
to free them from the shackles of a slave mentality
and to image more positively their racial identity . . .
not as slaves or coloreds or boys or mammies
but as Negroes, and later as blacks, as people of color,
as African Americans.*

Dudley Randall

(b. 1914)

A Different Image

Washington D.C. native Dudley Randall was educated at the University of Michigan, Washington State, and the University of Ghana. He founded The Broadside Press, one of the first small presses in America to work exclusively with black authors. He himself is a writer and poet.

In the poem that follows Randall speaks to the necessity for African Americans to redefine their identity in terms of a new image. The poem first appeared in a collection of poems by Randall titled Cities Burning.

The age
requires this task:
create
a different image;
re-animate
the mask.

Shatter the icons of slavery and fear.
Replace
the leer
of the minstrel's burnt-cork face
with a proud, serene
and classic bronze of Benin.

Marcus Garvey

(1887–1940)

---

from *The Philosophy and Opinions of
Marcus Garvey*
Speech Delivered on Emancipation Day
at Liberty Hall, New York City, N.Y. U.S.A.
January 1, 1922
&
The Future As I See It

*Born in Jamaica and educated at the University of
London, Marcus Garvey emigrated to America in 1916
and in the aftermath of the First World War founded
the Universal Negro Improvement Association.
Through the UNIA Garvey hoped to realize his vision
of redeeming Africa from European control by uniting
all her scattered children together into a mighty force
four hundred million strong. Garvey strove to make
African Americans take possession of themselves, their
future, and their continent. Repatriation figured significantly into his scheme, and the UNIA did in fact
establish a settlement in Liberia.*

The following pieces clarify Garvey's vision of a mighty united African people whose future includes the reclamation of their true homeland.

SPEECH DELIVERED ON EMANCIPATION DAY

Fifty-nine years ago Abraham Lincoln signed the Emancipation Proclamation declaring four million Negroes in this country free. Several years prior to that Queen Victoria of England signed the Emancipation Proclamation that set at liberty hundreds of thousands of West Indian Negro slaves.

West Indian Negroes celebrate their emancipation on the first day of August of every year. The American Negroes celebrate their emancipation on the first of January of every year. Tonight we are here to celebrate the emancipation of the slaves in this country.

We are the descendants of the men and women who suffered in this country for two hundred and fifty years under that barbarous, that brutal institution known as slavery. You who have not lost trace of your history will recall the fact that over three hundred years ago your fore-bears were taken from the great Continent of Africa and brought here for the purpose of using them as slaves. Without mercy, without any sympathy they worked our fore-bears. They suffered, they bled, they died. But with their sufferings, with their blood, which they shed in their death, they had a hope that one day their posterity would be free, and we are assembled here tonight as the children of their hope.

I trust each and every one of you therefore will realize that you have a duty which is incumbent upon you; a duty that you must perform, because our fore-bears who suffered, who bled, who died had hopes that are not yet completely realized. They hoped that we as their children would be free, but they also hoped that their country from whence they came would also be free to their children, their grand-children and great grand-children at some future time. It is for the freedom of that country—that Motherland of ours—that four and a half million Negroes, as members of the Universal Negro Improvement Association, are laboring today.

This race of ours gave civilization, gave art, gave science; gave literature to the world. But it has been the way with races and nations. The one race stands out prominently in the one century or in the one age; and in another century or age it passes off the stage of action, and another race takes its place. The Negro once occupied a high position in the world, scientifically, artistically and commercially, but in the balancing of the great scale of evolution, we lost our place and some one, other than ourselves occupies the stand we once held.

God never intended that man should enslave his fellow, and the price of such a sin or such a violation of Heaven's law must be paid by every one. As for me, because of the blessed past, because of the history that I know, so long as there is within me the breath of life and the spirit of God, I shall struggle on and urge others of our race to struggle on to see that justice is done to the black peoples of the world. Yes, we appreciate the sorrows of the past, and we are going to work in the present that the sorrows of our generation shall not be perpetuated in the future. On the contrary, we shall strive that by our labors, succeeding generations of our own shall call us blessed, even as we call the generation of the past blessed today. And they indeed were blest. They were blest with a patience not yet known to man. A patience that enabled them to endure the tortures and the sufferings of slavery for two hundred and fifty years. Why? Was it because they loved slavery so? No. It was because they loved this generation more—Isn't it wonderful. Transcendent? What then are you going to do to show your appreciation of this love, what gratitude are you going to manifest in return for what they have done for you? As for me, knowing the sufferings of my fore-fathers I shall give back to Africa that liberty that she once enjoyed hundreds of years ago, before her own sons and daughters were taken from her shores and brought in chains to this Western World.

No better gift can I give in honor of the memory of the love of my fore-parents for me, and in gratitude of the sufferings they endured that I might be free; no grander gift can I bear to the sacred memory of the generation past than a free and a redeemed Africa—a monument for all eternity—for all times.

As by the action of the world, as by the conduct of all the races and nations it is apparent that not one of them has the sense of justice, the sense of love, the sense of equity, the sense of charity, that would make men happy, and make God satisfied. It is apparent that it is left to the Negro to play such a part in human affairs—for when we look to the Anglo-Saxon we see him full of greed, avarice, no mercy, no love, no charity. We go from the white man to the yellow man, and we see the same unenviable characteristics in the Japanese. Therefore we must believe that the Psalmist had great hopes of this race of ours when he prophesied "Princes shall come out of Egypt and Ethiopia shall stretch forth her hands unto God."

If humanity is regarded as made up of the children of God and God loves all humanity (we all know that) then God will be more pleased with that race that protects all humanity than with the race that outrages the children of God.

And so tonight we celebrate this anniversary of our emancipation, we do it not with regret, on the contrary we do it with an abiding confidence, a hope and faith in ourselves and in our God. And the faith that we have is a faith that will ultimately take us back to that ancient place, that ancient position that we once occupied, when Ethiopia was in her glory.

THE FUTURE AS I SEE IT

It comes to the individual, the race, the nation, once in a life time to decide upon the course to be pursued as a career. The hour has now struck for the individual Negro as well as the entire race to decide the course that will be pursued in the interest of our own liberty.

We who make up the Universal Negro Improvement Association have decided that we shall go forward, upward and onward toward the great goal of human liberty. We have determined among ourselves that all barriers placed in the way of our progress must be removed, must be cleared away for we desire to see the light of a brighter day.

The Negro is Ready

The Universal Negro Improvement Association for five years has been proclaiming to the world the readiness of the Negro to carve out a pathway for himself in the course of life. Men of other races and nations have become alarmed at this attitude of the Negro in his desire to do things for himself and by himself. This alarm has become so universal that organizations have been brought into being here, there and everywhere for the purpose of deterring and obstructing this forward move of our race. Propaganda has been waged here, there and everywhere for the purpose of misinterpreting the intention of this organization; some have said that this organization seeks to create discord and discontent among the races; some say we are organized for the purpose of hating other people. Every sensible, sane and honest-minded person knows that the Universal Negro Improvement Association has no such intention. We are organized for the absolute purpose of bettering our condition, industrially, commercially, socially, religiously and politically. We are organized not to hate other men, but to lift ourselves, and to demand respect of all humanity. We have a program that we believe to be righteous; we believe it to be just, and we have made up our minds to lay down ourselves on the altar of sacrifice for the realization of this great hope of ours, based upon the foundation of righteousness. We declare to the world that Africa must be free, that the entire Negro race must be emancipated from industrial bondage, peonage and serfdom; we make no compromise, we make no apology in this our declaration. We do not desire to create offense on the part of other races, but we are determined that we shall be heard, that we shall be given the rights to which we are entitled.

The Propaganda Of Our Enemies

For the purpose of creating doubts about the work of the Universal Negro Improvement Association, many attempts have been made to cast shadow and gloom over our work. They have even written the most uncharitable things about our organization; they have spoken so unkindly of our effort, but what do we care? They spoke unkindly and uncharitably about all the reform movements that have helped in the betterment of humanity. They maligned the great movement of the Christian religion; they maligned the great liberation movements of America, of France, of England, of Russia; can we expect, then, to escape being maligned in this, our desire for the liberation of Africa and the freedom of four hundred million Negroes of the world?

We have unscrupulous men and organizations working in opposition to us. Some trying to capitalize the new spirit that has come to the Negro to make profit out of it to their own selfish benefit; some are trying to set back the Negro from seeing the hope of his own liberty, and thereby poisoning our people's mind against the motives of our organization; but every sensible far-seeing Negro in this enlightened age knows what propaganda means. It is the medium of discrediting that which you are opposed to, so that the propaganda of our enemies will be of little avail as soon as we are rendered able to carry to our peoples scattered throughout the world the true message of our great organization.

"Crocodiles" As Friends

Men of the Negro race, let me say to you that a greater future is in store for us; we have no cause to lose hope, to become faint-hearted. We must realize that upon ourselves depend our destiny, our future; we must carve out that future, that destiny, and we who make up the Universal Negro Improvement Association have pledged ourselves that nothing in the world shall stand in our way, nothing in the world shall discourage us, but opposition shall make us work harder, shall bring us closer together so that as one man the millions of us will march on toward that goal that we have set for ourselves.

The new Negro shall not be deceived. The new Negro refuses to take advice from anyone who has not felt with him, and suffered with him. We have suffered for three hundred years, therefore we feel that the time has come when only those who have suffered with us can interpret our feelings and our spirit. It takes the slave to interpret the feelings of the slave; it takes the unfortunate man to interpret the spirit of his unfortunate brother; and so it takes the suffering Negro to interpret the spirit of his comrade. It is strange that so many people are interested in the Negro now, willing to advise him how to act, and what organizations he should join, yet nobody was interested in the Negro to the extent of not making him a slave for two hundred and fifty years, reducing him to industrial peonage and serfdom after he was freed; it is strange that the same people can be so interested in the Negro now, as to tell him what organization he should follow and what leader he should support.

Whilst we are bordering on a future of brighter things, we are also at our danger period, when we must either accept the right philosophy, or go down by following deceptive propaganda which has hemmed us in for many centuries.

Deceiving The People

There is many a leader of our race who tells us that everything is well, and that all things will work out themselves and that a better day is coming. Yes, all of us know that a better day is coming; we all know that one day we will go home to Paradise, but whilst we are hoping by our Christian virtues to have an entry into Paradise we also realize that we are living on earth, and that the things that are practiced in Paradise are not practiced here. You have to treat this world as the world treats you; we are living in a temporal, material age, an age of activity, an age of racial, national selfishness. What else can you expect but to give back to the world what the world gives to you, and we are calling upon the four hundred million Negroes of the world to take a decided stand, a determined stand, that we shall occupy a firm position; that position shall be an emancipated race and a free nation of our own. We are determined that we shall have a free country; we are determined that we shall have a flag; we are determined that we shall have a government second to none in the world.

An Eye For An Eye

Men may spurn the idea, they may scoff at it; the metropolitan press of this country may deride us; yes, white men may laugh at the idea of Negroes talking about government; but let me tell you there is going to be a government, and let me say to you also that whatsoever you give, in like measure it shall be returned to you. The world is sinful, and therefore man believes in the doctrine of an eye for an eye, a tooth for a tooth. Everybody believes that revenge is God's, but at the same time we are men, and revenge sometimes springs up, even in the most Christian heart.

Why should man write down a history that will react against him? Why should man perpetrate deeds of wickedness upon his brother which will return to him in like measure? Yes, the Germans maltreated the French in the Franco-Prussian war of 1870, but the French got even with the Germans in 1918. It is history, and history will repeat itself. Beat the Negro, brutalize the Negro, kill the Negro, burn the Negro, imprison the Negro, scoff at the Negro, deride the Negro, it may come back to you one of these fine days, because the supreme destiny of man is in the hands of God. God is no respecter of persons, whether that person be white, yellow or black. Today the one race is up, tomorrow it has fallen; today the Negro seems to be the footstool of the other races and nations of the world; tomorrow the Negro may occupy the highest rung of the great human ladder.

But, when we come to consider the history of man, was not the Negro a power, was he not great once? Yes, honest students of history can recall the day when Egypt, Ethiopia and Timbuctoo towered in their civilizations, towered above Europe, towered above Asia. When Europe was inhabited by a race of cannibals, a race of savages, naked men, heathens and pagans, Africa was peopled with a race of cultured black men, who were masters in art, science and literature; men who were cultured and refined; men who, it was said, were like the gods. Even the great poets of old sang in beautiful sonnets of the delight it afforded the gods to be in companionship with the Ethiopians. Why, then, should we lose hope? Black men, you were once great; you shall be great again. Lose not courage, lose not faith, go forward. The thing to do is to get organized; keep separated and you will be exploited, you will be robbed, you will be killed. Get organized, and you will compel the world to respect you. If the world fails to give you consideration, because you are black men, because you are Negroes, four hundred millions of you shall, through organization, shake the pillars of the universe and bring down creation, even as Samson brought down the temple upon his head and upon the heads of the Philistines.

An Inspiring Vision

So Negroes, I say, through the Universal Negro Improvement Association, that there is much to live for. I have a vision of the future, and I see before me a picture of a redeemed Africa, with her dotted cities, with her beautiful civilization, with her millions of happy children, going to and fro. Why should I lose hope, why should I give up and take a back place in this age of progress? Remember that you are men, that God created you Lords of this creation. Lift up yourselves, men, take yourselves out of the mire and hitch your hopes to the stars; yes, rise as high as the very stars themselves. Let no man pull you down, let no man destroy your ambition, because man is but your companion, your equal; man is your brother; he is not your lord; he is not your sovereign master.

We of the Universal Negro Improvement Association feel happy; we are cheerful. Let them connive to destroy us; let them organize to destroy us; we shall fight the more. Ask me personally the cause of my success, and I say opposition; oppose me, and I fight the more, and if you want to find out the sterling worth of the Negro, oppose him, and under the leadership of the Universal Negro Improvement Association he shall fight his way to victory, and in the days to come, and I believe not far distant, Africa shall reflect a splendid demonstration of the worth of the Negro, of the determination of the Negro, to set himself free and to establish a government of his own.

Malcolm X

(1925–1965)

---

from *The Autobiography of Malcolm X*
1965

Malcolm K. Little was born in Omaha, Nebraska, and raised in Michigan. His father, a Baptist preacher active in Marcus Garvey's Universal Negro Improvement Association, was run over by a streetcar when Malcolm was six, and nine years later his mother was placed in a mental hospital for the rest of her life. Throughout his teens Malcolm mixed odd jobs with petty crime in Detroit, Boston, New Haven, and New York until he was sentenced in 1946 to an eight-year prison term in Massachusetts for larceny. In prison Malcolm K. Little was converted by an inmate to the Nation of Islam, and in 1952, forever renouncing his slave name Little, he became Malcolm X. Rising quickly in the Black Muslim ranks to the ministry of the New York mosque, he was second only to the NOI's national leader, Elijah Muhammad, when he left the

NOI in 1964. Thereupon he founded the Organization of Afro-American Unity. At an OAAU rally in Harlem on February 21, 1965, he was assassinated.

In the following excerpt from The Autobiography, *which was written with Alex Haley, Malcolm X illuminates the black nationalist goals he envisioned for his people and evaluates his own achievement.*

I kept having all kinds of troubles trying to develop the kind of Black Nationalist organization I wanted to build for the American Negro. Why Black Nationalism? Well, in the competitive American society, how can there ever be any white-black solidarity before there is first some black solidarity? If you will remember, in my childhood I had been exposed to the Black Nationalist teachings of Marcus Garvey—which, in fact, I had been told had led to my father's murder. Even when I was a follower of Elijah Muhammad, I had been strongly aware of how the Black Nationalist political, economic and social philosophies had the ability to instill within black men the racial dignity, the incentive, and the confidence that the black race needs today to get up off its knees, and to get on its feet, and get rid of its scars, and to take a stand for itself.

One of the major troubles that I was having in building the organization that I wanted—an all-black organization whose ultimate objective was to help create a society in which there could exist honest white-black brotherhood—was that my earlier public image, my old so-called "Black Muslim" image, kept blocking me. I was trying to gradually reshape that image. I was trying to turn a corner, into a new regard by the public, especially Negroes; I was no less angry than I had been, but at the same time the true brotherhood I had seen in the Holy World had influenced me to recognize that anger can blind human vision.

Every free moment I could find, I did a lot of talking to key people whom I knew around Harlem, and I made a lot of speeches, saying: "True Islam taught me that it takes *all* of the religious, political, economic, psychological, and racial ingredients, or characteristics, to make the Human Family and the Human Society complete.

"Since I learned the *truth* in Mecca, my dearest friends have come to include *all* kinds—some Christians, Jews, Buddhists, Hindus, agnostics, and even atheists! I have friends who are called capitalists, Socialists, and Communists! Some of my friends are moderates, conservatives, extremists—some are even Uncle Toms! My friends today are black, brown, red, yellow, and *white!*"

I said to Harlem street audiences that only when mankind would submit to the One God who created all—only then would mankind even approach the "peace" of which so much *talk* could be heard . . . but toward which so little *action* was seen.

I said that on the American racial level, we had to approach the black man's struggle against the white man's racism as a human problem, that we had to forget hypocritical politics and propaganda. I said that both races, as human beings, had the obligation, the responsibility, of helping to correct America's human problem. The well-meaning white people, I said, had to combat, actively and directly, the racism in other white people. And the black people had to build within themselves much greater awareness that along with equal rights there had to be the bearing of equal responsibilities.

I knew, better than most Negroes, how many white people truly wanted to see American racial problems solved. I knew that many whites were as frustrated as Negroes. I'll bet I got fifty letters some days from white people. The white people in meeting audiences would throng around me, asking me, after I had addressed them somewhere, "What *can* a sincere white person do?"

When I say that here now, it makes me think about that little co-ed I told you about, the one who flew from her New England college down to New York and came up to me in the Nation of Islam's restaurant in Harlem, and I told her that there was "nothing" she could do. I regret that I told her that. I wish that now I knew her name, or where I could telephone her, or write to her, and tell her what I tell white people now when they present themselves as being sincere, and ask me, one way or another, the same thing that she asked.

The first thing I tell them is that at least where my own particular Black Nationalist organization, the Organization of Afro-American Unity, is concerned, they can't *join* us. I have these very deep feelings that white people who want to join black organizations are really just taking the escapist way to salve their consciences. By visibly hovering near us, they are "proving" that they are "with us." But the hard truth is this *isn't* helping to solve America's racist problem. The Negroes aren't the racists. Where the really sincere white people have got to do their "proving" of themselves is not among the black *victims,* but out on the battle lines of where America's racism really *is*—and that's in their own home communities; America's racism is among their own fellow whites. That's where the sincere whites who really mean to accomplish something have got to work.

Aside from that, I mean nothing against any sincere whites when I say that as members of black organizations, generally whites' very presence subtly renders the black organization automatically less effective. Even the best white members will slow down the Negroes' discovery of what they need to do, and particularly of what they can do—for themselves, working by themselves, among their own kind, in their own communities.

I sure don't want to hurt anybody's feelings, but in fact I'll even go so far as to say that I never really trust the kind of white people who are always so anxious to hang around Negroes, or to hang around in Negro communities. I don't trust the kind of whites who love having Negroes always hanging around them. I don't know—this feeling may be a throwback to the years when I was hustling in Harlem and all of those red-faced, drunk whites in the afterhours clubs were always grabbing hold of some Negroes and talking about "I just want you to know you're just as good as I am—" And then they got back in their taxicabs and black limousines and went back downtown to the places where they lived and worked, where no blacks except servants had better get caught. But, anyway, I know that every time that whites join a black organization, you watch, pretty soon the blacks will be leaning on the whites to support it, and before you know it a black may be up front with a title, but the whites, because of their money, are the real controllers.

I tell sincere white people, "Work in conjunction with us—each of us working among our own kind." Let sincere white individuals find all other white people they can who feel as they do—and let them form their own all-white groups, to work trying to convert other white people who are thinking and acting so racist. Let sincere whites go and teach nonviolence to white people!

We will completely respect our white co-workers. They will deserve every credit. We will give them every credit. We will meanwhile be working among our own kind, in our own black communities—showing and teaching black men in ways that only other black men can—that the black man has got to help himself. Working separately, the sincere white people and sincere black people actually will be working together.

In our mutual sincerity we might be able to show a road to the salvation of America's very soul. It can only be salvaged if human rights and dignity, in full, are extended to black men. Only such real, meaningful actions as those which are sincerely motivated from a deep sense of humanism and moral responsibility can get at the basic causes that produce the racial explosions in America today. Otherwise, the racial explosions are only going to grow worse. Certainly nothing is ever going to be solved by throwing upon me and other so-called black "extremists" and "demagogues" the blame for the racism that is in America.

Sometimes, I have dared to dream to myself that one day, history may even say that my voice—which disturbed the white man's smugness, and his arrogance, and his complacency—that my voice helped to save America from a grave, possibly even a fatal catastrophe.

The goal has always been the same, with the approaches to it as different as mine and Dr. Martin Luther King's nonviolent marching, that dramatizes the brutality and the evil of the white man against defenseless blacks. And in the racial climate of this country today, it is anybody's guess which of the "extremes" in approach to the black man's problems might *personally* meet a fatal catastrophe first—"non-violent" Dr. King, or so-called "violent" me.

* * *

Anything I do today, I regard as urgent. No man is given but so much time to accomplish whatever is his life's work. My life in particular never has stayed fixed in one position for very long. You have seen how throughout my life, I have often known unexpected drastic changes.

I am only facing the facts when I know that any moment of any day, or any night, could bring me death. This is particularly true since the last trip that I made abroad. I have seen the nature of things that are happening, and I have heard things from sources which are reliable.

To speculate about dying doesn't disturb me as it might some people. I never have felt that I would live to become an old man. Even before I was a Muslim—when I was a hustler in the ghetto jungle, and then a criminal in prison, it always stayed on my mind that I would die a violent death. In fact, it runs in my family. My father and most of his brothers died by violence—my father because of what he believed in. To come right down to it, if I take the kind of things in which I believe, then add to that the kind of temperament that I have, plus the one hundred per cent dedication I have to whatever I believe in —these are ingredients which make it just about impossible for me to die of old age.

I have given to this book so much of whatever time I have because I feel, and I hope, that if I honestly and fully tell my life's account, read objectively it might prove to be a testimony of some social value.

I think that an objective reader may see how in the society to which I was exposed as a black youth here in America, for me to wind up in a prison was really just about inevitable. It happens to so many thousands of black youth.

I think that an objective reader may see how when I heard "The white man is the devil," when I played back what had been my own experiences, it was inevitable that I would respond positively; then the next twelve years of my life were devoted and dedicated to propagating that phrase among the black people.

I think, I hope, that the objective reader, in following my life —the life of only one ghetto-created Negro—may gain a better picture and understanding than he has previously had of the black ghettoes which are shaping the lives and the thinking of almost all of the 22 million Negroes who live in America.

Thicker each year in these ghettoes is the kind of teen-ager that I was—with the wrong kinds of heroes, and the wrong kinds of influences. I am not saying that all of them become the kind of parasite that I was. Fortunately, by far most do not. But still, the small fraction who do add up to an annual total of more and more costly, dangerous youthful criminals. The F.B.I. not long ago released a report of a shocking rise in crime each successive year since the end of World War II—ten to twelve per cent each year. The report did not say so in so many words, but I am saying that the majority of that crime increase is annually spawned in the black ghettoes which the American racist society permits to exist. In the 1964 "long, hot summer" riots in major cities across the United States, the socially disinherited black ghetto youth were always at the forefront.

In this year, 1965, I am certain that more—and worse—riots are going to erupt, in yet more cities, in spite of the conscience-salving Civil Rights Bill. The reason is that the *cause* of these riots, the racist malignancy in America, has been too long unattended.

I believe that it would be almost impossible to find anywhere in America a black man who has lived further down in the mud of human society than I have; or a black man who has been any more ignorant than I have been; or a black man who has suffered more anguish during his life than I have. But it is only after the deepest darkness that the greatest joy can come; it is only after slavery and prison that the sweetest appreciation of freedom can come.

For the freedom of my 22 million black brothers and sisters here in America, I do believe that I have fought the best that I knew how, and the best that I could, with the shortcomings that I have had. I know that my shortcomings are many.

My greatest lack has been, I believe, that I don't have the kind of academic education I wish I had been able to get—to have been a lawyer, perhaps. I do believe that I might have made a good lawyer. I have always loved verbal battle, and challenge. You can believe me that if I had the time right now, I would not be one bit ashamed to go back into any New York

City public school and start where I left off at the ninth grade, and go on through a degree. Because I don't begin to be academically equipped for so many of the interests that I have. For instance, I love languages. I wish I were an accomplished linguist. I don't know anything more frustrating than to be around people talking something you can't understand. Especially when they are people who look just like you. In Africa, I heard original mother tongues, such as Hausa, and Swahili, being spoken, and there I was standing like some little boy, waiting for someone to tell me what had been said; I never will forget how ignorant I felt.

Aside from the basic African dialects, I would try to learn Chinese, because it looks as if Chinese will be the most powerful political language of the future. And already I have begun studying Arabic, which I think is going to be the most powerful spiritual language of the future.

I would just like to *study*. I mean ranging study, because I have a wide-open mind. I'm interested in almost any subject you can mention. I know this is the reason I have come to really like, as individuals, some of the hosts of radio or television panel programs I have been on, and to respect their minds —because even if they have been almost steadily in disagreement with me on the race issue, they still have kept their minds open and objective about the truths of things happening in this world. Irv Kupcinet in Chicago, and Barry Farber, Barry Gray and Mike Wallace in New York—people like them. They also let me see that they respected my mind—in a way I know they never realized. The way I knew was that often they would invite my opinion on subjects off the race issue. Sometimes, after the programs, we would sit around and talk about all kinds of things, current events and other things, for an hour or more. You see, most whites, even when they credit a Negro with some intelligence, will still feel that all he can talk about is the race issue; most whites never feel that Negroes can contribute anything to other areas of thought, and ideas. You just notice how rarely you will ever hear whites asking any Negroes what they think about the problem of world health, or the space race to land men on the moon.

*   *   *

Every morning when I wake up, now, I regard it as having another borrowed day. In any city, wherever I go, making speeches, holding meetings of my organization, or attending to other business, black men are watching every move I make, awaiting their chance to kill me. I have said publicly many times that I know that they have their orders. Anyone who chooses not to believe what I am saying doesn't know the Muslims in the Nation of Islam.

But I am also blessed with faithful followers who are, I believe, as dedicated to me as I once was to Mr. Elijah Muhammad. Those who would hunt a man need to remember that a jungle also contains those who hunt the hunters.

I know, too, that I could suddenly die at the hands of some white racists. Or I could die at the hands of some Negro hired by the white man. Or it could be some brainwashed Negro acting on his own idea that by eliminating me he would be helping out the white man, because I talk about the white man the way I do.

Anyway, now, each day I live as if I am already dead, and I tell you what I would like for you to do. When I *am* dead—I say it that way because from the things I *know,* I do not expect to live long enough to read this book in its finished form—I want you to just watch and see if I'm not right in what I say: that the white man, in his press, is going to identify me with "hate."

He will make use of me dead, as he has made use of me alive, as a convenient symbol of "hatred"—and that will help him to escape facing the truth that all I have been doing is holding up a mirror to reflect, to show, the history of unspeakable crimes that his race has committed against my race.

You watch. I will be labeled as, at best, an "irresponsible" black man. I have always felt about this accusation that the black "leader" whom white men consider to be "responsible" is invariably the black "leader" who never gets any results. You only get action as a black man if you are regarded by the white man as "irresponsible." In fact, this much I had learned when I was just a little boy. And since I have been some kind of a "leader" of black people here in the racist society of America, I have been more reassured each time the white man resisted me, or attacked me harder—because each time made me more certain that I was on the right track in the American black man's best interests. The racist white man's opposition automatically made me know that I did offer the black man something worthwhile.

Yes, I have cherished my "demagogue" role. I know that societies often have killed the people who have helped to change those societies. And if I can die having brought any light, having exposed any meaningful truth that will help to destroy the racist cancer that is malignant in the body of America—then, all of the credit is due to Allah. Only the mistakes have been mine.

James Baldwin

(1924–1987)

The American Dream
and the American Negro

On March 7, 1965, The New York Times Magazine *published a slightly condensed transcript of a debate delivered at the Cambridge Union Society of Cambridge University in England to commemorate the one hundred fiftieth anniversary of its founding. Invited to speak for the proposition that "the American Dream is at the expense of the American Negro" was essayist and novelist James Baldwin; opposing the motion was William F. Buckley, Jr., editor of* The National Review. *Baldwin's remarks on that occasion follow.*

I find myself, not for the first time, in the position of a kind of Jeremiah. It would seem to me that the question before the house is a proposition horribly loaded, that one's response to that question depends on where you find yourself in the world, what your sense of reality is. That is, it depends on assumptions we hold so deeply as to be scarcely aware of them.

The white South African or Mississippi sharecropper or Alabama sheriff has at bottom a system of reality which compels them really to believe when they face the Negro that this woman, this man, this child must be insane to attack the system to which he owes his entire identity. For such a person, the proposition which we are trying to discuss here does not exist.

On the other hand, I have to speak as one of the people who have been most attacked by the Western system of reality. It comes from Europe. That is how it got to America. It raises the question of whether or not civilizations can be considered equal, or whether one civilization has a right to subjugate—in fact, to destroy—another.

Now, leaving aside all the physical factors one can quote—leaving aside the rape or murder, leaving aside the bloody catalogue of oppression which we are too familiar with anyway—what the system does to the subjugated is to destroy his sense of reality. It destroys his father's authority over him. His father can no longer tell him anything because his past has disappeared.

In the case of the American Negro, from the moment you are born every stick and stone, every face, is white. Since you have not yet seen a mirror, you suppose you are, too. It comes as a great shock around the age of 5, 6 or 7 to discover that the flag to which you have pledged allegiance, along with everybody else, has not pledged allegiance to you. It comes as a great shock to see Gary Cooper killing off the Indians and, although you are rooting for Gary Cooper, that the Indians are you.

It comes as a great shock to discover that the country which is your birthplace and to which you owe your life and identity has not, in its whole system of reality, evolved any place for you. The disaffection and the gap between people, only on the basis of their skins, begins there and accelerates throughout your whole lifetime. You realize that you are 30 and you are having a terrible time. You have been through a certain kind of mill and the most serious effect is again not the catalogue of disaster—the policeman, the taxi driver, the waiters, the landlady, the banks, the insurance companies, the millions of details 24 hours of every day which spell out to you that you are a worthless human being. It is not that. By that time you have begun to see it happening in your daughter, your son or your niece or your nephew. You are 30 by now and nothing you have done has helped you to escape the trap. But what is worse is that nothing you have done, and as far as you can tell nothing you *can* do, will save your son or your daughter from having the same disaster and from coming to the same end.

We speak about expense. There are several ways of addressing oneself to some attempt to find out what that word means here. From a very literal point of view, the harbors and the ports and the railroads of the country—the economy, especially in the South—could not conceivably be what they are if it had not been (and this is still so) for cheap labor. I am speaking very seriously, and this is not an overstatement: I picked cotton, I carried it to the market, I built the railroads under someone else's whip for nothing. For nothing.

The Southern oligarchy which has still today so very much power in Washington, and therefore some power in the world, was created by my labor and my sweat and the violation of my women and the murder of my children. This in the land of the free, the home of the brave. None can challenge that statement. It is a matter of historical record.

In the Deep South you are dealing with a sheriff or a landlord or a landlady or the girl at the Western Union desk. She doesn't know quite whom she is dealing with—by which I mean, if you are not part of a town and if you are a Northern nigger, it shows in millions of ways. She simply knows that it is an unknown quantity and she wants to have nothing to do with it. You have to wait a while to get your telegram. We have all been through it. By the time you get to be a man it is fairly easy to deal with.

But what happens to the poor white man's, the poor white woman's, mind? It is this: they have been raised to believe, and by now they helplessly believe, that no matter how terrible some of their lives may be and no matter what disaster over-

takes them, there is one consolation like a heavenly revelation
—at least they are not black. I suggest that of all the terrible
things that could happen to a human being that is one of the
worst. I suggest that what has happened to the white South-
erner is in some ways much worse than what has happened to
the Negroes there.

Sheriff Clark in Selma, Ala., cannot be dismissed as a total
monster; I am sure he loves his wife and children and likes to
get drunk. One has to assume that he is a man like me. But he
does not know what drives him to use the club, to menace with
the gun and to use the cattle prod. Something awful must have
happened to a human being to be able to put a cattle prod
against a woman's breasts. What happens to the woman is
ghastly. What happens to the man who does it is in some ways
much, much worse. Their moral lives have been destroyed by
the plague called color.

This is not being done 100 years ago, but in 1965 and in a
country which is pleased with what we call prosperity, with a
certain amount of social coherence, which calls itself a civilized
nation and which espouses the notion of freedom in the world.
If it were white people being murdered, the Government would
find some way of doing something about it. We have a civil
rights bill now. We had the 15th Amendment nearly 100 years
ago. If it was not honored then, I have no reason to believe that
the civil rights bill will be honored now.

The American soil is full of the corpses of my ancestors
through 400 years and at least three wars. Why is my freedom,
my citizenship in question now? What one begs the American
people to do, for all our sakes, is simply to accept our history.

It seems to me when I watch Americans in Europe that what
they don't know about Europeans is what they don't know
about me. They were not trying to be nasty to the French girl,
rude to the French waiter. They did not know that they hurt
their feelings, they didn't have any sense that this particular
man and woman were human beings. They walked over them
with the same sort of bland ignorance and condescension, the
charm and cheerfulness, with which they had patted me on the
head and which made them upset when *I* was upset.

When I was brought up I was taught in American history

books that Africa had no history and that neither had I. I was a savage about whom the least said the better, who had been saved by Europe and who had been brought to America. Of course, I believed it. I didn't have much choice. These were the only books there were. Everyone else seemed to agree. If you went out of Harlem the whole world agreed. What you saw was much bigger, whiter, cleaner, safer. The garbage was collected, the children were happy. You would go back home and it would seem, of course, that this was an act of God. You belonged where white people put you.

It is only since World War II that there has been a counter-image in the world. That image has not come about because of any legislation by any American Government, but because Africa was suddenly on the stage of the world and Africans had to be dealt with in a way they had never been dealt with before. This gave the American Negro, for the first time, a sense of himself not as a savage. It has created and will create a great many conundrums.

One of the things the white world does not know, but I think I know, is that black people are just like everybody else. We are also mercenaries, dictators, murderers, liars. We are human, too. Unless we can establish some kind of dialogue between those people who enjoy the American dream and those other people who have not achieved it, we will be in terrible trouble. This is what concerns me most. We are sitting in this room and we are all civilized; we can talk to each other, at least on certain levels, so that we can walk out of here assuming that the measure of our politeness has some effect on the world.

I remember when the ex-Attorney General, Mr. Robert Kennedy, said it was conceivable that in 40 years in America we might have a Negro President. That sounded like a very emancipated statement to white people. They were not in Harlem when this statement was first heard. They did not hear the laughter and bitterness and scorn with which this statement was greeted. From the point of view of the man in the Harlem barber shop, Bobby Kennedy only got here yesterday and now he is already on his way to the Presidency. We were here for 400 years and now he tells us that maybe in 40 years, if you are good, we may let you become President.

Perhaps I can be reasoned with, but I don't know—neither does Martin Luther King—none of us knows how to deal with people whom the white world has so long ignored, who don't believe anything the white world says and don't entirely believe anything I or Martin say. You can't blame them.

It seems to me that the City of New York has had, for example, Negroes in it for a very long time. The City of New York was able in the last 15 years to reconstruct itself, to tear down buildings and raise great new ones and has done nothing whatever except build housing projects, mainly in the ghettoes, for the Negroes. And of course the Negroes hate it. The children can't bear it. They want to move out of the ghettoes. If American pretensions were based on more honest assessments of life, it would not mean for Negroes that when someone says "urban renewal" some Negroes are going to be thrown out into the streets, which is what it means now.

It is a terrible thing for an entire people to surrender to the notion that one-ninth of its population is beneath them. Until the moment comes when we, the Americans, are able to accept the fact that my ancestors are both black and white, that on that continent we are trying to forge a new identity, that we need each other, that I am not a ward of America, I am not an object of missionary charity, I am one of the people who built the country—until this moment comes there is scarcely any hope for the American dream. If the people are denied participation in it, by their very presence they will wreck it. And if that happens it is a very grave moment for the West.

Adam Clayton Powell, Jr.

(1908–1972)

from *Adam by Adam*
Black Power and the Future of America

Like his father, Connecticut-born Adam Clayton Powell, Jr., studied for the ministry. After seminary he became an associate pastor at the Abyssinian Baptist Church in New York, where he established and maintained a powerful black political base for three decades. The dynamic Powell organized picket lines in ghetto streets, demanded that Harlem's white shopowners hire black employees, daily confronted white authority to seek justice and secure government services for his people, and in 1941 became the first black to serve on New York's city council. Four years later he was elected to Congress. Throughout his long, successful congressional career, and after it, Powell took politics to the pulpit of Harlem's Abyssinian Baptist Church where he fervently preached black power, pride, and dignity.

The following chapter from Powell's autobiography

discusses the future of the black power movement in America. Rejecting tokenism and stirring the racial consciousness of African Americans, he focuses on the use of economic force and political power to achieve equality.

Every single black leader in America with a strong national following has been bought off, assassinated, imprisoned, or exiled. While I know I was not directly responsible, in a way I have a deep sense of guilt concerning the assassinations of Martin Luther King, Jr., and Malcolm X.

Martin Luther King came to see me once in Washington, bringing with him Ralph Abernathy. Chuck Stone, my administrative assistant, and the chief investigator of the Education and Labor Committee, was also present.

King and I talked for about three hours. I told him that the concept of total nonviolence had become outmoded. I reminded him that when Gandhi died, even Nehru, his closest follower, gave up the concept in the course of the fratricidal war between the Hindus and Moslems that resulted in the creation of Pakistan. King then told me that he was giving up the concept of total nonviolence.

Following our talk I went on to California to speak on campuses there, and in the course of a press conference during my trip reported that Martin Luther King was giving up total nonviolence—as he had said in front of witnesses during our talk in Washington. King immediately called his own press conference and denied that he had made such a statement. My puzzlement over this action was dispelled several days later when he received a foundation grant for several hundred thousand dollars.

Subsequently, however, King preached a sermon at the Riverside Baptist Church in New York City, in which he did state as a matter of record that he could not continue his concept of total nonviolence as long—and I quote him—"as my nation is the greatest purveyor of violence in the world."

During our Washington talk King also did not tell me the truth regarding his financing, and Ralph Abernathy corrected him on that score. I had asked King, "Martin, how much money are you getting from white people?"

"None," he said, "except what comes in through the mails when we send out our form letters for appeals through the Southern Christian Leadership Conference."

"Martin, you forgot that just last week we got over a hundred thousand dollars from a foundation," Abernathy said.

No comment from Martin.

King later visited me several times at Bimini. One night we were with a crowd of Biminians and went into a restaurant for something to eat. After we were settled—all of us black—one of the younger fellows with us said, "Do you think Dr. King would preach us a little sermon? We've never heard him."

I said, "How about it, Martin? These young people have never heard you preach." So he leaned back and preached an old-fashioned Baptist sermon. While he was preaching, a stranger, whose identity we were never able to discover, came up to one of the men in our group and said to him, "Please tell Dr. King not to go to Memphis because if he does, he will be killed."

I passed this along to Dr. King, who apparently thought little of it. Two weeks later he was dead.

Malcolm X, one of the great minds we black people lost, was a dear friend of mine. As time went on we became extremely close because I was able to give him a better understanding of his religion. At the time we became acquainted he thought that Christianity was the white man's religion and that Islamism, or Muslimism was the black man's religion. I pointed to the Coptic cross in the Abyssinian Baptist Church and said to him, "This is where Christianity began—in Ethiopia. It wasn't until A.D. 329 that Constantine recognized Christianity, but long before that there was the Coptic Church."

I also taught Malcolm that his concepts of Muslimism were incorrect, and I urged him to go to the Arab countries and if possible to Mecca to find out what Islam really was. This he did. After his return from Mecca he held a press conference at which he stated that he had found outstanding leaders of the Muslim religion who were white, with blue eyes and blond hair, and that he knew he had been wrong in his previous thinking on that point. Evidently his changed attitude did not find favor with all his followers because two months after this Malcolm X was assassinated.

Stokely Carmichael had great charisma and showed great promise for the future of black people. An activist, he traveled to Communist countries where I, a United States Congressman, couldn't go. Eventually he became involved with my old friend Kwame Nkrumah, the deposed redeemer of Ghana. He lived with Nkrumah for some time and then returned to America, preaching Pan-Africanism, which is the gospel of Nkrumah. But his speeches did not go over too well; in fact, some audiences in the States and the Caribbean booed him when he spoke.

What we blacks are suffering from—and white America is suffering from also—is a fragmentation of leadership. There is no leader among blacks and there is no leader among whites.

Even the Black Panthers have no leadership left. Whether one agrees with them or not, one must give them due respect as being the first organization of black people since Nat Turner's to commit themselves to a willingness to die for the cause. And any time a man like J. Edgar Hoover can call the Panthers' 100,200 members a threat to the security of this vast nation of 200 millions plus, then you know they are a power.

Jesse Jackson is one of the brightest hopes for the future. Jackson, who worked for Dr. King in Chicago, setting up the successful Operation Breadbasket there, has brains, looks, charisma, and is a gifted orator besides. I see him as the only man on the horizon who can come forward and provide leadership, not only for black America but for blacks and whites together.

What, then, for the future? I believe—no, I know—that we are passing through a revolution. And I believe that we are also on the edge of a civil war. That war will be a war not of racism or regionalism but of young people, black and white, campus people, poor whites, Chicanos, and blacks—in all a group that will number 100 million by 1972.

Black people need to make a decision, however, before they achieve this unity of the majority—they need to decide what they are going to believe about integration and separatism. My own opinion is that we cannot afford the luxury of differences among ourselves now. But the one point on which we can all definitely afford to agree is unity on the basis of desegregation, regardless of whether we are joining with Black Muslims, Black Panthers, or the Negro bourgeoisie. After desegregation is accomplished, then we can afford the luxury of differences among ourselves.

BLACK POWER!
BLACK POWER!

During 1968, 1969, and 1970 I made more than one hundred speeches all over the United States. I spoke to entirely white audiences in the South and to entirely black audiences in the North. And I found that no phrase strikes more terror to the hearts of white Americans than Black Power.

Black Power was founded half a century ago by Marcus Garvey, the semiliterate immigrant from Jamaica, at whose feet I sat as a youngster and listened while he talked. I held the first National Black Power Conference in this Republic. Therefore I write with authority.

Black Power does not mean antiwhite unless whites make blacks antiwhite.

Black power does not mean violence, but it does not mean total nonviolence. It does not mean that you walk with a chip on your shoulder, but you walk letting the chips fly where they may.

Black Power means black dignity. Pride in being black. Pride that black is beautiful. Pride that blacks are not second-class citizens as our forefathers were.

Black Power means a complete separation from Negroes. Especially the Negro bourgeoisie or, as I call them, Negro bushies.

Black Power means pride in heritage. Pride in knowing that before the first white man, a savage in what is now England, could ever comb his matted locks, black men were carving statues, painting, creating astronomy, mathematics, and the alphabet.

Black Power means pride that the first man who died on Boston Common that America might be free was a black man, Crispus Attucks. Pride that a black man, Benjamin Banneker, planned the city of Washington, the capital of the Republic—and before him another black man from France, Pierre L'Enfant.

Black Power means that blacks have a willingness to die for their cause—no cause has ever been successful without the willingness of the people who believe in it to die for it, whether they died or not.

Black Power means we are no better—and above all no less —in terms of equality with any other ethnic group in the United States.

Black Power means we are going to lead our own black group and do not want any white leadership. Whites can help us with troops, maybe a corporal or sergeant, but above all no white generals. We will command our destiny. We ask those who want to help us to help us. With or without you, we're going to win.

Black Power means that we have paid the price in Watts, in Newark, in Detroit, in Harlem, in a hundred and three cities after Martin Luther King, Jr., was assassinated.

Black Power means we're not afraid of anyone even though others may have the weapons that we do not have—although some of the Black Power groups do have weapons.

Black Power means we are proud of our Black Panthers. We may not agree with them, because few people really understand them. But we are proud of any group that's willing to die for its cause.

Black Power means we are searching for truth always. Not the truth of J. Edgar Hoover's wiretapping of Black Panther Headquarters and infiltrating of Black Power movements. It means the kind of truth that we discovered on the scene in Chicago when we went to the Black Panther Headquarters. The truth that the Attorney General of Illinois had publicly denied—but that later made him dismiss the charges against the Black Panthers he had arrested.

The truth about Fred Hampton's assassination by the police of the city of Chicago. We saw the truth—the door with every bullet hole made from the outside in. Not one shot fired from the inside out. We saw the truth—that Fred Hampton was killed while he was sleeping; they came through an outside door on the back porch and shot him in the top of his head.

Black Power calls on all Americans to stop the genocide against the Black Panthers and black people everywhere.

Black Power says don't forget the executive secretary of the NAACP who was murdered in Mississippi. Don't forget the two white boys from Manhattan and a black soul brother who were bulldozed into the earth in Mississippi. Don't forget the assassination of Jack Kennedy. Don't forget the assassination of Bobby Kennedy.

Black Power says power to the people. The gaunt man who walked at midnight on Pennsylvania Avenue said it once—power to the people. He said the only government that would not perish from the earth would be a government of the people (power to the people), by the people (power to the people), and for the people (power to the people). But what does this power, this Black Power, come from? Let me tell you what I have been telling my brothers, what I call a Black Position Paper.

1. Black organizations must be black-led. To the extent to which black organizations are led by whites, to that precise extent is their black potential for ultimate control and direction diluted.

2. The black masses must finance their own organizations; at least such organizations must derive the main source of their funds from black people. No other ethnic or religious group in America permits others to control their organizations. This fact of organizational life is the crucible for black progress. Jews control Jewish organizations; there are no Italians or Irish on the board of directors of B'nai B'rith. Poles control Polish-American organizations. But the moment a black man seeks to dominate his own organization, he's labeled a "racist." And frightened black Uncle Toms quickly shun him to cuddle up to Mr. Charlie to prove their sniveling loyalty to the doctrine that "white must be right."

3. The black masses must demand and refuse to accept noth-

ing less than that proportionate percentage of the political spoils, such as jobs, elective offices, and appointments, that are equal to their proportion of the population and their voting strength. They must reject the shameful racial tokenism that characterizes the political life of America today. Where blacks provide 20 percent of the vote, they should have 20 percent of the jobs.

This is not true of other ethnic groups, who usually obtain political favors far in excess of their proportion. A good example for comparison are Chicago's Negroes and Polish-Americans. According to the 1960 census, there were 223,255 Polish-Americans and 812,637 Negroes in Chicago. As late as 1970 there were three Polish-American Congressmen from Chicago and only one Negro Congressman. Thus, with approximately one-fourth as many persons as Negroes, Polish-Americans nonetheless had three times as many Congressmen. That kind of inequity is not due to racial discrimination. It is due to racial apathy, stupidity, lethargy, indifference, ignorance, and lack of courage.

4. Black people must support and push black candidates for political office first, operating on the principle of "all other things being equal." This is a lesson Chicago Negroes might well learn. In a primary in the heavily black Sixth Congressional District, Chicago black people actually elected a dead white man over a live black woman. A young white candidate, who had going for him only the fact that he was young and white, defeated an intelligent, dedicated black woman who was backed by all major civil rights groups for alderman in a predominantly black ward.

5. Black leadership in the North and the South must differentiate between and work within the two-pronged thrust of the black revolution: economic self-sufficiency and political power. The Civil Rights Act of 1964 had absolutely no meaning for black people in New York, Chicago, or any of the Northern Cities. De jure school segregation, denial of the right to vote, or barriers to public accommodations are no longer sources of concern to Northern blacks. Civil rights in the North means more jobs, better education, manpower retraining, and development of new skills. As chairman of the House Committee on Education and Labor, I controlled all labor legislation, such as

the minimum wage, all education legislation, including aid to elementary schools and higher education, the manpower training and redevelopment program, vocational rehabilitation, and, of greater importance today, the "War on Poverty." This is legislative power. This is political power. I use myself as an example because this is the audacious power I urge every black woman and man to seek—the kind of political clout needed to achieve greater economic power and bring the black revolution into fruition.

6. Black masses must produce and contribute to the economy of the country in strength proportionate to their population. We must become a race of producers, not consumers. We must rid ourselves of the welfare paralysis that humiliates our human spirit.

7. Black communities of this country—whether New York's Harlem, Chicago's South and West Sides, or Philadelphia's North Side—must neither tolerate nor accept outside leadership, black or white. Each community must provide its own local leadership, strengthening the resources within its own local community.

8. The black masses should follow only those leaders who can sit at the bargaining table with the white power structure as equals and negotiate for a share of the loaf of bread, not beg for some of its crumbs. We must stop sending little boys whose organizations are controlled and financed by white businessmen to do a man's job. Because only those who are financially independent can be men. This is why earlier I called for black people to finance their own organizations and institutions. In so doing, the black masses guarantee the independence of their leadership.

9. This black leadership—the ministers, politicians, businessmen, doctors, and lawyers—must come back to the blacks who made them in the first place or be purged by the black masses. Black communities all over America today suffer from "absentee black leadership." The leaders have fled to the suburbs and, not unlike their white counterparts in black communities, use these communities to make their two dollars, then reject those who have made them in the first place as neighbors and social equals. This kind of double-dealing must stop.

10. Blacks must reject the white community's carefully se-

lected "ceremonial Negro leaders" and insist that the white community deal instead with the black leadership chosen by black communities. For every "ceremonial Negro leader" we permit to lead us, we are weakened and derogated just that much.

11. Blacks must distinguish between desegregation and integration. Desegregation removes all barriers and facilitates access to an open society. Integration accomplishes the same thing but has a tendency to denude the Negro of pride in himself. Blacks must seek desegregation, thereby retaining pride and participation in their own institutions, just as other groups, the Jews, Irish, Italians, and Poles have done. Negroes are the only group in America that has utilized the world "integration" in pursuing equality.

12. Demonstration and all continuing protest activity must always be nonviolent. Violence, even when it erupts recklessly in anger among our teen-agers, must be curbed and discouraged.

13. No black person over twenty-one must be permitted to participate in a demonstration, walk a picket line, or be part of any civil rights or community acvitity unless he or she is a registered voter.

14. Black people must continue to defy the laws of man when such laws conflict with the law of God. The law of God ordains that "there is neither Jew nor Greek, there is neither bond nor freedom, there is neither male nor female: for ye are all one." Equal in the eyes of God, but unequal in the eyes of man, black people must press forward at all times, climbing toward that higher ground of the harmonious society that shapes the laws of man to the laws of God.

15. Black people must discover a new and creative total involvement with ourselves. We must turn our energies inwardly toward our homes, our churches, our families, our children, our colleges, our neighborhoods, our businesses, and our communities. Our fraternal and social groups must become an integral part of this creative involvement by using their resources and energy toward constructive fund-raising and community activities. This is no time for cotillions and teas. These are the steps I urge all of America's 25 million black people to take as

we begin the dawn of a new day by walking together. And as we walk together hand in hand, firmly keeping the faith of our black forebears, we glory in what we have become and are today.

Shirley Chisholm

(b. 1924)

The 51% Minority

Born in Brooklyn, educated at Brooklyn College and then Columbia University, Shirley Chisholm served on the Bureau of Child Welfare for New York State from 1959 to 1964, when she was elected to the New York State legislature. In 1969 Representative Chisholm was the first black woman to serve in the Congress of the United States.

In the speech that follows—it was delivered in 1970 at the Conference on Women's Employment—Chisholm calls for more representation of women by women on all levels of government. As women compose a majority of the voters in America (a significant number of them being black women), Chisholm reasons, they should not be represented by so conspicuous a minority of women in political office. Chisholm thus weds a feminist vision of empowerment with her dream as an African-American woman.

. . . I am, as it is obvious, both black and a woman. And that is a good vantage point from which to view at least two elements of what is becoming a social revolution: the American black revolution and the women's liberation movement. But it is also a horrible disadvantage. It is a disadvantage because America as a nation is both racist and anti-feminist. Racism and anti-feminism are two of the prime traditions of this country. For any individual, breaking with social tradition is a giant step—a giant step because there are no social traditions which do not have corresponding social sanctions—the sole purpose of which are to protect the sanctity of those traditions.

That's when we ask the question, "Do women dare?" We're not asking whether women are capable of a break with tradition so much as we're asking whether they are capable of bearing the sanctions that will be placed upon them. . . .

Each—black male and black female, white male and white female—must escape first from their own intolerable trap before they can be fully effective in helping others to free themselves. Therein lies one of the major reasons that there are not more involved in the women's liberation movement. Women cannot, for the most part, operate independently of men because they often do not have sufficient economic freedom.

In 1966, the median earnings of women who worked full time for the whole year was less than the median income for males who worked full time for the whole year. In fact, white women workers made less than black male workers, and of course, black women workers made the least of all. Whether it is intentional or not, women are paid less than men for the same work, no matter what their chosen field of work. Whether it is intentional or not, employment for women is regulated more in terms of the jobs that are available to them. This is almost as true for white women as it is for black women. Whether it is intentional or not, when it becomes time for a high school girl to think about preparing for her career, her

counselors, whether they be male or female, will think first of
her so-called natural career—housewife and mother—and begin to program her for a field with which children and marriage will not unduly interfere.

That's exactly the same as the situation of the young black
students who the racist counselor advises to prepare for ser-
vice-oriented occupations, because he does not even think of
them entering the professions. And the response of the average young female is precisely the same as the response of the
average young black or Puerto Rican—tacit agreement—because the odds seem to be stacked against them.

This is not happening as much as it once did to young minority group people. It is not happening because they have been
radicalized, and the country is becoming sensitized to its racist
attitudes. Women must learn a lesson from that experience.
They must rebel. . . .

The law cannot do it for us. *We must do it for ourselves.*
Women in this country must become revolutionaries. We must
refuse to accept the old, the traditional roles and stereotypes.
. . . We must replace the old, negative thoughts about our
femininity with positive thoughts and positive action affirming
it, and more. But we must also remember that we will be breaking with tradition, and so we must prepare ourselves education-
ally, economically, and psychologically in order that we will be
able to accept and bear with the sanctions that society will
immediately impose upon us.

I'm a politician. . . . I have been in politics for 20 years, and
in that time I have learned a few things about the role of
women in power. And the major thing that I have learned is
that women are the backbone of America's political organizations. They are the letter writers, the envelope stuffers, the
telephone answerers; they're the campaign workers and the
organizers. Perhaps it is in America, more than any other country, that the inherent proof of the old bromide, "The power
behind the throne is a woman" is most readily apparent.

Let me remind you once again of the relatively few women
standard bearers on the American political scene. There are
only 10 United States Representatives; one Senator; no cabinet
members who are women; no women on the Supreme Court

and only a small percentage of lady judges at the federal court level who might be candidates.

It is true that at the state level the picture is somewhat brighter, just as it is true that the North presents a service that is somewhat more appealing to the black American when compared to the South. But even though in 1967 there were 318 women who were in the state legislatures, the percentage is not good when compared with the fact that in almost all 50 states, there are more women of voting age than there are men and that in each state, the number of women of voting age is increasing at a greater rate than the number of men. Nor is it an encouraging figure when compared with the fact that in 1966 there were not 318 women in the state legislatures, as now, but there were 328, which shows that there has been a decline. . . .

I have pointed out time and time again that the harshest discrimination that I have encountered in the political arena is anti-feminism, both from males and brain-washed, Uncle Tom females. When I first announced that I was running for the United States Congress, both males and females advised me, as they had when I ran for the New York State legislature, to go back to teaching—a woman's vocation—and leave the politics to the men.

And one of the major reasons that I will not leave the American scene—that is, voluntarily—is because the number of women in politics is declining. There are at least 2,000,000 more women than men of voting age, but the fact is that while we get out the vote, we also do not get out *to* vote. In 1964, for example, 72% of registered males voted, while only 67% of the registered females voted. We seem to want to become a political minority by choice. I believe that women have a special contribution to make to help bring order out of chaos in our nation today because they have special qualities of leadership which are greatly needed today. And these qualities are the patience, tolerance, and perseverance which have developed in many women because of suppression. And if we can add to these qualities a reservoir of information about the techniques of community action, we can indeed become effective harbingers for change.

Women must participate more in the legislative process, because even of the contributions that I have just mentioned, the single greatest contribution that women could bring to American politics would be a spirit of moral fervor, which is sorely needed in this nation today. But unfortunately, women's participation in politics is declining, as I have noted. . . .

Your time is now, my sisters. . . . New goals and new priorities, not only for this country, but for all of mankind must be set. Formal education will not help us do that. We must therefore depend upon informal learning. We can do that by confronting people with their humanity and their own inhumanity —confronting them wherever we meet them: in the church, in the classroom, on the floor of the Congress and the state legislatures, in the bars, and on the streets. We must reject not only the stereotypes that others hold of us, but also the stereotypes that we hold of ourselves.

In a speech made a few weeks ago to an audience that was predominately white and all female, I suggested the following, if they wanted to create change. You must start in your own homes, your own schools, and your own churches. I don't want you to go home and talk about integrated schools, churches, or marriages if the kind of integration you're talking about is black and white. I want you to go home and work for, fight for, the integration of male and female—human and human. . . .

Alex Haley

(1921–1992)

---

from *Roots*

Born in Ithaca, New York, Alex Haley worked for years as a shipboard cook for the United States Coast Guard. In his free time he wrote. Myriad rejection slips later he worked full time as a free-lance journalist, authoring such revelatory pieces as the Playboy *interview of Malcolm X in 1963. The following year he collaborated with Malcolm X on the now classic autobiography. Haley is best known, however, for the epic story of his family's African ancestry which was published in 1976 as* Roots.

Haley's quest for his roots began with the stories he heard as a child from his grandmothers and aunts about a particular ancestor who had come from Africa as a slave. The quest took Haley ultimately to a griot in Africa, where he discovered an ancient cultural heritage and a family history that had been obliterated by the slave experience. The excerpt included here de-

*scribes the moment in a village called Juffure, in the
back country of West Africa, that Haley's dream is realized and his life radically altered.*

Now over thirty years later the sole surviving one of the old
ladies who had talked the family narrative on the Henning front
porch was the youngest among them, Cousin Georgia Anderson. Grandma was gone, and all of the others too. In her eight-
ies now, Cousin Georgia lived with her son and daughter,
Floyd Anderson and Bea Neely, at 1200 Everett Avenue, Kansas City, Kansas. I hadn't seen her since my frequent visits
there of a few years before, then to offer what help I could to
my politically oriented brother, George. Successively out of the
U. S. Army Air Force, Morehouse College, then the University
of Arkansas Law School, George was hotly campaigning to become a Kansas state senator. The night of his victory party,
laughter flourished that actually why he'd won was . . .
Cousin Georgia. Having repetitively heard her campaign director son, Floyd, tell people of George's widely recognized integ-
rity, our beloved gray, bent, feisty Cousin Georgia had taken to
the local sidewalks. Rapping her walking cane at people's
doors, she had thrust before their startled faces a picture of
her grandnephew candidate, declaring, "Dat boy got mo' 'teg-
gity dan you can shake a stick at!"

Now I flew to Kansas City again, to see Cousin Georgia.

I think that I will never quite get over her instant response
when I raised the subject of the family story. Wrinkled and
ailing, she jerked upright in her bed, her excitement like boyhood front-porch echoes:

"Yeah, boy, dat African say his name was 'Kin-tay'! . . . He
say de guitar a *'ko,'* de river 'Kamby Bolongo,' an' he was chop-
pin' wood to make hisself a drum when dey cotched 'im!"

Cousin Georgia became so emotionally full of the old family
story that Floyd, Bea, and I had a time trying to calm her
down. I explained to her that I wanted to try to see if there was

any way that I could possibly find where our "Kin-tay" had
come from . . . which could reveal *our* ancestral tribe.

"You go 'head, boy!" exclaimed Cousin Georgia. "Yo' sweet
grandma an' all of 'em—dey up dere *watchin'* you!"

The thought made me feel something like . . . *My God!*

Soon after, I went to the National Archives in Washington,
D.C., and told a reading-room desk attendant that I was interested in Alamance County, North Carolina, census records just
after the Civil War. Rolls of microfilm were delivered. I began
turning film through the machine, feeling a mounting sense of
intrigue while viewing an endless parade of names recorded in
that old-fashioned penmanship of different 1800s census tak-
ers. After several of the long microfilm rolls, tiring, suddenly in
utter astonishment I found myself looking down there on:
"Tom Murray, black, blacksmith—," "Irene Murray, black,
housewife—" . . . followed by the names of Grandma's older
sisters—most of whom I'd listened to countless times on
Grandma's front porch. "Elizabeth, age 6"—nobody in the
world but my Great Aunt Liz! At the time of that census,
Grandma wasn't even born yet!

It wasn't that I hadn't believed the stories of Grandma and
the rest of them. You just *didn't* not believe my grandma. It was
simply so uncanny sitting staring at those names actually right
there in official U. S. Government records.

Then living in New York, I returned to Washington as often
as I could manage it—searching in the National Archives, in
the Library of Congress, in the Daughters of the American
Revolution Library. Wherever I was, whenever black library
attendants perceived the nature of my search, documents I'd
requested would reach me with a miraculous speed. From one
or another source during 1966, I was able to document at least
the highlights of the cherished family story; I would have given
anything to be able to tell Grandma—then I would remember
what Cousin Georgia had said, that she, all of them, were "up
there watchin'."

Now the thing was where, what, how could I pursue those
strange phonetic sounds that it was always said our African
ancestor had spoken. It seemed obvious that I had to reach as
wide a range of actual Africans as I possibly could, simply be-

cause so many different tribal tongues are spoken in Africa. There in New York City, I began doing what seemed logical: I began arriving at the United Nations around quitting time; the elevators were spilling out people who were thronging through the lobby on their way home. It wasn't hard to spot the Africans, and every one I was able to stop, I'd tell my sounds to. Within a couple of weeks, I guess I had stopped about two dozen Africans, each of whom had given me a quick look, a quick listen, and then took off. I can't say I blame them—me trying to communicate some African sounds in a Tennessee accent.

Increasingly frustrated, I had a long talk with George Sims, with whom I'd grown up in Henning, and who is a master researcher. After a few days, George brought me a list of about a dozen people academically renowned for their knowledge of African linguistics. One whose background intrigued me quickly was a Belgian Dr. Jan Vansina. After study at the University of London's School of African and Oriental Studies, he had done his early work living in African villages and written a book called *La Tradition Orale.* I telephoned Dr. Vansina where he now taught at the University of Wisconsin, and he gave me an appointment to see him. It was a Wednesday morning that I flew to Madison, Wisconsin, motivated by my intense curiosity about some strange phonetic sounds . . . and with no dream in this world of what was about to start happening. . . .

That evening in the Vansinas' living room, I told him every syllable I could remember of the family narrative heard since little boyhood—recently buttressed by Cousin Georgia in Kansas City. Dr. Vansina, after listening intently throughout, then began asking me questions. Being an oral historian, he was particularly interested in the physical transmission of the narrative down across generations.

We talked so late that he invited me to spend the night, and the next morning Dr. Vansina, with a very serious expression on his face, said, "I wanted to sleep on it. The ramifications of phonetic sounds preserved down across your family's generations can be immense." He said that he had been on the phone with a colleague Africanist, Dr. Philip Curtin; they both felt certain that the sounds I'd conveyed to him were from the

"Mandinka" tongue. I'd never heard that word; he told me that it was the language spoken by the Mandingo people. Then he guess translated certain of the sounds. One of them probably meant cow or cattle; another probably meant the baobab tree, generic in West Africa. The word *ko,* he said, could refer to the *kora,* one of the Mandingo people's oldest stringed instruments, made of a halved large dried gourd covered with goatskin, with a long neck, and twenty-one strings with a bridge. An enslaved Mandingo might relate the *kora* visually to some among the types of stringed instruments that U.S. slaves had.

The most involved sound I had heard and brought was Kamby Bolongo, my ancestor's sound to his daughter Kizzy as he had pointed to the Mattaponi River in Spotsylvania County, Virginia. Dr. Vansina said that without question, *bolongo* meant, in the Mandinka tongue, a moving water, as a river; preceded by "Kamby," it could indicate the Gambia River.

I'd never heard of it.

An incident happened that would build my feeling—especially as more uncanny things occurred—that, yes, they were up there watchin' . . .

I was asked to speak at a seminar held at Utica College, Utica, New York. Walking down a hallway with the professor who had invited me, I said I'd just flown in from Washington and why I'd been there. "The Gambia? If I'm not mistaken, someone mentioned recently that an outstanding student from that country is over at Hamilton."

The old, distinguished Hamilton College was maybe a half hour's drive away, in Clinton, New York. Before I could finish asking, a Professor Charles Todd said, "You're talking about Ebou Manga." Consulting a course roster, he told me where I could find him in an agricultural economics class. Ebou Manga was small of build, with careful eyes, a reserved manner, and black as soot. He tentatively confirmed my sounds, clearly startled to have heard me uttering them. Was Mandinka his home tongue? "No, although I am familiar with it." He was a Wolof, he said. In his dormitory room, I told him about my quest. We left for The Gambia at the end of the following week.

Arriving in Dakar, Senegal, the next morning, we caught a light plane to small Yundum Airport in The Gambia. In a passenger van, we rode into the capital city of Banjul (then Bath-

urst). Ebou and his father, Alhaji Manga—Gambians are
mostly Moslem—assembled a small group of men knowledgeable in their small country's history, who met with me in the
lounge of the Atlantic Hotel. As I had told Dr. Vansina in Wisconsin, I told these men the family narrative that had come
down across the generations. I told them in a reverse progres-
sion, backward from Grandma through Tom, Chicken George,
then Kizzy saying how her African father insisted to other
slaves that his name was "Kin-tay," and repetitively told her
phonetic sounds identifying various things, along with stories
such as that he had been attacked and seized while not far
from his village, chopping wood.

When I had finished, they said almost with wry amusement,
"Well, of course 'Kamby Bolongo' would mean Gambia River;
anyone would know that." I told them hotly that no, a great
many people *wouldn't* know it! Then they showed a much
greater interest that my 1760s ancestor had insisted his name
was "Kin-tay." "Our country's oldest villages tend to be named
for the families that settled those villages centuries ago," they
said. Sending for a map, pointing, they said, "Look, here is the
village of Kinte-Kundah. And not too far from it, the village of
Kinte-Kundah Janneh-Ya."

Then they told me something of which I'd never have
dreamed: of very old men, called *griots,* still to be found in the
older back-country villages, men who were in effect living,
walking archives of oral history. A senior *griot* would be a man
usually in his late sixties or early seventies; below him would
be progressively younger *griots*—and apprenticing boys, so a
boy would be exposed to those *griots'* particular line of narrative for forty or fifty years before he could qualify as a senior
griot, who told on special occasions the centuries-old histories
of villages, of clans, of families, of great heroes. Throughout
the whole of black Africa such oral chronicles had been
handed down since the time of the ancient forefathers, I was
informed, and there were certain legendary *griots* who could
narrate facets of African history literally for as long as three
days without ever repeating themselves.

Seeing how astounded I was, these Gambian men reminded
me that every living person ancestrally goes back to some time
and some place where no writing existed; and then human

memories and mouths and ears were the only ways those human beings could store and relay information. They said that
we who live in the Western culture are so conditioned to the
"crutch of print" that few among us comprehend what a trained
memory is capable of.

Since my forefather had said his name was "Kin-tay"—properly spelled "Kinte," they said—and since the Kinte clan was
old and well known in The Gambia, they promised to do what
they could to find a *griot* who might be able to assist my
search.

Back in the United States, I began devouring books on African history. It grew quickly into some kind of obsession to
correct my ignorance concerning the earth's second-largest
continent. It embarrasses me to this day that up to then my
images about Africa had been largely derived or inferred from
Tarzan movies and my very little authentic knowledge had
come from only occasional leafings through the *National Geo-
graphic*. All of a sudden now, after reading all day, I'd sit on the
edge of my bed at night studying a map of Africa, memorizing
the different countries' relative positions and the principal waters where slave ships had operated.

After some weeks, a registered letter came from The Gambia; it suggested that when possible, I should come back. But
by now I was stony broke—especially because I'd been invest-
ing very little of my time in writing.

Once at a *Reader's Digest* lawn party, cofounder Mrs. DeWitt
Wallace had told me how much she liked an "Unforgettable
Character" I had written—about a tough old seadog cook who
had once been my boss in the U. S. Coast Guard—and before
leaving, Mrs. Wallace volunteered that I should let her know if
I ever needed some help. Now I wrote to Mrs. Wallace a rather
embarrassed letter, briefly telling her the compulsive quest I'd
gotten myself into. She asked some editors to meet with me
and see what they felt, and invited to lunch with them, I talked
about nonstop for nearly three hours. Shortly afterward, a letter told me that the *Reader's Digest* would provide me with a
three-hundred-dollar monthly check for one year, and plus that
—my really vital need—"reasonable necessary travel expenses."

I again visited Cousin Georgia in Kansas City—something

had urged me to do so, and I found her quite ill. But she was thrilled to hear both what I had learned and what I hoped to learn. She wished me Godspeed, and I flew then to Africa.

The same men with whom I had previously talked told me now in a rather matter-of-fact manner that they had caused word to be put out in the back country, and that a *griot* very knowledgeable of the Kinte clan had indeed been found—his name, they said, was "Kebba Kanji Fofana." I was ready to have a fit. "Where *is* he?" They looked at me oddly: "He's in his village."

I discovered that if I intended to see this *griot,* I was going to have to do something I'd never have dreamed I'd ever be doing —organizing what seemed, at least to me then, a kind of minisafari! It took me three days of negotiating through unaccustomed endless African palaver finally to hire a launch to get upriver; to rent a lorry and a Land-Rover to take supplies by a roundabout land route; to hire finally a total of fourteen people, including three interpreters and four musicians, who had told me that the old *griots* in the back country wouldn't talk without music in the background.

In the launch *Baddibu,* vibrating up the wide, swift "Kamby Bolongo," I felt queasily, uncomfortably alien. Did they all have me appraised as merely another pith helmet? Finally ahead was James Island, for two centuries the site of a fort over which England and France waged war back and forth for the ideal vantage point to trade in slaves. Asking if we might land there a while, I trudged amid the crumbling ruins yet guarded by ghostly cannon. Picturing in my mind the kinds of atrocities that would have happened there, I felt as if I would like to go flailing an ax back through that facet of black Africa's history. Without luck I tried to find for myself some symbol remnant of an ancient chain, but I took a chunk of mortar and a brick. In the next minutes before we returned to the *Baddibu,* I just gazed up and down that river that my ancestor had named for his daughter far across the Atlantic Ocean in Spotsylvania County, Virginia. Then we went on, and upon arriving at a little village called Albreda, we put ashore, our destination now on foot the yet smaller village of Juffure, where the men had been told that this *griot* lived.

There is an expression called "the peak experience"—that

which emotionally, nothing in your life ever transcends. I've had mine, that first day in the back country of black West Africa.

When we got within sight of Juffure, the children who were playing outside gave the alert, and the people came flocking from their huts. It's a village of only about seventy people. Like most back-country villages, it was still very much as it was two hundred years ago, with its circular mud houses and their conical thatched roofs. Among the people as they gathered was a small man wearing an off-white robe, a pillbox hat over an aquiline-featured black face, and about him was an aura of "somebodiness" until I knew he was the man we had come to see and hear.

As the three interpreters left our party to converge upon him, the seventy-odd other villagers gathered closely around me, in a kind of horseshoe pattern, three or four deep all around; had I stuck out my arms, my fingers would have touched the nearest ones on either side. They were all staring at me. The eyes just raked me. Their foreheads were furrowed with their very intensity of staring. A kind of visceral surging or a churning sensation started up deep inside me; bewildered, I was wondering what on earth was this . . . then in a little while it was rather as if some full-gale force of realization rolled in on me: Many times in my life I had been among crowds of people, but never where *every one was jet black!*

Rocked emotionally, my eyes dropped downward as we tend to do when we're uncertain, insecure, and my glance fell upon my own hands' brown complexion. This time more quickly than before, and even harder, another gale-force emotion hit me: I felt myself some variety of a hybrid . . . I felt somehow impure among the pure; it was a terribly shaming feeling. About then, abruptly the old man left the interpreters. The people immediately also left me now to go crowding about him.

One of my interpreters came up quickly and whispered in my ears, "They stare at you so much because they have never here seen a black American." When I grasped the significance, I believe that hit me harder than what had already happened. They hadn't been looking at me as an individual, but I represented in their eyes a symbol of the twenty-five millions of us black people whom they had never seen, who lived beyond an ocean.

The people were clustered thickly about the old man, all of them intermittently flicking glances toward me as they talked animatedly in their Mandinka tongue. After a while, the old man turned, walked briskly through the people, past my three interpreters, and right up to me. His eyes piercing into mine, seeming to feel I should understand his Mandinka, he expressed what they had all decided they *felt* concerning those unseen millions of us who lived in those places that had been slave ships' destinations—and the translation came: "We have been told by the forefathers that there are many of us from this place who are in exile in that place called America—and in other places."

The old man sat down, facing me, as the people hurriedly gathered behind him. Then he began to recite for me the ancestral history of the Kinte clan, as it had been passed along orally down across centuries from the forefathers' time. It was not merely conversational, but more as if a scroll were being read; for the still, silent villagers, it was clearly a formal occasion. The *griot* would speak, bending forward from the waist, his body rigid, his neck cords standing out, his words seeming almost physical objects. After a sentence or two, seeming to go limp, he would lean back, listening to an interpreter's translation. Spilling from the *griot's* head came an incredibly complex Kinte clan lineage that reached back across many generations: who married whom; who had what children; what children then married whom; then their offspring. It was all just unbelievable. I was struck not only by the profusion of details, but also by the narrative's biblical style, something like: "—and so-and-so took as a wife so-and-so, and begat . . . and begat . . . and begat . . ." He would next name each begat's eventual spouse, or spouses, and their averagely numerous offspring, and so on. To date things the *griot* linked them to events, such as "—in the year of the big water"—a flood—"he slew a water buffalo." To determine the calendar date, you'd have to find out when that particular flood occurred.

Simplifying to its essence the encyclopedic saga that I was told, the *griot* said that the Kinte clan had begun in the country called Old Mali. Then the Kinte men traditionally were blacksmiths, "who had conquered fire," and the women mostly were potters and weavers. In time, one branch of the clan moved into the country called Mauretania; and it was from Mauretania that one son of this clan, whose name was Kairaba Kunta Kinte —a *marabout,* or holy man of the Moslem faith—journeyed down into the country called The Gambia. He went first to a village called Pakali N'Ding, stayed there for a while, then went to a village called Jiffarong, and then to the village of Juffure.

In Juffure, Kairaba Kunta Kinte took his first wife, a Mandinka maiden whose name was Sireng. And by her he begot two sons, whose names were Janneh and Saloum. Then he took a second wife; her name was Yaisa. And by Yaisa, he begot a son named Omoro.

Those three sons grew up in Juffure until they became of age. Then the elder two, Janneh and Saloum, went away and founded a new village called Kinte-Kundah Janneh-Ya. The youngest son, Omoro, stayed on in Juffure village until he had thirty rains—years—of age, then he took as his wife a Mandinka maiden named Binta Kebba. And by Binta Kebba, roughly between the years 1750 and 1760, Omoro Kinte begat four sons, whose names were, in the order of their birth, Kunta, Lamin, Suwadu, and Madi.

The old *griot* had talked for nearly two hours up to then, and perhaps fifty times the narrative had included some detail about someone whom he had named. Now after he had just named those four sons, again he appended a detail, and the interpreter translated—

"About the time the King's soldiers came"—another of the *griot's* time-fixing references—"the eldest of these four sons, Kunta, went away from his village to chop wood . . . and he was never seen again. . . ." And the *griot* went on with his narrative.

I sat as if I were carved of stone. My blood seemed to have congealed. This man whose lifetime had been in this backcountry African village had no way in the world to know that he had just echoed what I had heard all through my boyhood years on my grandma's front porch in Henning, Tennessee . . . of an African who always had insisted that his name was "Kin-tay"; who had called a guitar a *"ko,"* and a river within the state of Virginia, "Kamby Bolongo"; and who had been kid-

naped into slavery while not far from his village, chopping
wood, to make himself a drum.

I managed to fumble from my dufflebag my basic notebook,
whose first pages containing grandma's story I showed to an
interpreter. After briefly reading, clearly astounded, he spoke
rapidly while showing it to the old *griot,* who became agitated;
he got up, exclaiming to the people, gesturing at my notebook
in the interpreter's hands, and *they* all got agitated.

I don't remember hearing anyone giving an order, I only
recall becoming aware that those seventy-odd people had
formed a wide human ring around me, moving counterclock-
wise, chanting softly, loudly, softly; their bodies close together,
they were lifting their knees high, stamping up reddish puffs of
the dust. . . .

The woman who broke from the moving circle was one of
about a dozen whose infant children were within cloth slings
across their backs. Her jet-black face deeply contorting, the
woman came charging toward me, her bare feet slapping the
earth, and snatching her baby free, she thrust it at me almost
roughly, the gesture saying "Take it!" . . . and I did, clasping
the baby to me. Then she snatched away her baby; and another
woman was thrusting her baby, then another, and another . . .
until I had embraced probably a dozen babies. I wouldn't learn
until maybe a year later, from a Harvard University professor,
Dr. Jerome Bruner, a scholar of such matters, "You didn't
know you were participating in one of the oldest ceremonies of
humankind, called 'The laying on of hands'! In their way, they
were telling you 'Through this flesh, which is us, we are you,
and you are us!' "

Later the men of Juffure took me into their mosque built of
bamboo and thatch, and they prayed around me in Arabic. I
remember thinking, down on my knees, "After I've found out
where I came from, I can't understand a word they're saying."
Later the crux of their prayer was translated for me: "Praise be
to Allah for one long lost from us whom Allah has returned."

Since we had come by the river, I wanted to return by land.
As I sat beside the wiry young Mandingo driver who was leaving dust pluming behind us on the hot, rough, pitted, back-
country road toward Banjul, there came from somewhere into
my head a staggering awareness . . . that *if* any black Ameri-

can could be so blessed as I had been to know only a few
ancestral clues—could he or she know *who* was either the pa-
ternal or maternal African ancestor or ancestors, and about
where that ancestor lived when taken, and finally about *when*
the ancestor was taken—then only those few clues might well
see that black American able to locate some wizened old black
griot whose narrative could reveal the black American's ancestral clan, perhaps even the very village.

In my mind's eye, rather as if it were mistily being projected
on a screen, I began envisioning descriptions I had read of how
collectively millions of our ancestors had been enslaved. Many
thousands were individually kidnaped, as my own forebear
Kunta had been, but into the millions had come awake screaming in the night, dashing out into the bedlam of raided villages,
which were often in flames. The captured able survivors were
linked neck-by-neck with thongs into processions called "cof-
fles," which were sometimes as much as a mile in length. I
envisioned the many dying, or left to die when they were too
weak to continue the torturous march toward the coast, and
those who made it to the beach were greased, shaved, probed
in every orifice, often branded with sizzling irons; I envisioned
them being lashed and dragged toward the longboats; their
spasms of screaming and clawing with their hands into the
beach, biting up great choking mouthfuls of the sand in their
desperation efforts for one last hold on the Africa that had
been their home; I envisioned them shoved, beaten, jerked
down into slave ships' stinking holds and chained onto shelves,
often packed so tightly that they had to lie on their sides like
spoons in a drawer. . . .

My mind reeled with it all as we approached another, much
larger village. Staring ahead, I realized that word of what had
happened in Juffure must have left there well before I did. The
driver slowing down, I could see this village's people thronging
the road ahead; they were waving, amid their cacophony of
crying out something; I stood up in the Land-Rover, waving
back as they seemed grudging to open a path for the Land-
Rover.

I guess we had moved a third of the way through the village
when it suddenly registered in my brain what they were all
crying out . . . the wizened, robed elders and younger men,

the mothers and the naked tar-black children, they were all waving-up at me; their expressions buoyant, beaming, all were crying out together, *"Meester Kinte! Meester Kinte!"*

Let me tell you something: I am a man. A sob hit me somewhere around my ankles; it came surging upward, and flinging my hands over my face, I was just bawling, as I hadn't since I was a baby. *"Meester Kinte!"* I just felt like I was weeping for all of history's incredible atrocities against fellowmen, which seems to be mankind's greatest flaw. . . .

Flying homeward from Dakar, I decided to write a book. My own ancestors' would automatically also be a symbolic saga of all African-descent people—who are without exception the seeds of someone like Kunta who was born and grew up in some black African village, someone who was captured and chained down in one of those slave ships that sailed them across the same ocean, into some succession of plantations, and since then a struggle for freedom.

In New York, my waiting telephone messages included that in a Kansas City Hospital, our eighty-three-year-old Cousin Georgia had died. Later, making a time-zone adjustment, I discovered that she passed away within the very hour that I had walked into Juffure Village. I think that as the last of the old ladies who talked the story on Grandma's front porch, it had been her job to get me to Africa, then she went to join the others up there watchin'.

In fact, I see starting from my little boyhood, a succession of related occurrences that finally when they all joined have caused this book to exist. Grandma and the others drilled the family story into me. Then, purely by the fluke of circumstances, when I was cooking on U. S. Coast Guard ships at sea, I began the long trial-and-error process of teaching myself to write. And because I had come to love the sea, my early writing was about dramatic sea adventures gleaned out of yellowing old maritime records in the U. S. Coast Guard's Archives. I couldn't have acquired a much better preparation to meet the maritime research challenges that this book would bring.

Always, Grandma and the other old ladies had said that a ship brought the African to "somewhere called 'Naplis." I knew they had to have been referring to Annapolis, Maryland. So I felt now that I had to try to see if I could find *what* ship had sailed to Annapolis from the Gambia River, with her human cargo including "the African," who would later insist that "Kintay" was his name, after his massa John Waller had given him the name "Toby."

I needed to determine a time around which to focus search for this ship. Months earlier, in the village of Juffure, the *griot* had timed Kunta Kinte's capture with "about the time the King's soldiers came."

Returning to London, midway during a second week of searching in records of movement assignments for British military units during the 1760s, I finally found that "King's soldiers" *had* to refer to a unit called "Colonel O'Hare's forces." The unit was sent from London in 1767 to guard the then British-operated Fort James Slave Fort in the Gambia River. The *griot* had been so correct that I felt embarrassed that, in effect, I had been checking behind him.

I went to Lloyds of London. In the office of an executive named Mr. R. C. E. Landers, it just poured out of me what I was trying to do. He got up from behind his desk and he said, "Young man, Lloyds of London will give you all of the help that we can." It was a blessing, for through Lloyds, doors began to be opened for me to search among myriad old English maritime records.

I can't remember any more exhausting experience than my first six weeks of seemingly endless, futile, day-after-day of searching in an effort to isolate and then pin down a specific slave ship on a specific voyage from within cartons upon cartons, files upon files of old records of thousands of slave-ship triangular voyages among England, Africa, and America. Along with my frustration, the more a rage grew within me the more I perceived to what degree the slave trade, in its time, was regarded by most of its participants simply as another major industry, rather like the buying, selling, and shipment of livestock today. Many records seemed never to have been opened after their original storage, apparently no one had felt occasion to go through them.

I hadn't found a single ship bound from The Gambia to Annapolis, when in the seventh week, one afternoon about two-thirty, I was studying the 1,023rd sheet of slave-ship records. A wide rectangular sheet, it recorded the Gambia River entrances and exits of some thirty ships during the years 1766 and 1767. Moving down the list, my eyes reached ship No. 18, and automatically scanned across its various data heading entries.

On July 5, 1767—the year "the King's soldiers came"—a ship named *Lord Ligonier,* her captain, a Thomas E. Davies, had sailed from the Gambia River, her destination Annapolis. . . .

I don't know why, but oddly my internal emotional reaction was delayed. I recall passively writing down the information, I turned in the records, and walked outside. Around the corner was a little tea shop. I went in and ordered a tea and cruller. Sitting, sipping my tea, it suddenly hit me that quite possibly that ship brought Kunta Kinte!

I still owe the lady for the tea and cruller. By telephone, Pan American confirmed their last seat available that day to New York. There simply wasn't time to go by the hotel where I was staying; I told a taxi driver, "Heathrow Airport!" Sleepless through that night's crossing of the Atlantic, I was seeing in my mind's eye the book in the Library of Congress, Washington D.C., that I had to get my hands on again. It had a light brown cover, with darker brown letters—*Shipping in the Port of Annapolis,* by Vaughan W. Brown.

From New York, the Eastern Airlines shuttle took me to Washington; I taxied to the Library of Congress, ordered the book, almost yanked it from the young man who brought it, and went riffling through it . . . and there it was, confirmation! The *Lord Ligonier* had cleared Annapolis' customs officials on September 29, 1767.

Renting a car, speeding to Annapolis, I went to the Maryland Hall of Records and asked archivist Mrs. Phebe Jacobsen for copies of any local newspaper published around the first week of October 1767. She soon produced a microfilm roll of the Maryland *Gazette.* At the projection machine, I was halfway through the October 1 issue when I saw the advertisement in the antique typeface: "JUST IMPORTED, In the ship *Lord Ligonier,* Capt. Davies, from the River Gambia, in Africa, and to be sold by the subscribers, in Annapolis, for cash, or good bills of exchange on Wednesday the 7th of October next, A Cargo of CHOICE HEALTHY SLAVES. The said ship will take tobacco to London on liberty at 6s. Sterling per ton." The advertisement was signed by John Ridout and Daniel of St. Thos. Jenifer.

On September 29, 1967, I felt I should be nowhere else in the world except standing on a pier at Annapolis—and I was; it was two hundred years to the day after the *Lord Ligonier* had landed. Staring out to seaward across those waters over which my great-great-great-great grandfather had been brought, again I found myself weeping.

The 1766–67 document compiled at James Fort in the Gambia River had included that the *Lord Ligonier* had sailed with 140 slaves in her hold. How many of them had lived through the voyage? Now on a second mission in the Maryland Hall of Records, I searched to find a record of the ship's cargo listed upon her arrival in Annapolis—and found it, the following inventory, in old-fashioned script: 3,265 "elephants' teeth," as ivory tusks were called; 3,700 pounds of beeswax; 800 pounds of raw cotton; 32 ounces of Gambian gold; and 98 "Negroes." Her loss of 42 Africans en route, or around one third, was average for slaving voyages.

I realized by this time that Grandma, Aunt Liz, Aunt Plus, and Cousin Georgia also had been *griots* in their own ways. My notebooks contained their centuries-old story that our African had been sold to "Massa John Waller," who had given him the name "Toby." During his fourth escape effort, when cornered he had wounded with a rock one of the pair of professional slave-catchers who caught him, and they had cut his foot off. "Massa John's brother, Dr. William Waller," had saved the slave's life, then indignant at the maiming, had bought him from his brother. I dared to hope there might actually exist some kind of an actual documenting record.

I went to Richmond, Virginia. I pored through microfilmed legal deeds filed within Spotsylvania County, Virginia, after September 1767, when the *Lord Ligonier* had landed. In time, I found a lengthy deed dated September 5, 1768, in which John Waller and his wife Ann transferred to William Waller land and goods, including 240 acres of farmland . . . and then on the second page, "and also one Negro man slave named Toby."

My God!

In the twelve years since my visit to the Rosetta Stone, I have traveled half a million miles, I suppose, searching, sifting, checking, crosschecking, finding out more and more about the people whose respective oral histories had proved not only to be correct, but even to connect on both sides of the ocean. Finally I managed to tear away from yet more researching in order to push myself into actually writing this book. To develop Kunta Kinte's boyhood and youth took me a long time, and having come to know him well, I anguished upon his capture. When I began trying to write of his, or all of those Gambians' slave-ship crossing, finally I flew to Africa and canvassed among shipping lines to obtain passage on the first possible freighter sailing from any black African port directly to the United States. It turned out to be the Farrell Lines' *African Star*. When we put to sea, I explained what I hoped to do that might help me write of my ancestor's crossing. After each late evening's dinner, I climbed down successive metal ladders into her deep, dark, cold cargo hold. Stripping to my underwear, I lay on my back on a wide rough bare dunnage plank and forced myself to stay there through all ten nights of the crossing, trying to imagine what did he see, hear, feel, smell, taste— and above all, in knowing Kunta, what things did he think? My crossing of course was ludicrously luxurious by any comparison to the ghastly ordeal endured by Kunta Kinte, his companions, and all those other millions who lay chained and shackled in terror and their own filth for an average of eighty to ninety days, at the end of which awaited new physical and psychic horrors. But anyway, finally I wrote of the ocean crossing— from the perspective of the human cargo.

Finally I've woven our whole seven generations into this book that is in your hands. In the years of the writing, I have also spoken before many audiences of how *Roots* came to be, naturally now and then someone asks, "How much of *Roots* is fact and how much is fiction?" To the best of my knowledge and of my effort, every lineage statement within *Roots* is from either my African or American families' carefully preserved oral history, much of which I have been able conventionally to corroborate with documents. Those documents, along with the myriad textural details of what were contemporary indigenous lifestyles, cultural history, and such that give *Roots* flesh have come from years of intensive research in fifty-odd libraries, archives, and other repositories on three continents.

Since I wasn't yet around when most of the story occurred, by far most of the dialogue and most of the incidents are of necessity a novelized amalgam of what I *know* took place together with what my researching led me to plausibly *feel* took place.

I think now that not only are Grandma, Cousin Georgia, and those other ladies "up there watchin'," but so are all of the others: Kunta and Bell; Kizzy; Chicken George and Matilda; Tom and Irene; Grandpa Will Palmer; Bertha; Mama—and now, as well, the most recent one to join them, Dad. . . .

IV

The Promised Land

Stealthy night journeys, secret messages,
narrow escapes, and dark borders
were written into African-American history
as thousands of fugitive slaves found
in the free states and Canada their Canaan
or, as they also called it, their Promised Land.

Robert Hayden
(b. 1913)

Runagate Runagate

Poet and teacher, formerly a professor in the English department at the University of Michigan, Robert Hayden was born in Detroit. In the poem that follows, in language alternately heroic and vernacular, Hayden draws images from slave narratives, the Bible, spirituals, and folk tunes as he invokes the names of abolitionists to convey the desire for freedom laced by the taste of fear as it might have been experienced by fugitive slaves in their escape on the Undergound Railroad to a "mythic North."

"Runagate Runagate" was included in Hayden's 1966 volume of Selected Poems.

I.

Runs falls rises stumbles on from darkness into darkness
and the darkness thicketed with shapes of terror
and the hunters pursuing and the hounds pursuing
and the night cold and the night long and the river
to cross and the jack-muh-lanterns beckoning beckoning
and blackness ahead and when shall I reach that
      somewhere
morning and keep on going and never turn back and
      keep on going

      Runagate
                  Runagate
                              Runagate

Many thousands rise and go
many thousands crossing over

                                    O mythic North
                        O star-shaped yonder Bible city

Some go weeping and some rejoicing
some in coffins and some in carriages
some in silks and some in shackles

      Rise and go or fare you well

No more auction block for me
no more driver's lash for me

      If you see my Pompey, 30 yrs of age,
      new breeches, plain stockings, negro shoes;
      if you see my Anna, likely young mulatto

branded E on the right cheek, R on the left,
catch them if you can and notify subscriber.
Catch them if you can, but it won't be easy.
They'll dart underground when you try to catch them,
plunge into quicksand, whirlpools, mazes,
turn into scorpions when you try to catch them.

And before I'll be a slave
I'll be buried in my grave

North star and bonanza gold
I'm bound for the freedom, freedom-bound
and oh Susyanna don't you cry for me

Runagate

Runagate

II.

Rises from their anguish and their power,

Harriet Tubman,

woman of earth, whipscarred,
a summoning, a shining

Mean to be free

And this was the way of it, brethren brethren,
way we journeyed from Can't to Can.
Moon so bright and no place to hide,
the cry up and the patterollers riding,
hound dogs belling in bladed air.
And fear starts a-murbling, Never make it,
we'll never make it. *Hush that now,*
and she's turned upon us, levelled pistol
glinting in the moonlight:
Dead folks can't jaybird-talk, she says:
you keep on going now or die, she says.

Wanted   Harriet Tubman   alias The General
alias Moses   Stealer of Slaves

In league with Garrison   Alcott   Emerson
Garrett   Douglass   Thoreau   John Brown

Armed and known to be Dangerous

Wanted   Reward   Dead or Alive

   Tell me, Ezekiel, oh tell me do you see
   mailed Jehovah coming to deliver me?

Hoot-owl calling in the ghosted air,
five times calling to the hants in the air.
Shadow of a face in the scary leaves,
shadow of a voice in the talking leaves:
Come ride-a my train

Oh that train, ghost-story train
through swamp and savanna movering movering,
over trestles of dew, through caves of the wish,
Midnight Special on a sabre track movering movering,
first stop Mercy and the last Hallelujah.

Come ride-a my train

   Mean mean mean to be free.

Harriet Tubman

(1821–1913)

On Liberty or Death

Harriet Tubman was born in bondage in Rochester County, Maryland. Harriet Tubman was born to be free. Leaving behind her the husband and two children who refused to follow her, Harriet Tubman made her escape across the Mason-Dixon Line to freedom. She then made her people's freedom her cause. Working through the Underground Railroad, Tubman risked nineteen long and dangerous runs in the dead of deep southern nights to lead fugitive slaves to their liberty in Canada. Her deliverance of more than three hundred slaves to "the Promised Land" in a single decade earned her the name of Moses, and for her fearless leadership she was also often called the General.

The brief statement by Tubman that is included here appears in the book Harriet Tubman, The Moses of Her People *by Sarah Bradford.*

There was one of two things I had a *right* to, liberty, or death; if I could not have one, I would have the other; for no man should take me alive; I should fight for my liberty as long as my strength lasted, and when the time came for me to go, the Lord would let them take me.

Richard Wright

(1908–1960)

---

from *Black Boy*

This passage from Richard Wright's autobiography recounts the moment of a fifteen-year-old black boy's flight towards the promise of the North and, as significantly, his escape fifty years after the abolition of slavery from the cultural bondage imposed upon blacks in a white South where he would always only be a "nigger" who couldn't learn his "place" in life.

The accidental visit of Aunt Maggie to Memphis formed a practical basis for my planning to go north. Aunt Maggie's husband, the "uncle" who had fled from Arkansas in the dead of night, had deserted her; and now she was casting about for a living. My mother, Aunt Maggie, my brother, and I held long conferences, speculating on the prospects of jobs and the cost of apartments in Chicago. And every time we conferred, we defeated ourselves. It was impossible for all four of us to go at once; we did not have enough money.

Finally sheer wish and hope prevailed over common sense and facts. We discovered that if we waited until we were prepared to go, we would never leave, we would never amass enough money to see us through. We would have to gamble. We finally decided that Aunt Maggie and I would go first, even though it was winter, and prepare a place for my mother and brother. Why wait until next week or next month? If we were going, why not go at once?

Next loomed the problem of leaving my job cleanly, smoothly, without arguments or scenes. How could I present the fact of leaving to my boss? Yes, I would pose as an innocent boy; I would tell him that my aunt was taking me and my paralyzed mother to Chicago. That would create in his mind the impression that I was not asserting my will; it would block any expression of dislike on his part for my act. I knew that southern whites hated the idea of Negroes leaving to live in places where the racial atmosphere was different.

It worked as I had planned. When I broke the news of my leaving two days before I left—I was afraid to tell it sooner for fear that I would create hostility on the part of the whites with whom I worked—the boss leaned back in his swivel chair and gave me the longest and most considerate look he had ever given me.

"Chicago?" he repeated softly.

"Yes, sir."

"Boy, you won't like it up there," he said.

"Well, I have to go where my family is, sir," I said.

The other white office workers paused in their tasks and listened. I grew self-conscious, tense.

"It's cold up there," he said.

"Yes, sir. They say it is," I said, keeping my voice in a neutral tone.

He became conscious that I was watching him and he looked away, laughing uneasily to cover his concern and dislike.

"Now, boy," he said banteringly, "don't you go up there and fall into that lake."

"Oh, no, sir," I said, smiling as though there existed the possibility of my falling accidentally into Lake Michigan.

He was serious again, staring at me. I looked at the floor.

"You think you'll do any better up there?" he asked.

"I don't know, sir."

"You seem to've been getting along all right down here," he said.

"Oh, yes, sir. If it wasn't for my mother's going, I'd stay right here and work," I lied as earnestly as possible.

"Well, why not stay? You can send her money," he suggested.

He had trapped me. I knew that staying now would never do. I could not have controlled my relations with the whites if I had remained after having told them that I wanted to go north.

"Well, I want to be with my mother," I said.

"You want to be with your mother," he repeated idly. "Well, Richard, we enjoyed having you with us."

"And I enjoyed working here," I lied.

There was silence; I stood awkwardly, then moved to the door. There was still silence; white faces were looking strangely at me. I went upstairs, feeling like a criminal. The word soon spread through the factory and the white men looked at me with new eyes. They came to me.

"So you're going north, hunh?"

"Yes, sir. My family's taking me with 'em."

"The North's no good for your people, boy."

"I'll try to get along, sir."

"Don't believe all the stories you hear about the North."

"No, sir. I don't."

"You'll come back here where your friends are."

"Well, sir. I don't know."

"How're you going to act up there?"

"Just like I act down here, sir."

"Would you speak to a white girl up there?"

"Oh, no, sir. I'll act there just like I act here."

"Aw, no, you won't. You'll change. Niggers change when they go north."

I wanted to tell him that I was going north precisely to change, but I did not.

"I'll be the same," I said, trying to indicate that I had no imagination whatever.

As I talked I felt that I was acting out a dream. I did not want to lie, yet I had to lie to conceal what I felt. A white censor was standing over me and, like dreams forming a curtain for the safety of sleep, so did my lies form a screen of safety for my living moments.

"Boy, I bet you've been reading too many of them damn books."

"Oh, no, sir."

I made my last errand to the post office, put my bag away, washed my hands, and pulled on my cap. I shot a quick glance about the factory; most of the men were working late. One or two looked up. Mr. Falk, to whom I had returned my library card, gave me a quick, secret smile. I walked to the elevator and rode down with Shorty.

"You lucky bastard," he said bitterly.

"Why do you say that?"

"You saved your goddamn money and now you're gone."

"My problems are just starting," I said.

"You'll never have any problems as hard as the ones you had here," he said.

"I hope not," I said. "But life is tricky."

"Sometimes I get so goddamn mad I want to kill everybody," he spat in a rage.

"You can leave," I said.

"I'll never leave this goddamn South," he railed. "I'm always saying I am, but I won't . . . I'm lazy. I like to sleep too goddamn much. I'll die here. Or maybe they'll kill me."

I stepped from the elevator into the street, half expecting someone to call me back and tell me that it was all a dream, that I was not leaving.

This was the culture from which I sprang. This was the terror from which I fled.

The next day when I was already in full flight—aboard a northward bound train—I could not have accounted, if it had been demanded of me, for all the varied forces that were making me reject the culture that had molded and shaped me. I was leaving without a qualm, without a single backward glance.

The face of the South that I had known was hostile and forbidding, and yet out of all the conflicts and the curses, the blows and the anger, the tension and the terror, I had somehow gotten the idea that life could be different, could be lived in a fuller and richer manner. As had happened when I had fled the orphan home, I was now running more away from something than toward something. But that did not matter to me. My mood was: I've got to get away; I can't stay here.

But what was it that always made me feel that way? What was it that made me conscious of possibilities? From where in this southern darkness had I caught a sense of freedom? Why was it that I was able to act upon vaguely felt notions? What was it that made me feel things deeply enough for me to try to order my life by my feelings? The external world of whites and blacks, which was the only world that I had ever known, surely had not evoked in me any belief in myself. The people I had met had advised and demanded submission. What, then, was I after? How dare I consider my feelings superior to the gross environment that sought to claim me?

It had been only through books—at best, no more than vicarious cultural transfusions—that I had managed to keep myself alive in a negatively vital way. Whenever my environment had failed to support or nourish me, I had clutched at books; consequently, my belief in books had risen more out of a sense of desperation than from any abiding conviction of their ultimate value. In a peculiar sense, life had trapped me in a realm of emotional rejection; I had not embraced insurgency through open choice. Existing emotionally on the sheer, thin margin of southern culture, I had felt that nothing short of life itself hung upon each of my actions and decisions; and I had grown used to change, to movement, to making many adjustments.

In the main, my hope was merely a kind of self-defence, a conviction that if I did not leave I would perish, either because of possible violence of others against me, or because of my possible violence against them. The substance of my hope was formless and devoid of any real sense of direction, for in my southern living I had seen no looming landmark by which I could, in a positive sense, guide my daily actions. The shocks of southern living had rendered my personality tender and swollen, tense and volatile, and my flight was more a shunning

of external and internal dangers than an attempt to embrace
what I felt I wanted.

It had been my accidental reading of fiction and literary criticism that had evoked in me vague glimpses of life's possibilities. Of course, I had never seen or met the men who wrote the
books I read, and the kind of world in which they lived was as
alien to me as the moon. But what enabled me to overcome my
chronic distrust was that these books—written by men like
Dreiser, Masters, Mencken, Anderson, and Lewis—seemed
defensively critical of the straitened American environment.
These writers seemed to feel that America could be shaped
nearer to the hearts of those who lived in it. And it was out of
these novels and stories and articles, out of the emotional impact of imaginative constructions of heroic or tragic deeds, that
I felt touching my face a tinge of warmth from an unseen light;
and in my leaving I was groping toward that invisible light,
always trying to keep my face so set and turned that I would
not lose the hope of its faint promise, using it as my justifica-
tion for action.

The white South said that it knew "niggers," and I was what
the white South called a "nigger." Well, the white South had
never known me—never known what I thought, what I felt.
The white South said that I had a "place" in life. Well, I had
never felt my "place"; or, rather, my deepest instincts had always made me reject the "place" to which the white South had
assigned me. It had never occurred to me that I was in any way
an inferior being. And no word that I had ever heard fall from
the lips of southern white men had ever made me really doubt
the worth of my own humanity. True, I had lied. I had stolen. I
had struggled to contain my seething anger. I had fought. And
it was perhaps a mere accident that I had never killed . . . But
in what other ways had the South allowed me to be natural, to
be real, to be myself, except in rejection, rebellion, and aggres-
sion?

Not only had the southern whites not known me, but, more
important still, as I had lived in the South I had not had the
chance to learn who I was. The pressure of southern living
kept me from being the kind of person that I might have been.
I had been what my surroundings had demanded, what my
family—conforming to the dictates of the whites above them—

had exacted of me, and what the whites had said that I must be. Never being fully able to be myself, I had slowly learned that the South could recognize but a part of a man, could accept but a fragment of his personality, and all the rest—the best and deepest things of heart and mind—were tossed away in blind ignorance and hate.

I was leaving the South to fling myself into the unknown, to meet other situations that would perhaps elicit from me other responses. And if I could meet enough of a different life, then, perhaps, gradually and slowly I might learn who I was, what I might be. I was not leaving the South to forget the South, but so that some day I might understand it, might come to know what its rigors had done to me, to its children. I fled so that the numbness of my defensive living might thaw out and let me feel the pain—years later and far away—of what living in the South had meant.

Yet, deep down, I knew that I could never really leave the South, for my feelings had already been formed by the South, for there had been slowly instilled into my personality and consciousness, black though I was, the culture of the South. So, in leaving, I was taking a part of the South to transplant in alien soil, to see if it could grow differently, if it could drink of new and cool rains, bend in strange winds, respond to the warmth of other suns, and, perhaps, to bloom . . . And if that miracle ever happened, then I would know that there was yet hope in that southern swamp of despair and violence, that light could emerge even out of the blackest of the southern night. I would know that the South too could overcome its fear, its hate, its cowardice, its heritage of guilt and blood, its burden of anxiety and compulsive cruelty.

With ever watchful eyes and bearing scars, visible and invisible, I headed North, full of a hazy notion that life could be lived with dignity, that the personalities of others should not be violated, that men should be able to confront other men without fear or shame, and that if men were lucky in their living on earth they might win some redeeming meaning for their having struggled and suffered here beneath the stars.

Claude Brown

(b. 1937)

---

from *Manchild in the Promised Land*

Born and raised in New York City, Claude Brown became a writer after graduating from Howard University and the law school at Stanford University. Best known for his autobiographical Manchild in the Promised Land *and the author of* The Children of Harlem, *Brown has also written several plays for the American Negro Theater Guild.*

The first passage that follows, the Foreword to Manchild in the Promised Land, *presents the irony of Brown's title in that the Promised Land his parents, formerly sharecroppers in the South, dreamed of and sought is in fact a ghetto slum. The second passage defines the frustration of second-generation urban blacks who have been born into the nightmare of this ghetto—a dreamless and treacherous world where the outmoded cultural attitudes of their still unemancipated parents bear no relevance to the reality they encounter daily on the cruel urban streets of New York.*

I want to talk about the first Northern urban generation of Negroes. I want to talk about the experiences of a misplaced generation, of a misplaced people in an extremely complex, confused society. This is a story of their searching, their dreams, their sorrows, their small and futile rebellions, and their endless battle to establish their own place in America's greatest metropolis—and in America itself.

The characters are sons and daughters of former Southern sharecroppers. These were the poorest people of the South, who poured into New York City during the decade following the Great Depression. These migrants were told that unlimited opportunities for prosperity existed in New York and that there was no "color problem" there. They were told that Negroes lived in houses with bathrooms, electricity, running water, and indoor toilets. To them, this was the "promised land" that Mammy had been singing about in the cotton fields for many years.

Going to New York was good-bye to the cotton fields, good-bye to "Massa Charlie," good-bye to the chain gang, and, most of all, good-bye to those sunup-to-sundown working hours. One no longer had to wait to get to heaven to lay his burden down; burdens could be laid down in New York.

So, they came, from all parts of the South, like all the black chillun o' God following the sound of Gabriel's horn on that long-overdue Judgment Day. The Georgians came as soon as they were able to pick train fare off the peach trees. They came from South Carolina where the cotton stalks were bare. The North Carolinians came with tobacco tar beneath their finger-nails.

They felt as the Pilgrims must have felt when they were coming to America. But these descendants of Ham must have been twice as happy as the Pilgrims, because they had been catching twice the hell. Even while planning the trip, they sang spirituals as "Jesus Take My Hand" and "I'm On My Way" and chanted, "Hallelujah, I'm on my way to the promised land!"

It seems that Cousin Willie, in his lying haste, had neglected to tell the folks down home about one of the most important aspects of the promised land: it was a slum ghetto. There was a tremendous difference in the way life was lived up North. There were too many people full of hate and bitterness crowded into a dirty, stinky, uncared-for closet-size section of a great city.

Before the soreness of the cotton fields had left Mama's back, her knees were getting sore from scrubbing "Goldberg's" floor. Nevertheless, she was better off; she had gone from the fire into the frying pan.

The children of these disillusioned colored pioneers inherited the total lot of their parents—the disappointments, the anger. To add to their misery, they had little hope of deliverance. For where does one run to when he's already in the promised land?

When I went uptown now, I always had a definite purpose. I was going up to see Pimp to try and get him interested in something. I would take him out to the Flatbush section of Brooklyn and to Brighton, and we'd just walk. We'd walk around in Washington Heights. Sometimes on Sundays I liked to take him bike riding with me and show him other parts of New York City, hoping he could really get to see something outside of Harlem.

I was kind of worried about him now, because he was at that age, fifteen, where it was time to start doing something to be older and get into street life and do the things that the other cats out there were doing.

He knew that I was playing piano. I'd bring him down to my place sometimes and play for him. I'd take him to joints like the Five Spot. I showed him Connie's. He kind of liked it, but it didn't really impress him. He'd say things like, "Yeah, I'm gonna learn to blow a trumpet; I like a trumpet," but I knew that this wasn't really his thing.

I knew he had problems now. He had that problem of staying home and taking all that stuff from Dad. Mama had told me that he had had a fight with Dad. He was fighting back now. He was declaring his independence. I couldn't say anything. I didn't know what to do when he started complaining about how Dad and Mama and Papa, my grandfather, were still in the woods and he was growing up. He was getting away from all that old down-home stuff, and he didn't go for hearing it all the time around the house. I knew he was right, because I'd had the same feeling. You feel as though they're trying to make something out of you that you couldn't be and didn't want to be if you could, as though they're trying to raise you as a farm boy in New York, in Harlem.

I knew he was right, but I couldn't agree with him. I couldn't say, "Yeah, man. You got to get outta there." I wasn't sure that he was ready to leave, and I didn't have anyplace for him to go.

He would come down to my place after he'd had a fight with Dad and stay for a night. I knew Mama was all upset, because she'd get on the phone and start calling until he got there. She'd be real upset every time he stayed out after twelve o'clock. She was afraid that he was going to run away. She'd had her troubles with me, and I guess she figured history was repeating itself. Mama had really been through something with me, and I knew this. She had not had any trouble out of Carole and Margie. She'd always said she hoped she wouldn't have any grandsons, because if she had it all to do over again, she'd never have any boys.

I knew she had one reason for saying that, but I didn't want her to have another. I was trying to cool Pimp. I didn't feel that this cat was really ready to make it out on his own. He'd been a good boy all his life, and good boys weren't supposed to be pulling up and leaving home at fifteen.

I had to stop him from coming down to my place, because he was liking it too much. He'd come down, I'd give him money to go to school, money to blow. It was better than being home, because he didn't have anybody to answer to. I never asked him where he'd been or where he was going. He could stay out as late as he wanted to. Cats were always jamming at my place, all the young jazz musicians, the cats playing at the joints around where I lived. They'd be coming up all times of the night, getting high smoking pot and having jam sessions.

There'd be all kinds of bitches up there. We'd be partying

way into the wee hours. This was a hip life, the way he saw it, and he wanted to get in. But I knew he wasn't ready for anything like this. It might have had a bad effect on him. The last thing I had to worry about was having my morals corrupted. But Pimp was younger, and he wasn't ready for this thing, the way I saw it. I was afraid for him, so I had to pull a mean trick on him to stop him from coming.

One night he came down, and he said he was tired of Mama and Dad and wanted me to look for a place for him. This was about twelve-thirty.

I said, "Okay, man," and pretended that I was serious about finding him a place. It was a cold night. I said, "Look, I only have one blanket." I put him in the little room across from me, and he almost froze. The next morning, he was in a hurry to get out of there and get back uptown to his warm bed.

I still didn't think he was ready, and more than that, I just didn't want him to hurt Mama as much as I had. I decided to go up there and talk to him, find out just what was going on. I could ask Mama about it, but she'd say, "That boy just thinks he's grown; he's gon fight his daddy, and he gon go outta here and stay as late as he wants." Mama couldn't understand Pimp any more than he could understand her.

I tried to talk to her. I said, "Look, Mama, Pimp grew up here in New York City. He's kind of different. He didn't grow up on all that salt pork, collard greens, and old-time religion. You can't make a chitterlin' eater out of him now."

Mama said, "Now, look here, nigger, you ate a whole lot of chitterlin's yourself, and chitterlin's wasn't too good for you back there in the early forties when your daddy wasn't doing too good on his job."

"Look, Mama, why don't you listen sometime, just for a little while. I'm telling you your son's got problems, Mama. It's not problems down on the farm. He's got problems here in New York City. And the only way he's going to solve these problems is that you try and help him."

"Oh, boy, sometimes I don't know what's wrong with you. You gon get involved in all that psychology you're always talkin' about and go stone crazy."

"Yeah, Mama, forget it." I just couldn't talk to her.

This day that I'd come up to talk was right after a big snowstorm. It was pretty cold; there was a lot of snow in the street. Traffic was moving at a snail's pace, almost at a standstill. Mama was complaining about how cold it was.

"Mama, why don't you complain to the landlord about this?"

"I called the office of the renting agency twice, and they said he wasn't in. When I called the third time, I spoke to him, but he said that it wasn't any of his problem, and I'd have to fix it up myself. I ain't got no money to be gettin' these windows relined."

"Mama, that's a whole lot of stuff. I know better than that. Why don't you go up to the housing commission and complain about it?"

"I ain't got no time to be goin' no place complainin' about nothin'. I got all this housework to do, and all this cookin'; I got to be runnin' after Pimp."

"Look, Mama, let's you and me go up there right now. I'm gonna write out a complaint, and I want you to sign it."

"I got all this washin' to do."

"Mama, you go on and you wash. I'm gon wait for you; I'm gon help you wash."

Mama started washing the clothes. As soon as she finished that, she had to put the pot on the stove. Then she had to fix some lunch. As soon as she finished one thing, she would find another thing that she had to do right away. She just kept stalling for time.

Finally, after waiting for about three hours, when she couldn't find anything else to do, I said, "Look, Mama, come on, let's you and me go out there."

We went over to 145th Street. We were going to take the crosstown bus to Broadway, to the temporary housing-commission office.

We were waiting there. Because of the snowstorm, the buses weren't running well, so we waited there for a long time. Mama said, "Look, we'd better wait and go some other time."

I knew she wanted to get out of this, and I knew if I let her go and put it off to another time, it would never be done. I said, "Mama, we can take a cab."

"You got any money?"

"No."

"I ain't got none either. So we better wait until another time."

"Look, Mama, you wait right here on the corner. I'm going across the street to the pawnshop, and when I get back, we'll take a cab."

She waited there on the corner, and I went over to the pawnshop and pawned my ring. When I came back, we took a cab to Broadway and 145th Street, to the temporary housing-commission office. When I got there, I told one of the girls at the window that I wanted to write out a complaint against a tenement landlord.

She gave me a form to fill out and said I had to make out two copies. I sat down and started writing. It seemed like a whole lot to Mama, because Mama didn't do too much writing. She used a small sheet of paper even when she wrote a letter.

She kept bothering me while I was writing. She said, "Boy, what's all that you puttin' down there? You can't be saying nothin' that ain't the truth. Are you sure you know what you're talking about? Because I'm only complaining about the window, now, and it don't seem like it'd take that much writing to complain about just the one window."

"Mama, you're complaining about all the windows. Aren't all the windows in the same shape?"

"I don't know."

"Well, look here, Mama, isn't it cold in the whole house?"

"Yeah."

"When was the last time the windows were lined?"

"I don't know. Not since we lived in there."

"And you been livin' there seventeen years. Look, Mama, you got to do something."

"Okay, just don't put down anything that ain't true." She kept pulling on my arm.

"Look, Mama, I'm gonna write out this thing. When I finish I'll let you read it, and if there's anything not true in it, I'll cross it out. Okay?"

"Okay, but it just don't seem like it take all that just to write out one complaint."

I had to write with one hand and keep Mama from pulling on me with the other hand. When I finished it, I turned in the two complaint forms, and we left. Mama kept acting so scared, it really got on my nerves. I said, "Look, Mama, you ain't got nothin' to be scared of."

She said she wasn't scared, but she just wanted to stay on the good side of the landlord, because sometimes she got behind in the rent.

"Yeah, Mama, but you can't be freezin' and catching colds just because sometimes you get behind in the rent. Everybody gets behind in the rent, even people who live on Central Park West and Park Avenue. They get behind in the rent. They're not freezin' to death just because they're behind in the rent."

"Boy, I don't know what's wrong with you, but you're always ready to get yourself into something or start some trouble."

"Yeah, Mama, if I'm being mistreated, I figure it's time to start some trouble."

"Boy, I just hope to God that you don't get yourself into something one day that you can't get out of."

"Mama, everybody grows into manhood, and you don't stop to think about that sort of thing once you become a man. You just do it, even if it's trouble that you can't get out of. You don't stop to think. Look, forget about it, Mama. Just let me worry about the whole thing."

"Okay, you do the worryin', but the landlord ain't gon come down there in Greenwich Village and put you out. He gon put us out."

"Mama, he ain't gon put nobody out, don't you believe me?" I pinched her on the cheek, and she got a smile out.

After a couple of days, I came back uptown. I asked Mama, "What about the windows?"

"Nothin' about the windows."

"What you mean 'nothin' about the windows'?" I was getting a little annoyed, because she just didn't seem to want to be bothered. I said, "You mean they didn't fix the windows yet? You didn't hear from the landlord?"

"No, I didn't hear from the landlord."

"Well, we're going back up to the housing commission."

"What for?"

"Because we're gon get something done about these windows."

"But something's already been done."

"What's been done, if you didn't hear anything from the landlord?"

"Some man came in here yesterday and asked me what windows."

"What man?"

"I don't know what man."

"Well, what did he say? Didn't he say where he was from?"

"No, he didn't say anything. He just knocked on the door and asked me if I had some windows that needed relining. I said, 'Yeah,' and he asked me what windows, so I showed him the three windows in the front."

"Mama, you didn' show him all the others?"

"No, because that's not so bad, we didn't need them relined."

"Mama, oh, Lord, why didn't you show him the others?"

"Ain't no sense in trying to take advantage of a good thing."

"Yeah, Mama. I guess it was a good thing to you."

I thought about it. I thought about the way Mama would go down to the meat market sometimes, and the man would sell her some meat that was spoiled, some old neck bones or some pig tails. Things that weren't too good even when they weren't spoiled. And sometimes she would say, "Oh, those things aren't too bad." She was scared to take them back, scared to complain until somebody said, "That tastes bad." Then she'd go down there crying and mad at him, wanting to curse the man out. She had all that Southern upbringing in her, that business of being scared of Mr. Charlie. Everybody white she saw was Mr. Charlie.

Pimp was still in this thing, and I was afraid for him. I knew it was a hard thing for him to fight. I suppose when I was younger, I fought it by stealing, by not being at home, by getting into trouble. But I felt that Pimp was at a loss as to what to do about it. It might have been a greater problem for him.

It seemed as though the folks, Mama and Dad, had never heard anything about Lincoln or the Emancipation Proclamation. They were going to bring the South up to Harlem with them. I knew they had had it with them all the time. Mama would be telling Carole and Margie about the root workers down there, about somebody who had made a woman leave her husband, all kinds of nonsense like that.

I wanted to say, "Mama, why don't you stop tellin' those girls all that crazy shit?" But I couldn't say anything, because they wouldn't believe me, and Mama figured she was right. It seemed as though Mama and Dad were never going to get out of the woods until we made them get out.

Many times when I was there, Mama would be talking all that nonsense about the woods and about some dead person who had come back. Her favorite story was the time her mother came back to her and told her everything was going to be all right and that she was going to get married in about three or four months. I wanted to say, "Look, Mama, we're in New York. Stop all that foolishness."

She and Dad had been in New York since 1935. They were in New York, but it seemed like their minds were still down there in the South Carolina cotton fields. Pimp, Carole, and Margie had to suffer for it. I had to suffer for it too, but because I wasn't at home as much as the others, I had suffered less than anybody else.

I could understand Pimp's anxieties about having to listen to Grandpapa, who was now living with Mama and Dad, talk that old nonsense about how good it was on the chain gang. He'd tell us about the time he ran away from the chain gang. He stayed on some farm in Georgia for about two or three weeks, but he got lonesome for his family. He knew if he went home, they would be waiting for him, so he went back to the chain gang. The white man who was in charge of the chain gang gave him his old job back and said something like, "Hello there, Brock. Glad to see you back." He said they'd treated him nice. I couldn't imagine them treating him nice, because I didn't know anybody in the South who was treated nice, let alone on a chain gang. Still, Papa said the chain gang was good. I wanted to smack him. If he weren't my grandfather, I would have.

I felt sorry for Pimp, and I wished I were making a whole lot of money and could say, "Come on, man. Live with me and get away from that Harlem scene, and perhaps you can do something." But before he made the move from Harlem, he'd have to know where he was going, every step of the way, all by himself.

He was lost in that house. Nobody there even really knew he was alive. Mama and Dad were only concerned about the numbers coming out. Papa, since he was so old, would just sit around and look for the number in Ching Chow's ear in the newspaper comic section. When the number came out, he'd say, "I knew that number was comin'. I could've told you before."

I used to watch Pimp sometimes when I'd go up there. Papa would be talking this stuff about the number, and it seemed to be just paining Pimp. It hadn't bothered me that much. But I suppose it couldn't have. I used to be kind of glad that they were involved in this stuff. I guess I had an arrogant attitude toward the family. I saw them all as farmers. It made me feel good that they were involved in this stuff, because then they couldn't be aware of what I was doing and what was going down. The more they got involved in that old voodoo, the farther they got away from me and what I was doing out in the street.

Papa used to make me mad with, "Who was that old boy you was with today, that old tar-black boy?" Mama used to say things like that about people too, but I never felt that she was really color struck. Sometimes I used to get mad when she'd say things about people and their complexion, but she always treated all the people we brought up to the house real nice, regardless of whether they were dark- or light-skinned.

I knew that Pimp was at an age when he'd be bringing his friends around, and Papa would be talking that same stuff about, "Who's that black so-and-so?" If you brought somebody to the house who was real light-skinned, Papa would say, "They're nice," or "They're nice lookin'." All he meant was that the people were light-skinned.

I remember one time when Papa was telling his favorite story about how he could have passed for white when he first came to New York and moved down on the Lower East Side. He became a janitor of a building there. He said everybody thought he was white until they saw Uncle McKay, Mama's brother and Papa's son. He was about my complexion or a little lighter than I was, but anybody could tell he was colored. Papa said if it wasn't for McKay, he could have passed for white. This story used to get on my nerves, and I thought it was probably bothering Pimp now too. Sometimes I wanted to tell him, "Shit, man, why don't you just go on some place where you can pass for white, if that's the way you feel about it? And stop sitting here with all us real colored niggers and talkin' about it." But if I'd ever said that, Mama would have been mad at me for the rest of my life.

I wondered if it was good for him to be around all that old crazy talk, because I imagined that all my uncles who were dark-skinned—Uncle McKay, Uncle Ted, Uncle Brother—felt that Papa didn't care too much for them because they were dark-skinned, and I supposed that Pimp might have gotten that feeling too. I had the feeling that this wasn't anyplace for kids to be around, with some crazy old man talking all that stuff about light skin and how he could have passed for white and calling people black.

Many times, Mama and I talked about Pimp. She'd say, "I don't know what's gon happen to that boy." She'd always be telling him he was going to get into trouble.

I wanted to say, "Why don't you leave him alone and stop talking that?"

She'd say, "That boy's gon be up in Warwick just as sure as I'm livin'."

I said, "Mama, look, don't be puttin' the bad mouth on him." I could tell her about the bad mouth, because this was something she knew, and she'd get mad. This was the only way to stop her from talking that stuff sometimes.

She'd say, "Boy, what's wrong with you? You think I'd put some bad mouth on my children?" She'd get real excited about it.

I'd say, "Look, Mama, that's just what you're doin'. The police ain't sayin' he's goin' to Warwick; the judge ain't said he's goin' to Warwick; nobody's sayin' he's goin' to Warwick but you."

She'd say, "I'm trying to stop him from goin' out of here gettin' into some trouble."

I said, "Mama, ain't nobody talkin' about him goin' out of here gettin' into some trouble. Ain't nobody talkin' about him doin' nothin' but you. You're the only one who says he's gonna get in trouble. You're the only one who says the police gon get him soon and that he's gonna go to Warwick. Nobody's sayin' it but you; and all that amounts to is the bad mouth, because you're saying it before anything's happening."

Tears would come to her eyes, and she'd stop talking about it. That was good, because all I wanted to do was stop her from talking that nonsense about Pimp getting in trouble and going to Warwick and all that kind of foolishness. I knew that talking about the bad mouth would bother her. I didn't like to be mean to Mama, but this was something she understood. I knew she had all these boogeyman ideas in her head.

With Dad, I suppose it was just as bad at home. He would never read anything but the *Daily News,* and he always read about somebody cutting up somebody or killing somebody. He liked to read about the people in the neighborhood, and he'd point the finger at them. He'd say, "There goes another one." Just let it be one of my friends and, oh, man, he'd ride Pimp about it.

He'd say, "You remember that old no-good boy Sonny use to hang out with? He went to the chair last night," or "He got killed in a stickup someplace." He'd tell him, "You remember that old boy Sonny Boy use to bring up here years ago?" Pimp would never answer. "Well, they found him around there in the backyard on 146th Street dead, with a needle in his arm, last night. All of 'em just killin' theirselves. They ain't no damn good, and they ain't never had no sense. They didn't have enough sense to go out there and get a job like somebody who knows something, and act halfway decent. They just gon hang out around here and rob the decent people, and break into people's houses. Somebody had to kill them, if they didn't kill theirselves. So I suppose they just might as well go ahead and use too much of that stuff and kill theirselves, no-good damn bums, old triflin', roguish dope addicts. They all ought to kill theirselves."

He'd be preaching this at Pimp as though he were one of them. It bothered Pimp. It would bother anybody. Dad never messed with me with this sort of thing. I was on my own, I was clean, and I was certain that I had as much money in my pocket as he had, if not more. I was his equal, and he couldn't run down all that nonsense to me.

V

A Vision of the World United

To begin living together in multicultural harmony
demands a vision beyond the reach of irony . . .
a vision that crosses color lines,
overrides international boundaries,
and breaks down ethnic barriers.

Zora Neale Hurston

(1903–1960)

---

from *Dust Tracks on the Road*
Looking Things Over

*Folklorist, anthropologist, playwright, and novelist
Zora Neale Hurston was born in Eatonville, Florida, a
town incorporated and managed by blacks, where her
father was a minister and town leader. Hurston
worked at Columbia University with Franz Boas (considered by many to be the father of American anthro-
pology) and was awarded a Guggenheim fellowship.
Besides her novels and plays she wrote nonfiction
books on black culture and folklore.*

In the following excerpt from her autobiography,
Dust Tracks on the Road, *Hurston not only looks at the
past—and concludes that grandsons cannot be held
presently accountable for the actions of their grandfa-
thers—but also looks forward to a better, more noble
future bred of tolerance and dedicated to harmony
among all the peoples who compose one human race.*

Well, that is the way things stand up to now. I can look back and see sharp shadows, high lights, and smudgy inbetweens. I have been in Sorrow's kitchen and licked out all the pots. Then I have stood on the peaky mountain wrappen in rainbows, with a harp and a sword in my hands.

What I had to swallow in the kitchen has not made me less glad to have lived, nor made me want to low-rate the human race, nor any whole sections of it. I take no refuge from myself in bitterness. To me, bitterness is the under-arm odor of wishful weakness. It is the graceless acknowledgement of defeat. I have no urge to make any concessions like that to the world as yet. I might be like that some day, but I doubt it. I am in the struggle with the sword in my hands, and I don't intend to run until you run me. So why give off the smell of something dead under the house while I am still in there tussling with my sword in my hand?

If tough breaks have not soured me, neither have my glory-moments caused me to build any altars to myself where I can burn incense before God's best job of work. My sense of humor will always stand in the way of my seeing myself, my family, my race or my nation as the whole intent of the universe. When I see what we really are like, I know that God is too great an artist for we folks on my side of the creek to be all of His best works. Some of His finest touches are among us, without doubt, but some more of His masterpieces are among those folks who live over the creek.

So looking back and forth in history and around the temporary scene, I do not visualize the moon dripping down in blood, nor the sun batting his fiery eyes and laying down in the cradle of eternity to rock himself into sleep and slumber at instances of human self-bias. I know that the sun and the moon must be used to sights like that by now. I too yearn for universal justice, but how to bring it about is another thing. It is such a complicated thing, for justice, like beauty, is in the eye of the beholder. There is universal agreement on the principle, but the application brings on the fight. Oh, for some disinterested party to pass on things! Somebody will hurry to tell me that we voted God to the bench for that. But the lawyers who interpret His opinions, make His decisions sound just like they made them up themselves. Being an idealist, I too wish that the world was better than I am. Like all the rest of my fellow men, I don't want to live around people with no more principles than I have. My inner fineness is continually outraged at finding that the world is a whole family of Hurstons.

Seeing these things, I have come to the point by trying to make the day at hand a positive thing, and realizing the uselessness of gloominess.

Therefore, I see nothing but futility in looking back over my shoulder in rebuke at the grave of some white man who has been dead too long to talk about. That is just what I would be doing in trying to fix the blame for the dark days of slavery and the Reconstruction. From what I can learn, it was sad. Certainly. But my ancestors who lived and died in it are dead. The white men who profited by their labor and lives are dead also. I have no personal memory of those times, and no responsibility for them. Neither has the grandson of the man who held my folks. So I see no need in button-holing that grandson like the Ancient Mariner did the wedding guest and calling for the High Sheriff to put him under arrest.

I am not so stupid as to think that I would be bringing this descendant of a slave-owner any news. He has heard just as much about the thing as I have. I am not so humorless as to visualize this grandson falling out on the sidewalk before me, and throwing an acre of fits in remorse because his old folks held slaves. No, indeed! If it happened to be a fine day and he had had a nice breakfast, he might stop and answer me like this:

"In the first place, I was not able to get any better view of social conditions from my grandmother's womb than you could from your grandmother's. Let us say for the sake of argument that I detest the institution of slavery and all that it implied, just as much as you do. You must admit that I had no more power to do anything about it in my unborn state than you had in yours. Why fix your eyes on me? I respectfully refer you to my ancestors, and bid you a good day."

If I still lingered before him, he might answer me further by asking questions like this:

"Are you so simple as to assume that the Big Surrender (Southerners, both black and white speak of Lee's surrender to Grant as the Big Surrender) banished the concept of human slavery from the earth? What is the principle of slavery? Only the literal buying and selling of human flesh on the block? That was only an outside symbol. Real slavery is couched in the desire and the efforts of any man or community to live and advance their interests at the expense of the lives and interests of others. All of the outward signs come out of that. Do you not realize that the power, prestige and prosperity of the greatest nations on earth rests on colonies and sources of raw materials? Why else are great wars waged? If you have not thought, then why waste up time with your vapid accusations? If you have, then why single *me* out?" And like Pilate, he will light a cigar, and stroll on off without waiting for an answer.

Anticipating such an answer, I have no intention of wasting my time beating on old graves with a club. I know that I cannot pry aloose the clutching hand of Time, so I will turn all my thoughts and energies on the present. I will settle for from now on.

And why not? For me to pretend that I am Old Black Joe and waste my time on his problems, would be just as ridiculous as for the government of Winston Churchill to bill the Duke of Normandy the first of every month, or for the Jews to hang around the pyramids trying to picket Old Pharaoh. While I have a handkerchief over my eyes crying over the landing of the first slaves in 1619, I might miss something swell that is going on in 1942. Furthermore, if somebody were to consider my grandmother's ungranted wishes, and give *me* what *she* wanted, I would be too put out for words.

What do I want, then? I will tell you in a parable. A Negro deacon was down on his knees praying at a wake held for a sister who had died that day. He had his eyes closed and was going great guns, when he noticed that he was not getting any more "amens" from the rest. He opened his eyes and saw that everybody else was gone except himself and the dead woman.

Then he saw the reason. The supposedly dead woman was trying to sit up. He bolted for the door himself, but it slammed shut so quickly that it caught his flying coat-tails and held him sort of static. "Oh, no Gabriel!" the deacon shouted, "dat aint no way for you to do. I can do my own running, but you got to 'low me the same chance as the rest."

I don't know any more about the future than you do. I hope that it will be full of work, because I have come to know by experience that work is the nearest thing to happiness that I can find. No matter what else I have among the things that humans want, I go to pieces in a short while if I do not work. What all my work shall be, I don't know that either, every hour being a stranger to you until you live it. I want a busy life, a just mind and a timely death.

But if I should live to be very old, I have laid plans for that so that it will not be too tiresome. So far, I have never used coffee, liquor, nor any form of stimulant. When I get old, and my joints and bones tell me about it, I can sit around and write for myself, if for nobody else, and read slowly and carefully the mysticism of the East, and re-read Spinoza with love and care. All the while my days can be a succession of coffee cups. Then when the sleeplessness of old age attacks me, I can have a likker bottle snug in my pantry and sip away and sleep. Get mellow and think kindly of the world. I think I can be like that because I have known the joy and pain of deep friendship. I have served and been served. I have made some good enemies for which I am not a bit sorry. I have loved unselfishly, and I have fondled hatred with the red-hot tongs of Hell. That's living.

I have no race prejudice of any kind. My kinfolks, and my "skin-folks" are dearly loved. My own circumference of everyday life is there. But I see their same virtues and vices everywhere I look. So I give you all my right hand of fellowship and love, and hope for the same from you. In my eyesight, you lose nothing by not looking just like me. I will remember you all in my good thoughts, and I ask you kindly to do the same for me. Not only just me. You, who play the zig-zag lightning of power over the world, with the grumbling thunder in your wake, think kindly of those who walk in the dust. And you who walk in humble places, think kindly too, of others. There has been no proof in the world so far that you would be less arrogant if you held the lever of power in your hands. Let us all be kissing-friends. Consider that with tolerance and patience, we godly demons may breed a noble world in a few hundred generations or so. Maybe all of us who do not have the good fortune to meet, or meet again, in this world, will meet at a barbecue.

Paul Robeson

(1898–1976)

from *Here I Stand*
Love Will Find Out the Way

*From the outset of his theatrical career the cele-
brated singer and actor Paul Robeson traveled widely
in Europe, and in 1927 he settled in London for twelve
years. His experience outside the racially segregated
United States played a significant role in the shaping
of his identity both as a uniquely talented, individual
artist and as an African-American man. As the citizen
of a world where no doors were barred by color lines,
Robeson discovered in the many peoples he encountered a common humanity that, he believed, bound all
men and women everywhere together.*

*In this chapter from his autobiography Robeson re-
lates a variety of anecdotes from his travels abroad
that afforded him a faith in the human possibility of
racial harmony.*

My experiences abroad, in the twelve years (1927–1939) that I made my home in London, brought me to understand that, no matter where else I might travel, my home-ground must be America. That point came up during the Congressional committee hearing when, after I had said that "in Russia I felt for the first time like a full human being—no color prejudice like in Mississippi, no color prejudice like in Washington," one of the committee members angrily demanded: "Why did you not stay in Russia?"

"Because my father was a slave," I retorted, "and my people died to build this country, and I am going to stay right here and have a part of it, just like you. And no fascist-minded people will drive me from it. Is that clear?"

Well, let me here try to make it clear how I came to feel that way. It was in Britain—among the English, Scottish, Welsh and Irish people of that land—that I learned that the essential character of a nation is determined not by the upper classes, but by the common people, and that the common people of all nations are truly brothers in the great family of mankind. If in Britain there were those who lived by plundering the colonial peoples, there were also the many millions who earned their bread by honest toil. And even as I grew to feel more Negro in spirit, or African as I put it then, I also came to feel a sense of oneness with the white working people whom I came to know and love.

This belief in the oneness of humankind, about which I have often spoken in concerts and elsewhere, has existed within me side by side with my deep attachment to the cause of my own race. Some people have seen a contradiction in this duality: white people who have seen me as a "citizen of the world," singing the songs of many lands in the languages of those peoples, have wondered sometimes how I could be so partisan for the colored people; and Negroes, on the other hand, have wondered why I have often expressed a warm affection for peoples who seem remote and foreign to them. I do not think,

however, that my sentiments are contradictory; and in England
I learned that there truly is a kinship among us all, a basis for
mutual respect and brotherly love.

My first glimpse of this concept came through song, and that
is not strange, for the songs that have lived through the years
have always been the purest expressions of the heart of humanity. Early in my professional musical career I had the great
good fortune to become associated with Lawrence Brown, an
extraordinarily gifted Negro composer and arranger, and over
the years this association grew into a successful partnership
and personal friendship. It was this musician who clarified my
instinctive feeling that the simple, beautiful songs of my childhood, heard every Sunday in church and every day at home
and in the community—the great poetic song-sermons of the
Negro preacher and the congregation, the work songs and
blues of my father's folk from the plantations of North Carolina
—should become important concert material. Lawrence
Brown, who also knew and played the folk music of other peoples, as well as the great classics of Western song literature
(many of which are based on folk themes), was firm in his
conviction that our music—Negro music of African and American derivation—was in the tradition of the world's great folk
music. And so for my first five years as a singer my repertoire
consisted entirely of my people's songs.

Then I went on to learn the songs of other peoples, and in
Britain there was at hand the riches of English, Welsh and
Gaelic folk-songs. And as I sang these lovely melodies I felt
that they, too, were close to my heart and expressed the same
soulful quality that I knew in Negro music. Others had noted
this kinship before me, and in his autobiography Frederick
Douglass, recalling the songs "both merry and sad" that he
had heard as a plantation slave, wrote: "Child as I was, these
wild songs depressed my spirit. Nowhere outside of dear old
Ireland, in the days of want and famine, have I heard sounds so
mournful." (Douglass had visited Ireland in 1847.) And in Scotland, Marjory Kennedy-Fraser, a noted contemporary authority
on Gaelic folk-song, has suggested that Negro song is a direct
product of her own people's culture. Without going into a discussion here of that claim, it is interesting to note Miss Ken-

nedy-Fraser's viewpoint, expressed in the foreword to one of
her collections, *Songs of the Hebrides:*

> As I write, I am on a short visit to the American Middle
> West, and Dvorak's use of Negro melodies in his New
> World Symphony comes to mind. The Celts, alike of Scot-
> land and Ireland, claim no inconsiderable share in the
> best of so-called Negro melodies of America, Hebridean
> younger sons, among others, becoming planters in the
> South two centuries ago, and taking with them Gaelic
> nurses with Celtic croons. And the Negroes learnt not
> only the croons but also the Gaelic tongue. And a woman
> of the Isles arriving in the South, it is told, had the fear on
> her that day, for did she not think that the blackness of
> the Gaelic-speaking Negro was the blackness of the sun
> on one of her own folk!

Nevertheless, as we know, an appreciation of another people's art cannot by itself bridge the gulf which separates one
people from another. Lovers of African sculpture can be quite
indifferent to the people whose hands have wrought those masterpieces, and here in America there have been many who
have appreciated—and appropriated—Negro music while
showing an utter disregard for its creators. In my case, the
tender beauty of their folk-songs drew me spiritually close to
the common peoples of Europe; but it was the ominous drum-
beat of current history that brought me to stand physically
among them.

The years that I lived abroad witnessed the rise of fascism:
the crash of martial music and the sound of marching jack-
boots drowned out the songs of peace and brotherhood. In
1933 Hitler rose to power in Germany and the raucous voice of
the "Master Race" heralded the coming horror. In Italy a self-
styled Caesar, who wore not toga but blackshirt, set out to win
an empire; and in 1935 Mussolini's fascist legions marched
against Ethiopia, and bomber and tank triumphed over musket
and spear. At Geneva the League of Nations was deaf to Haile
Selassie's desperate plea for sanctions against the aggressor as
they were deaf to Litvinov's warning that peace was indivisible.

Then, the next year, came Spain—the attack on the Spanish
Republic by the fascist traitor Franco, backed by the armed

might of Hitler and Mussolini. It was a dress rehearsal for World War II: the rubble of the Spanish village of Guernica, leveled by air bombardment, was the pattern of destruction that soon would come upon Rotterdam and Warsaw, Coventry and Stalingrad—and finally, to Berlin itself. The Western powers were calm and unmoving in the face of the agony of Ethiopia and Spain. The governments that had refused to vote sanctions against Fascist Italy imposed an embargo on arms for Republican Spain; and they were indifferent to the Nazi terror unleashed in Germany against Social Democrats and Communists, liberals and trade unionists, Jews and other so-called "inferior races."

In England, in the great country houses where I had often been welcomed as guest, having tea and exchanging smiles with Lord and Lady This-and-that, a quiet serenity prevailed. Hitler and Mussolini?—well, they might very well be "bounders," uncouth fellows really and quite unacceptable socially, but upper-class England was rather pleased by what the dictators were doing. After all, the Nazi-fascist partnership was based on the "anti-Comintern Pact" and they were out to save all the great houses of Europe from the menace of "Bolshevism"; and in Germany and Italy there was no longer any nonsense from Labor, and business went ahead much better with no trade unions. As for war, well, that was all nicely taken care of at the Munich Conference where Czechoslovakia was sacrificed to Hitler, and if the Nazis did march, they would surely go eastward—and that wouldn't be bad at all, would it?

But in Britain the umbrella of appeasement that was held high by Chamberlain did not obscure the portents seen in the skies by the common people, and everywhere they rallied for anti-fascist action. The heart of this movement was the forces of Labor—the trade unions, the cooperatives, the political parties of the Left—but other broad sections of the population were involved, including many from the middle class and people from the arts, sciences and professions. And so it was that I, as an artist, was drawn into that movement and I came to see that the struggle against fascism must take first place over every other interest.

In a radio broadcast that I made from the Continent to a great London rally in defense of Spain, I explained my stand:

Every artist, every scientist, must decide *now* where he
stands. He has no alternative. There is no standing above
the conflict on Olympian heights. There are no impartial
observers. Through the destruction, in certain countries,
of the greatest of man's literary heritage, through the
propagation of false ideas of racial and national superiority, the artist, the scientist, the writer is challenged. The
struggle invades the formerly cloistered halls of our uni-
versities and other seats of learning. The battlefront is
everywhere. There is no sheltered rear.

And I saw, too, that the struggle for Negro rights was an
inseparable part of the anti-fascist struggle and I said:

The artist must elect to fight for Freedom or for Slavery. I have made my choice. I had no alternative. The
history of this era is characterized by the degradation of
my people—despoiled of their lands, their culture destroyed, denied equal protection of the law, and deprived
of their rightful place in the respect of their fellows.
Not through blind faith or coercion, but conscious of
my course, I take my place with you. I stand with you in
unalterable support of the lawful government of Spain,
duly and regularly chosen by its sons and daughters.

I went to Spain in 1938, and that was a major turning point in
my life. There I saw that it was the working men and women of
Spain who were heroically giving "their last full measure of
devotion" to the cause of democracy in that bloody conflict, and
that it was the upper class—the landed gentry, the bankers and
industrialists—who had unleashed the fascist beast against
their own people. From the ranks of the workers of other lands
volunteers had come to help in the epic defense of Madrid, and
in Spain I sang with my whole heart and soul for these gallant
fighters of the International Brigade. A new, warm feeling for
my homeland grew within me as I met the men of the Abraham
Lincoln Battalion—the thousands of brave young Americans
who had crossed the sea to fight and die that another "government of the people, by the people and for the people shall not
perish from the earth." My heart was filled with admiration
and love for these white Americans, and there was a sense of

great pride in my own people when I saw that there were Negroes, too, in the ranks of the Lincoln men in Spain. Some of them, like Oliver Laws and Milton Herndon, were to be among the heavy casualties suffered by the volunteers and would be buried with their white comrades in the Spanish earth . . . a long way from home. From home? Yes, from America, my own home, and I knew in my heart that I would surely return there some day.

Spain—the anti-fascist struggle and all that I learned in it—brought me back to America. For another year I remained in Britain, and the more I became part of the Labor movement the more I came to realize that my home should be in America. I recall how a friend in Manchester deepened my understanding of the oneness of mankind as he explained how closely together the two of us were bound by the web of history and human suffering and aspiration. He told me of the life of bitter hardship and toil which his father and grandfather had known in the mills of that great textile center in England, and of how the cotton which his forefathers wove linked them with other toilers whose sweat and toil produced that cotton in faraway America—the Negro slaves, my own people, my own father. The workers of Manchester had supported the side of Abolition in the American Civil War, though the Union blockade of the South cut off the supply of cotton and resulted in greater hardship for them, while at the same time the mill-owners and their government had supported the side of Slavery. So here was a further insight and understanding of those forces in world life which make for common interests and make real the concept of international brotherhood.

The miners of Wales, who gave great support to the anti-fascist movement, welcomed me when I came to sing in behalf of aid to Spain and invited me into their union halls and into their homes. The Welsh miners, and other workers whom I met throughout England and Scotland, made it clear that there was a closer bond between us than the general struggle to preserve democracy from its fascist foes. At the heart of that conflict, they pointed out, was a class division, and although I was famous and wealthy, the fact was I came from a working-class people like themselves and therefore, they said, my place was with them in the ranks of Labor.

Well, there were not just bosses in America, I reflected; there were workers, too. If I had found the hand of brotherhood here among these working people of Britain, I ought to be able to find that hand in America as well. Above all, I must be among the Negro people during the great world crisis that was looming, and be part of their struggles for the new world a-coming that they sought. I would bring them, I planned, a message about Africa and would try to build a unity between them and their struggling kinfolk in the colonies. As artist and citizen, as a Negro and a friend of Labor, there should be plenty for me to do at home. I returned in 1939. . . .

In these last seven years, during which I have been cut off from personal contact with my friends in other lands, I have often reflected on the truth expressed in the words of a song that I have sung at many a concert—"Love will find out the way." By mail, by telephone and telegram, and through friends who have visited abroad, I have received many warm messages of friendship and good cheer from people throughout the world. And through the written word, by recordings and filmed interviews I have tried to keep in touch with audiences abroad whose numerous invitations for concert, stage and film appearances I was not free to accept.

A great joy during the period when I was not even permitted to travel to Canada (for which no passport is required from the United States), were the concerts at the border that were sponsored by the metal miners of Canada. In 1952 I had been invited to attend the Canadian convention of their union, the Mine, Mill and Smelter Workers, and when the State Department barred me from coming to them, the miners arranged for a concert to be held at Peace Arch Park, on the border between the State of Washington and the Province of British Columbia. I shall always remember that concert on May 18, 1952, when 30,000 Canadians came from many miles away to hear me, to demonstrate their friendship and to protest against all barriers to cultural exchange.

For three more years these concerts were held at that border, until finally the State Department was forced to retreat from its arbitrary and illegal ban on my travel to places which require no passport. The hand of brotherhood—yes, I found that hand in Canada, too.

Only a few weeks ago—this autumn of 1957—I had the wonderful experience of singing once again for the miners of Wales. They had sponsored an Eisteddfod—a traditional cultural festival of the Welsh people—and arrangements were made for me to sing for them by telephone. I cannot say how deeply I was moved on this occasion, for here was an audience that had adopted me as kin and though they were unseen by me I never felt closer to them. A few days later I received a letter from the National Union of Mineworkers, South Wales area, which said:

> The trans-Atlantic transmission was a huge success, not only from the standpoint of reception but more so, from the inspiring effect it had upon the five thousand or more people gathered at our Eisteddfod. If you could only have seen this great body of people clinging to every note and word, you would have known the extent of the feeling that exists in Wales for you and for your release from the bondage now forced upon you.
>
> W. Paynter, President.

The first of such concerts-by-telephone had been arranged earlier in the year, on May 26, when I sang to an audience of a thousand in London. That concert was held in connection with a conference sponsored by the National Paul Robeson Committee, a group of distinguished people in Britain whose statements and activities are quite unknown in our country. Indeed, we have yet to see a single line on that subject in the general "free press" of our land, including the New York *Times* which boasts that through its far-flung newsgathering facilities it gives its readers "all the news that's fit to print." So, presumably, the news that more than a score of Members of Parliament are sponsors of that committee, and that many other prominent persons—writers, scholars, actors, lawyers, trade union leaders, titled personages, etc.—are also associated with that movement, is deemed bad for Americans to read and so it has been completely suppressed.

During the past seven years many people in Britain have

spoken as individuals and through their organizations for my right to visit them again—as numerous others have in many other lands—and in March of 1956 a national movement was launched at a conference in Manchester. In a speech on that occasion, Mr. R. W. Casasola, president of the Foundry Workers Union, said that

> . . . we are assembled in 1956 to ask that a little book be given to a gentleman with his photo in it and the statement that he is an American by birth. Here where the Chartists met to map the first struggle for the free vote, we launch a struggle for the right of all human beings to leave their country at any time and return at any time. America must get back to the principles of the Mayflower pilgrims, who sailed from this country seeking freedom, before its name stinks all over the world.

I sent a message to that conference in which I tried to express that which no words could ever truly express—my heart-felt gratitude for all that the British people were doing in this case, and I said:

> It is deeply moving for me to know that you and so many others throughout Britain are speaking out in behalf of my right to travel, my right to resume my career as an international artist which I began some thirty years ago. Though I must send you these words from afar, I can say that never have I felt closer to you than I do today. The warmth of your friendship reaches out across the barriers which temporarily separate us and rekindles the memories of many happy years that I spent among you.

In this message I recalled the last time I had been in Manchester, when the people there rallied to support the rights of my people in America:

> And I remember so well my last visit to Manchester in 1949—the warmth of your welcome at the Arena—the thousands who assembled to support our struggle in America to save the lives of the "Trenton Six." That struggle, as you know, was won; the Negro youths who had

been sentenced to die in the electric chair were freed. The people of Manchester and other British cities, and people of many lands, had a great share in that victory.

In the spring of 1957 I was overjoyed to hear that the British Actors' Equity Association, at their annual meeting in London, had passed a resolution in favor of my coming to England. Here are a few lines from the report on that action published in the London *Times:*

. . . Mr. Guy Verney moved a resolution that the Council support the efforts being made to enable Mr. Robeson to sing here. Neither the English theatre nor the world could afford to waste a talent like Mr. Robeson's for an "irrelevant reason" . . . Mr. Verney said that so far as he knew there was no sinister international underground movement putting forward the resolution, which was a request by artists to be enabled to hear, and work with, a great international artist. . . . The composite resolution was carried.

On May 4, 1957, the *Manchester Guardian* printed the following report:

A letter signed by 27 M.P.'s [Members of Parliament] states that the Cooperative Party and the British Actors' Equity Association have added their support to the campaign to invite Mr. Robeson to sing in Britain and to ask the U. S. Government to allow him to come. The letter states that because of his political views—"which we regard as wholly irrelevant to the issue of freedom of travel and of the arts, although we do not necessarily agree with any of them"—Mr. Robeson's Government saw fit to deny the right to hear him to millions of British people who wanted to do so. In effect, since he was "blacklisted" in his own country, Mr. Robeson was barred from practicing his profession. The signatories believe that there was "never a more vital time for free countries to uphold their professions with regard to freedom of travel, as solemnly undertaken in the U.N. Declaration of Human Rights." The letter concludes: "Is this not doubly important in the case of so outstanding an artist as Paul Robeson, who properly belongs to all humanity?"

Recently I received a letter, dated October 16, 1957, from Mr. Glen Byam Shaw, C.B.E., Director of the Shakespeare Memorial Theatre, inviting me to take part in their 1958 season at Stratford-upon-Avon. Such an invitation is truly a great honor to anyone in the theatre anywhere, but will the State Department permit me to go? Certainly I shall make still another request for a passport, as I have done in response to the many invitations that have come from countries other than Britain—for concert appearances on the Continent and elsewhere, for a role in a Soviet film production, and other similar offers.

In the next chapter I will deal with the issues in my passport case, but here I would like to relate another experience in my efforts to function somehow, despite all barriers, as an international artist.

Friends in Europe were working on an important cultural project—a film sponsored by the World Federation of Trade Unions—and they wanted me to record a song to be used in the production. That was the gist of a letter that came to me in the summer of 1954. The letter was brief and few details were given. The words and music of the song were enclosed, but the lyricist and composer were unnamed. The lyrics were in German, but the song was to be sung in English. The various verses and choruses were to be sung in the precise number of seconds specified for each; and I was to sing unaccompanied (no doubt an orchestra would be put "under" my voice in the finished version).

It was a song for peace and freedom, a song of brotherhood for working people of all lands—of course I would do it.

But how? I remembered how it was in London and Hollywood when I sang for films . . . the elaborate, soundproof studios with perfect acoustics, the director, his assistant, the sound engineers, the conductor with his earphones, the orchestra in full array, the small army of technicians and propmen, the clutter of expensive equipment—and the only thing I had to do was sing! Evidently this would have to be a little different. Now I must be some sort of associate producer here in New York for a film being made somewhere in Europe. Well, all right. . . .

Producer Robeson's first task was not difficult: he instructed Singer Robeson to get busy learning the song. Time was short and the singer could practice it in German until the producer could find someone to write the English version. As I did not then have a house of my own, the "studio" for this production would be my brother's home in Harlem—the parsonage of the church where he is pastor. And soon there could be heard in his study the new song that I was practicing:

Old Man Mississippi wütet,
Schleppt uns unser Vieh weg und das Land sogar . . .

It was a stirring song of six mighty rivers—the Mississippi, the Ganges, the Nile, the Yangtse, the Volga, the Amazon—and of the people who toil in their fertile valleys; and there was beauty and passion in the German lyrics. But English lyrics were required, and one day when a friend, the writer Lloyd Brown, stopped by during one of the rehearsals, I told him about the project. Would he like to help out by putting the words into English? He agreed, and soon there was a new version to be practiced:

Old Man Mississippi rages,
Robs us of our cattle, plunders field and shore . . .

Fine . . . the singer was ready now with words and music, but what about making the recording, Mr. Producer? Time is short, you said.

Here was another problem. The large recording companies belong to Big Business and would flatly refuse to rent their studios for such a job; and the smaller companies would be afraid. Then, too, there were recent experiences of sabotage done by recording engineers whose ears, keenly attuned to the snarls of McCarthy, were deaf to a singer of Peace.

My son had the answer. Paul, Jr., is an electrical engineer, and in recent years has become quite expert in making recordings. He would be the sound engineer for this job; and his portable equipment would be set up in the parsonage for the recording session.

Conditions were not exactly ideal when we came to make the recording. The small children in the household could be admonished to be silent *(Sh! Uncle Paul is trying to make a record!),* and the telephone disconnected lest it ring, but who could guarantee that a taxi would not honk on the busy street outside and spoil a perfect "take"? Under the circumstances it would have been forgivable had the producer shown signs of being disconcerted, but in this case he was too busy playing the part of singer and keeping an eye on his son who stood across the room, frowning with fierce concentration at a stop watch in one hand, the other poised overhead to signal the split-second when each verse must end.

Well, taxis did honk, and a small boy shouted, and an airliner roared over the roof, and the six rivers of the song became sixty through all the re-takes—but finally the job was done. The mighty rivers now ran their courses on a thin ribbon of magnetic tape that was packed into a little box and sent across the sea. . . .

Months later we were delighted to read clippings from the European press which told of a new documentary film titled "Song of the Rivers," made by the great Dutch moviemaker, Joris Ivens. It was, said the critics, "a masterpiece," "a monumental work," "a hymn to Man, honoring labor and assailing colonialism." The reviewers described as "magnificent" the score, composed for the film by . . . Shostakovich! And the "unknown" lyricist was the famous German writer, Bertolt Brecht. The commentary was written by Vladimir Pozner, the noted French novelist; and Picasso was making a poster to publicize the film!

Masters of culture, champions of peace—what a wonderful film-making company I had become associated with! And there was a warm glow of appreciation for the invitation they had sent me, making it possible for a Negro American to join with Hollander and Russian and German and Frenchman and all the others in creative work for peace and liberation.

A year later, when I had the chance to visit Canada, I was very happy to see, in a trade union hall, this film which had carried the song from a house in Harlem to audiences around the world. Millions in many lands have seen "Song of the Rivers," and heard the commentary in Arabic, Japanese, Persian, Chinese, Czech, Slovak, Polish, English, Russian, French and many other languages; but people in the United States have been denied that opportunity.

But we know that such films for peace shall one day be welcomed to our land again, and singers of peace shall be given passports to travel abroad. No barriers can stand against the mightiest river of all—the people's will for peace and freedom now surging in floodtide throughout the world!

Martin Luther King, Jr.

(1929–1968)

A Christmas Sermon on Peace

In the four years following the March on Washington the nightmares of black poverty, increased racist violence against African Americans, urban riots, a presidential assassination, and a war in Vietnam deferred the dream that Martin Luther King, Jr., had articulated that day in August 1963. In this sermon delivered at the Ebenezer Baptist Church of Atlanta in 1967, less than four months before his death, King reaffirms his faith in that summer's dream—the dream of a world that recognizes and respects all its peoples, whatever their colors; his vision of a future that restores human hope, extirpates injustice, and resonates with peace.

Peace on earth . . .

This Christmas season finds us a rather bewildered human race. We have neither peace within nor peace without. Everywhere paralyzing fears harrow people by day and haunt them by night. Our world is sick with war; everywhere we turn we see its ominous possibilities. And yet, my friends, the Christmas hope for peace and goodwill toward all men can no longer be dismissed as a kind of pious dream of some utopian. If we don't have goodwill toward men in this world, we will destroy ourselves by the misuse of our own instruments and our own power. Wisdom born of experience should tell us that war is obsolete. There may have been a time when war served as a negative good by preventing the spread and growth of an evil force, but the very destructive power of modern weapons of warfare eliminates even the possibility that war may any longer serve as a negative good. And so, if we assume that life is worth living, if we assume that mankind has a right to survive, then we must find an alternative to war—and so let us this morning explore the conditions for peace. Let us this morning think anew on the meaning of that Christmas hope: "Peace on Earth, Good Will toward Men." And as we explore these conditions, I would like to suggest that modern man really go all out to study the meaning of nonviolence, its philosophy and its strategy.

We have experimented with the meaning of nonviolence in our struggle for racial justice in the United States, but now the time has come for man to experiment with nonviolence in all areas of human conflict, and that means nonviolence on an international scale.

Now let me suggest first that if we are to have peace on earth, our loyalties must become ecumenical rather than sectional. Our loyalties must transcend our race, our tribe, our class, and our nation; and this means we must develop a world perspective. No individual can live alone; no nation can live alone, and as long as we try, the more we are going to have war in this world. Now the judgment of God is upon us, and we must either learn to live together as brothers or we are all going to perish together as fools.

Yes, as nations and individuals, we are interdependent. I have spoken to you before of our visit to India some years ago. It was a marvelous experience; but I say to you this morning that there were those depressing moments. How can one avoid being depressed when one sees with one's own eyes evidences of millions of people going to bed hungry at night? How can one avoid being depressed when one sees with one's own eyes thousands of people sleeping on the sidewalks at night? More than a million people sleep on the sidewalks of Bombay every night; more than half a million sleep on the sidewalks of Calcutta every night. They have no houses to go into. They have no beds to sleep in. As I beheld these conditions, something within me cried out: "Can we in America stand idly by and not be concerned?" And an answer came: "Oh, no!" And I started thinking about the fact that right here in our country we spend millions of dollars every day to store surplus food; and I said to myself: "I know where we can store that food free of charge— in the wrinkled stomachs of the millions of God's children in Asia, Africa, Latin America, and even in our own nation, who go to bed hungry at night."

It really boils down to this: that all life is interrelated. We are all caught in an inescapable network of mutuality, tied into a single garment of destiny. Whatever affects one directly, affects all indirectly. We are made to live together because of the interrelated structure of reality. Did you ever stop to think that you can't leave for your job in the morning without being dependent on most of the world? You get up in the morning and go to the bathroom and reach over for the sponge, and that's handed to you by a Pacific islander. You reach for a bar of soap, and that's given to you at the hands of a Frenchman. And then you go into the kitchen to drink your coffee for the morning, and that's poured into your cup by a South American. And maybe you want tea: that's poured into your cup by a Chinese. Or maybe you're desirous of having cocoa for breakfast, and that's poured into your cup by a West African. And then you reach over for your toast, and that's given to you at the hands of an English-speaking farmer, not to mention the baker. And before you finish eating breakfast in the morning, you've depended on more than half of the world. This is the way our universe is structured, this is its interrelated quality. We aren't going to have peace on earth until we recognize this basic fact of the interrelated structure of all reality.

Now let me say, secondly, that if we are to have peace in the world, men and nations must embrace the nonviolent affirmation that ends and means must cohere. One of the great philosophical debates of history has been over the whole question of means and ends. And there have always been those who argued that the end justifies the means, that the means really aren't important. The important thing is to get to the end, you see.

So, if you're seeking to develop a just society, they say, the important thing is to get there, and the means are really unimportant; any means will do so long as they get you there—they may be violent, they may be untruthful means; they may even be unjust means to a just end. There have been those who have argued this throughout history. But we will never have peace in the world until men everywhere recognize that ends are not cut off from means, because the means represent the ideal in the making, and the end in process, and ultimately you can't reach good ends through evil means, because the means represent the seed and the end represents the tree.

It's one of the strangest things that all the great military geniuses of the world have talked about peace. The conquerors of old who came killing in pursuit of peace, Alexander, Julius Caesar, Charlemagne, and Napoleon, were akin in seeking a peaceful world order. If you will read *Mein Kampf* closely enough, you will discover that Hitler contended that everything he did in Germany was for peace. And the leaders of the world today talk eloquently about peace. Every time we drop our bombs in North Vietnam, President Johnson talks eloquently about peace. What is the problem? They are talking about peace as a distant goal, as an end we seek, but one day we must come to see that peace is not merely a distant goal we seek, but that it is a means by which we arrive at that goal. We must pursue peaceful ends through peaceful means. All of this is saying that, in the final analysis, means and ends must co-

here because the end is pre-existent in the means, and ultimately destructive means cannot bring about constructive
ends.

Now let me say that the next thing we must be concerned
about if we are to have peace on earth and goodwill toward
men is the nonviolent affirmation of the sacredness of all human life. Every man is somebody because he is a child of God.
And so when we say "Thou shalt not kill," we're really saying
that human life is too sacred to be taken on the battlefields of
the world. Man is more than a tiny vagary of whirling electrons
or a wisp of smoke from a limitless smoldering. Man is a child
of God, made in His image, and therefore must be respected as
such. Until men see this everywhere, until nations see this
everywhere, we will be fighting wars. One day somebody
should remind us that, even though there may be political and
ideological differences between us, the Vietnamese are our
brothers, the Russians are our brothers, the Chinese are our
brothers; and one day we've got to sit down together at the
table of brotherhood. But in Christ there is neither Jew nor
Gentile. In Christ there is neither male nor female. In Christ
there is neither Communist nor capitalist. In Christ, somehow,
there is neither bound nor free. We are all one in Christ Jesus.
And when we truly believe in the sacredness of human personality, we won't exploit people, we won't trample over people
with the iron feet of oppression, we won't kill anybody.

There are three words for "love" in the Greek New Testa-
ment; one is the word *"eros." Eros* is a sort of aesthetic, romantic love. Plato used to talk about it a great deal in his dialogues,
the yearning of the soul for the realm of the divine. And there
is and can always be something beautiful about *eros,* even in its
expressions of romance. Some of the most beautiful love in all
of the world has been expressed this way.

Then the Greek language talks about *"philos,"* which is another word for love, and *philos* is a kind of intimate love between personal friends. This is the kind of love you have for
those people that you get along with well, and those whom you
like on this level you love because you are loved.

Then the Greek language has another word for love, and
that is the word *"agapē." Agapē* is more than romantic love, it is
more than friendship. *Agapē* is understanding, creative, re-

demptive goodwill toward all men. *Agapē* is an overflowing love which seeks nothing in return. Theologians would say that it is the love of God operating in the human heart. When you rise to love on this level, you love all men not because you like them, not because their ways appeal to you, but you love them because God loves them. This is what Jesus meant when He said, "Love your enemies." And I'm happy that He didn't say, "Like your enemies," because there are some people that I find it pretty difficult to like. Liking is an affectionate emotion, and I can't like anybody who would bomb my home. I can't like anybody who would exploit me. I can't like anybody who would trample over me with injustices. I can't like them. I can't like anybody who threatens to kill me day in and day out. But Jesus reminds us that love is greater than liking. Love is understanding, creative, redemptive goodwill toward all men. And I think this is where we are, as a people, in our struggle for racial justice. We can't ever give up. We must work passionately and unrelentingly for first-class citizenship. We must never let up in our determination to remove every vestige of segregation and discrimination from our nation, but we shall not in the process relinquish our privilege to love.

I've seen too much hate to want to hate, myself, and I've seen hate on the faces of too many sheriffs, too many white citizens' councilors, and too many Klansmen of the South to want to hate, myself; and every time I see it, I say to myself, hate is too great a burden to bear. Somehow we must be able to stand up before our most bitter opponents and say: "We shall match your capacity to inflict suffering by our capacity to endure suffering. We will meet your physical force with soul force. Do to us what you will and we will still love you. We cannot in all good conscience obey your unjust laws and abide by the unjust system, because noncooperation with evil is as much a moral obligation as is cooperation with good, and so throw us in jail and we will still love you. Bomb our homes and threaten our children, and, as difficult as it is, we will still love you. Send your hooded perpetrators of violence into our communities at the midnight hour and drag us out on some wayside road and leave us half-dead as you beat us, and we will still love you. Send your propaganda agents around the country, and make it appear that we are not fit, culturally and otherwise, for integration, and we'll still love you. But be assured that we'll wear you down by our capacity to suffer, and one day we will win our freedom. We will not only win freedom for ourselves; we will so appeal to your heart and conscience that we will win you in the process, and our victory will be a double victory."

If there is to be peace on earth and goodwill toward men, we must finally believe in the ultimate morality of the universe, and believe that all reality hinges on moral foundations. Something must remind us of this as we once again stand in the Christmas season and think of the Easter season simultaneously, for the two somehow go together. Christ came to show us the way. Men love darkness rather than the light, and they crucified Him, and there on Good Friday on the Cross it was still dark, but then Easter came, and Easter is an eternal reminder of the fact that the truth-crushed earth will rise again. Easter justifies Carlyle in saying, "No lie can live for ever." And so this is our faith, as we continue to hope for peace on earth and goodwill toward men: let us know that in the process we have cosmic companionship.

In 1963, on a sweltering August afternoon, we stood in Washington, D.C., and talked to the nation about many things. Toward the end of that afternoon, I tried to talk to the nation about a dream that I had had, and I must confess to you today that not long after talking about that dream I started seeing it turn into a nightmare. I remember the first time I saw that dream turn into a nightmare, just a few weeks after I had talked about it. It was when four beautiful, unoffending, innocent Negro girls were murdered in a church in Birmingham, Alabama. I watched that dream turn into a nightmare as I moved through the ghettos of the nation and saw my black brothers and sisters perishing on a lonely island of poverty in the midst of a vast ocean of material prosperity, and saw the nation doing nothing to grapple with the Negroes' problem of poverty. I saw that dream turn into a nightmare as I watched my black brothers and sisters in the midst of anger and understandable outrage, in the midst of their hurt, in the midst of their disappointment, turn to misguided riots to try to solve that problem. I saw that dream turn into a nightmare as I watched the war in Vietnam escalating, and as I saw so-called military advisers, 16,000 strong, turn into fighting soldiers until today over 500,000 American boys are fighting on Asian soil. Yes, I am personally the victim of deferred dreams, of blasted hopes, but in spite of that I close today by saying I still have a dream, because, you know, you can't give up in life. If you lose hope, somehow you lose that vitality that keeps life moving, you lose that courage to be, that quality that helps you to go on in spite of all. And so today I still have a dream.

I have a dream that one day men will rise up and come to see that they are made to live together as brothers. I still have a dream this morning that one day every Negro in this country, every colored person in the world, will be judged on the basis of the content of his character rather than the color of his skin, and every man will respect the dignity and worth of human personality. I still have a dream today that one day the idle industries of Appalachia will be revitalized, and the empty stomachs of Mississippi will be filled, and brotherhood will be more than a few words at the end of a prayer, but rather the first order of business on every legislative agenda. I still have a dream today that one day justice will roll down like water, and righteousness like a mighty stream. I still have a dream today that in all of our state houses and city halls men will be elected to go there who will do justly and love mercy and walk humbly with their God. I still have a dream today that one day war will come to an end, that men will beat their swords into plowshares and their spears into pruning hooks, that nations will no longer rise up against nations, neither will they study war any more. I still have a dream today that one day the lamb and the lion will lie down together and every man will sit under his own vine and fig tree and none shall be afraid. I still have a dream today that one day every valley shall be exalted and every mountain and hill will be made low, the rough places will be made smooth and the crooked places straight, and the glory of the Lord shall be revealed, and all flesh shall see it together. I still have a dream that with this faith we will be able to adjourn the councils of despair and bring new light into the dark chambers of pessimism. With this faith we will be able to speed up the day when there will be peace on earth and goodwill toward men. It will be a glorious day, the morning stars will sing together, and the sons of God will shout for joy.

Bayard Rustin

(1910–1988)

from *Down the Line*
Reflections on the Death
of Martin Luther King, Jr.

*Bayard Rustin was raised by his mother and grand-
parents in West Chester, Pennsylvania. He attended
City College of New York. A civil rights activist, he
worked closely with Martin Luther King, Jr., in the
Montgomery bus boycott and the Southern Christian
Leadership Conference. He assisted A. Philip Randolph in organizing the March on Washington. He
served as the first field secretary of the Congress of Racial Equality and, from 1964, as the executive director
of the A. Philip Randolph Institute. Placing the African-American struggle for equality in the context of a
larger movement for human rights and social reform,
Rustin also worked on behalf of the Japanese interned
during World War II, the Free India Committee, and
the All African Peoples Congress.*

In the following piece written shortly after the assassination of Martin Luther King, Jr., Rustin pays tribute to the man who inspired America with his vision of the world united.

The murder of Dr. Martin Luther King, Jr., has thrust a lance into the soul of America. The pain is most shattering to the Negro people. We have lost a valiant son, a symbol of hope, and an eloquent spirit that inspired masses of people. Such a man does not appear often in the history of social struggle. When his presence signifies that greatness can inhabit a black skin, those who must deny this possibility stop at nothing to remove it. Dr. King now joins a long list of victims of desperate hate in the service of insupportable lies, myths, and stereotypes.

For me, the death of Dr. King brings deep personal grief. I had known and worked with him since the early days of the Montgomery bus protest in 1955, through the founding of the Southern Christian Leadership Conference, the Prayer Pilgrimage in 1957, the youth marches for integrated schools in 1958 and 1959, and the massive March on Washington in 1963.

Though his senior by twenty years, I came to admire the depth of his faith in nonviolence, in the ultimate vindication of the democratic process, and in the redeeming efficacy of social commitment and action. And underlying this faith was a quiet courage grounded in the belief that the triumph of justice, however long delayed, was inevitable. Like so many others, I watched his spirit take hold in the country, arousing long-slumbering consciences and giving shape to a new social movement. With that movement came new hopes, aspirations, and expectations. The stakes grew higher.

At such a time, so great a loss can barely be sustained by the Negro people. But the tragedy and shame of April 4 darken the entire nation as it teeters on the brink of crisis. And let no one mistake the signs: our country is in deadly serious trouble. This needs to be said because one of the ironies of life in an advanced industrialized society is that many people can go about their daily business without being directly affected by the ominous rumblings at the bottom of the system.

Yet we are at one of the great crossroads in our history, and the alternatives before us grow more stark with every summer's violence. In moments like these there is a strong temptation to succumb to utter despair and helpless cynicism. It is indeed hard to maintain a clear perspective, a reliable sense of where events are heading. But this is exactly what we are called upon to do. Momentous decisions are about to be made —consciously or by default—and the consequences will leave not one corner of this land, nor any race or class, untouched.

Where, then, do we go from here?

We are a house divided. Of this Dr. King's murder is a stunning reminder. Every analysis, strategy, and proposal for a way out of the American dilemma must begin with the recognition that a perilous polarization is taking place in our society. Part of it is no doubt due to the war in Vietnam, part to the often remarked generation gap. But generations come and go and so do foreign policies. The issue of race, however, has been with us since our earliest beginnings as a nation. I believe it is even deeper and sharper than the other points of contention. It has bred fears, myths, and violence over centuries. It is the source of dark and dangerous irrationality, a current of social pathology running through our history and dimming our brighter achievements.

Most of the time the reservoir of racism remains stagnant. But —and this has been true historically for most societies—when major economic, social, or political crises arise, the backwaters are stirred and latent racial hostility comes to the surface. Scapegoats must be found, simple targets substituted for complex problems. The frustration and insecurity generated by these problems find an outlet in notions of racial superiority and inferiority. Very often we find that the most virulent hostility to Negroes exists among ethnic groups that only recently "made it" themselves or that are still near the bottom of the ladder. They need to feel that somebody is beneath them. (This is a problem which the labor movement has had to face more acutely perhaps than any comparable institution in American life. And it's a problem which some of labor's middle-class critics have not had to cope with at all.)

Negroes are reacting to this hostility with a counter-hostility. Some say the white man has no soul; others say he is barbaric, uncivilized; others proclaim him racially inferior. As is so often the case, such a *reaction* is the exaggerated obverse of the original *action*.

And in fact it incorporates elements of white stereotypes of Negroes. ("Soul," for example, so far as it is definable, seems to consist in part of rhythm, spontaneity, pre-industrial sentimentality, a footloose antiregimentation, etc.—qualities attributed to Negroes by many whites, though in different words.)

This reaction among Negroes is not so new as many white people think. What is new is the intensity with which it is felt among some Negroes and the violent way it has been expressed in recent years. For this, the conservatives and reactionaries would blame the civil rights movement and the federal government. And in the very specific sense, we must conclude that they are right.

One effect of the civil rights struggle in the past ten years has been to convince a generation of young Negroes that their place in society is no longer predetermined at birth. We demonstrated that segregationist barriers could be toppled, that social relations were not fixed for all time, that change was on the agenda. The federal government reinforced this new consciousness with its many pronouncements that racial integration and equality were the official goals of American society.

The reactionaries would tell us that these hopes and promises were unreasonable to begin with and should never have been advanced. They equate stability with the preservation of the established hierarchy of social relations, and chaos with the reform of that unjust arrangement. The fact is that the promises were reasonable, justified, and long overdue. Our task is not to rescind them—how do you rescind the promise of equality?—but to implement them fully and vigorously.

This task is enormously complicated by the polarization now taking place on the race issue. We are caught in a vicious cycle: inaction on the poverty and civil rights fronts foments rioting in the ghettos; the rioting encourages vindictive inaction. Militancy, extremism, and violence grow in the black community; racism, reaction, and conservatism gain ground in the white community.

Personal observation and the law of numbers persuade me that a turn to the right comprises the larger part of the polarization. This, of course, is a perilous challenge not only to the Negro but also to the labor movement, to liberals and civil libertarians, to all of the forces for social progress. We must meet that challenge in 1968.

Meanwhile, a process of polarization is also taking place within the Negro community and, with the murder of Dr. King, it is likely to be accelerated.

Ironically and sadly, this will occur precisely because of the broad support Dr. King enjoyed among Negroes. That support cut across ideological and class lines. Even those Negro spokesmen who could not accept, and occasionally derided, Dr. King's philosophy of nonviolence and reconciliation, admired and respected his unique national and international position. They were moved by his sincerity and courage. Not, perhaps, since the days of Booker T. Washington—when 90 per cent of all Negroes lived in the South and were occupationally and socially more homogeneous than today—had any one man come so close to being *the* Negro leader. He was a large unifying force and his assassination leaves an enormous vacuum. The diverse strands he linked together have fallen from his hands.

The murder of Dr. King tells Negroes that if one of the greatest among them is not safe from the assassin's bullet, then what can the least of them hope for? In this context, those young black militants who have resorted to violence feel vindicated. "Look what happened to Dr. King," they say. "He was nonviolent; he didn't hurt anybody. And look what they did to him. If we have to go down, let's go down shooting. Let's take whitey with us."

Make no mistake about it: a great psychological barrier has now been placed between those of us who have urged nonviolence as the road to social change and the frustrated, despairing youth of the ghettos. Dr. King's assassination is only the latest example of our society's determination to teach young Negroes that violence pays. We pay no attention to them until they take to the streets in riotous rebellion. Then we make minor concessions—not enough to solve their basic problems, but enough to persuade them that we know they exist. "Besides," the young militants will tell you, "this country was built on violence. Look at what we did to the Indians. Look at our television and movies. And look at Vietnam. If the cause of the Vietnamese is worth taking up guns for, why isn't the cause of the black man right here in Harlem?"

These questions are loaded and oversimplified, to be sure, and they obscure the real issues and the programmatic direction we must take to meet them. But what we must answer is the bitterness and disillusionment that give rise to these questions. If our answers consist of mere words, they will fall on deaf ears. They will not ring true until ghetto-trapped Negroes experience significant and tangible progress in the daily conditions of their lives—in their jobs, income, housing, education, health care, political representation, etc. This must be understood by those often well-meaning people who, frightened by the polarization, would retreat from committed action into homilies about racial understanding.

We are indeed a house divided. But the division between race and race, class and class, will not be dissolved by massive infusions of brotherly sentiment. The division is not the result of bad sentiment and therefore will not be healed by rhetoric. Rather the division and the bad sentiments are both reflections of vast and growing inequalities in our socioeconomic system —inequalities of wealth, of status, of education, of access to political power. Talk of brotherhood and "tolerance" (are we merely to "tolerate" one another?) might once have had a cooling effect, but increasingly it grates on the nerves. It evokes contempt not because the values of brotherhood are wrong— they are more important now than ever—but because it just does not correspond to the reality we see around us. And such talk does nothing to eliminate the inequalities that breed resentment and deep discontent.

The same is true of most "black power" sloganeering, in which I detect powerful elements of conservatism. Leaving aside those extremists who call for violent revolution, the black power movement embraces a diversity of groups and ideologies. It contains a strong impulse toward withdrawal from social struggle and action, a retreat back into the ghetto, avoidance of contact with the white world. This impulse may, I fear, be strengthened by the assassination of Dr. King.

This brand of black power has much in common with the conservative white American's view of the Negro. It stresses self-help ("Why don't those Negroes pull themselves up by their own bootstraps like my ancestors did?"). It identifies the Negro's main problems in psychological terms, calls upon him to develop greater self-respect and dignity by studying Negro history and culture and by building independent institutions.

In all of these ideas there is some truth. But taken as a whole, the trouble with this thinking is that it assumes that the Negro can solve his problems by himself, in isolation from the rest of the society. The fact is, however, that the Negro did not create these problems for himself and he cannot solve them by himself.

Dignity and self-respect are not abstract virtues that can be cultivated in a vacuum. They are related to one's job, education, residence, mobility, family responsibilities, and other circumstances that are determined by one's economic and social status in the society. Whatever deficiencies in dignity and self-respect may be laid to the Negro are the consequence of generations of segregation, discrimination, and exploitation. Above all, in my opinion, these deficiencies result from systematic exclusion of the Negro from the economic mainstream.

This exclusion cannot be reversed—but only perpetuated—by gilding the ghettos. A "separate but equal" economy for black Americans is impossible. In any case, the ghettos do not have the resources needed for massive programs of abolishing poverty, inferior education, slum housing, and the other problems plaguing the Negro people. These resources must come primarily from the federal government, which means that the fate of the Negro is unavoidably tied to the political life of this nation.

It is time, therefore, that all of us, black and white alike, put aside rhetoric that obscures the real problems. It is precisely

because we have so long swept these incendiary problems under the rug that they are now exploding all around us, insisting
upon our attention. We can divert our eyes no longer.

The life and death of Martin Luther King are profoundly symbolic. From the Montgomery bus protest to the Memphis sanitation workers strike, his career embodies the internal development, the unfolding, the evolution of the modern civil rights
struggle.

That struggle began as a revolt against segregation in public
accommodations—buses, lunch counters, libraries, schools,
parks. It was aimed at ancient and obsolete institutional arrangements and mores left over from an earlier social order in
the South, an order that was being undermined and transformed by economic and technological forces.

As the civil rights movement progressed, winning victory
after victory in public accommodations and voting rights, it
became increasingly conscious that these victories would not
be secure or far-reaching without a radical improvement in the
Negro's socioeconomic position. And so the movement
reached out of the South into the urban centers of the North
and West. It moved from public accommodations to employment, welfare, housing, education—to find a host of problems
the nation had let fester for a generation.

But these were not problems that affected the Negro alone
or that could be solved easily with the movement's traditional
protest tactics. These injustices were imbedded not in ancient
and obsolete institutional arrangements but in the priorities of
powerful vested interests, in the direction of public policy, in
the allocation of our national resources. Sit-ins could integrate
a lunch counter, but massive social investments and imaginative public policies were required to eliminate the deeper inequalities.

Dr. King came to see that this was too big a job for the Negro
alone, that it called for an effective coalition with the labor
movement. As King told the AFL-CIO convention in 1961:

Negroes are almost entirely a working people. There
are pitifully few Negro millionaires and few Negro em-

ployers. Our needs are identical with labor's needs—decent wages, fair working conditions, livable housing, old age security, health and welfare measures, conditions in which families can grow, have education for their children and respect in the community.

That is why Negroes support labor's demands and fight laws which curb labor.

That is why the labor-hater and labor-baiter is virtually always a twin-headed creature spewing anti-Negro epithets from one mouth and anti-labor propaganda from the other mouth.

The duality of interest of labor and Negroes makes any crisis which lacerates you, a crisis from which we bleed. As we stand on the threshold of the second half of the twentieth century, a crisis confronts us both. Those who in the second half of the nineteenth century could not tolerate organized labor have had a rebirth of power and seek to regain the despotism of that era while retaining the wealth and privileges of the twentieth century.

. . . The two most dynamic and cohesive liberal forces in the country are the labor movement and the Negro freedom movement.

. . . I look forward confidently to the day when all who work for a living will be one, with no thought to their separateness as Negroes, Jews, Italians, or any other distinctions.

This will be the day when we shall bring into full realization the American dream—a dream yet unfulfilled. A dream of equality of opportunity, of privilege and property widely distributed; a dream of a land where men will not take necessities from the many to give luxuries to the few; a dream of a land where men will not argue that the color of a man's skin determines the content of his character; a dream of a nation where all our gifts and resources are held not for ourselves alone but as instruments of service for the rest of humanity; the dream of a country where every man will respect the dignity and worth of human personality—that is the dream.

And so Dr. King went to Memphis to help 1,300 sanitation workers—almost all of them black—to win union recognition, dues checkoff, higher wages, and better working conditions.

And in the midst of this new phase of his work he was assassinated. Since then, the sanitation workers have won their fight. But the real battle is just beginning.

The Report of the National Advisory Commission on Civil Disorders is the latest in a series of documents—official, semiofficial, and unofficial—that have sought to arouse the American people to the great dangers we face and to the price we are likely to pay if we do not multiply our efforts to eradicate poverty and racism.

The recent recommendations parallel those urged by civil rights and labor groups over the years. The legislative work of the Leadership Conference on Civil Rights, of the National Association for the Advancement of Colored People, and of the AFL-CIO has been vital to the progress we have made so far. This work is now proceeding effectively on a broad coordinated basis. It has pinpointed the objectives for which the entire nation must strive.

We have got to provide meaningful work at decent wages for every employable citizen. We must guarantee an adequate income for those unable to work. We must build millions of low-income housing units, tear down the slums, and rebuild our cities. We need to build schools, hospitals, mass transit systems. We need to construct new, integrated towns. As President Johnson has said, we need to build a "second America" between now and the year 2000.

It is in the context of this national reconstruction that the socioeconomic fate of the Negro will be determined. Will we build into the second America new, more sophisticated forms of segregation and exploitation or will we create a genuine open, integrated, and democratic society? Will we have a more equitable distribution of economic resources and political power, or will we sow the seeds of more misery, unrest, and division?

Because of men like Martin Luther King, it is unlikely that the American Negro can ever again return to the old order. But it is up to us, the living, black and white, to realize Dr. King's dream.

This means, first of all, to serve notice on the 90th Congress that its cruel indifference to the plight of our cities and of the

poor—even after the martyrdom of Dr. King—will not be tolerated by the American people. In an economy as fabulously pro-
ductive as ours, a balanced budget cannot be the highest virtue
and, in any case, it cannot be paid for by the poor.

Next, I believe, we must recognize the magnitude of the
threat we face in an election year from a resurgence of the
rightwing backlash forces. This threat will reach ever greater
proportions if this summer sees massive violence in the cities.
The Negro-labor-liberal coalition, whatever differences now exist within and among its constituent forces, must resolve to
unite this fall in order to defeat racism and reaction at the polls.
Unless we so resolve, we may find ourselves in a decade of
vindictive and mean conservative domination.

We owe it to Martin Luther King not to let this happen. We
owe it to him to preserve and extend his victories. We owe it to
him to fulfill his dreams. We owe it to his memory and to our
futures.

Alice Walker

(b. 1944)

---

from *In Search of Our
Mothers' Gardens*
Saving the Life That Is Your Own:
The Importance of Models in the
Artist's Life

*Critically acclaimed novelist, essayist, short story
writer, and poet Alice Walker was born in Eatonton,
Georgia. Best known for the Pulitzer Prize-winning
novel* The Color Purple, *Walker measures her own
growth as a writer by the unsung if not neglected or
totally ignored artistry of other African-American
women who saved their lives in their work. And beyond
her own particular experience, beyond the lives of all
those African-American women who wrote down and
told their stories, beyond all writers black and white,
man or woman, Third World or mainstream, godless
or on wings of spirit rising, lies "one immense story—
the same story, for the most part—with different parts*

of this story coming from a multitude of different per-spectives," as Walker envisions it, and in that immen-sity all our storytellers connect. In their story are all our worlds united.

There is a letter Vincent Van Gogh wrote to Emile Bernard that is very meaningful to me. A year before he wrote the letter, Van Gogh had had a fight with his domineering friend Gauguin, left his company, and cut off, in desperation and an-guish, his own ear. The letter was written in Saint-Remy, in the South of France, from a mental institution to which Van Gogh had voluntarily committed himself.

I imagine Van Gogh sitting at a rough desk too small for him, looking out at the lovely Southern light, and occasionally glanc-ing critically next to him at his own paintings of the landscape he loved so much. The date of the letter is December 1889. Van Gogh wrote:

> However hateful painting may be, and however cumber-some in the times we are living in, if anyone who has chosen this handicraft pursues it zealously, he is a man of duty, sound and faithful.
>
> Society makes our existence wretchedly difficult at times, hence our impotence and the imperfection of our work.
>
> . . . I myself am suffering under an absolute lack of models.
>
> But on the other hand, there are beautiful spots here. I have just done five size 30 canvasses, olive trees. And the reason I am staying on here is that my health is improving a great deal.
>
> What I am doing is hard, dry, but that is because I am trying to gather new strength by doing some rough work, and I'm afraid abstractions would make me soft.

Six months later, Van Gogh—whose health was "improving a great deal"—committed suicide. He had sold one painting during his lifetime. Three times was his work noticed in the press. But these are just details.

The real Vincent Van Gogh is the man who has "just done five size 30 canvasses, olive trees." To me, in context, one of the most moving and revealing descriptions of how a real artist thinks. And the knowledge that when he spoke of "suffering under an absolute lack of models" he spoke of that lack in terms of both the intensity of his commitment and the quality and singularity of his work, which was frequently ridiculed in his day.

The absence of models, in literature as in life, to say nothing of painting, is an occupational hazard for the artist, simply because models in art, in behavior, in growth of spirit and intellect—even if rejected—enrich and enlarge one's view of existence. Deadlier still, to the artist who lacks models, is the curse of ridicule, the bringing to bear on an artist's best work, especially his or her most original, most strikingly deviant, only a fund of ignorance and the presumption that, as an artist's critic, one's judgment is free of the restrictions imposed by prejudice, and is well informed, indeed, about all the art in the world that really matters.

What is always needed in the appreciation of art, or life, is the larger perspective. Connections made, or at least attempted, where none existed before, the straining to encompass in one's glance at the varied world the common thread, the unifying theme through immense diversity, a fearlessness of growth, of search, of looking, that enlarges the private and the public world. And yet, in our particular society, it is the narrowed and narrowing view of life that often wins.

Recently, I read at a college and was asked by one of the audience what I considered the major difference between the literature written by black and by white Americans. I had not spent a lot of time considering this question, since it is not the difference between them that interests me, but, rather, the way black writers and white writers seem to me to be writing one immense story—the same story, for the most part—with different parts of this immense story coming from a multitude of different perspectives. Until this is generally recognized, literature will always be broken into bits, black and white, and there will always be questions, wanting neat answers, such as this.

Still, I answered that I thought, for the most part, white American writers tended to end their books and their characters' lives as if there were no better existence for which to struggle. The gloom of defeat is thick.

By comparison, black writers seem always involved in a moral and/or physical struggle, the result of which is expected to be some kind of larger freedom. Perhaps this is because our literary tradition is based on the slave narratives, where escape for the body and freedom for the soul went together, or perhaps this is because black people have never felt themselves guilty of global, cosmic sins.

This comparison does not hold up in every case, of course, and perhaps does not really hold up at all. I am not a gatherer of statistics, only a curious reader, and this has been my impression from reading many books by black and white writers.

There are, however, two books by American women that illustrate what I am talking about: *The Awakening,* by Kate Chopin, and *Their Eyes Were Watching God,* by Zora Neale Hurston.

The plight of Mme Pontellier is quite similar to that of Janie Crawford. Each woman is married to a dull, society-conscious husband and living in a dull, propriety-conscious community. Each woman desires a life of her own and a man who loves her and makes her feel alive. Each woman finds such a man.

Mme Pontellier, overcome by the strictures of society and the existence of her children (along with the cowardice of her lover), kills herself rather than defy the one and abandon the other. Janie Crawford, on the other hand, refuses to allow society to dictate behavior to her, enjoys the love of a much younger, freedom-loving man, and lives to tell others of her experience.

When I mentioned these two books to my audience, I was not surprised to learn that only one person, a young black poet in the first row, had ever heard of *Their Eyes Were Watching God* (*The Awakening* they had fortunately read in their "Women in Literature" class), primarily because it was written by a black woman, whose experience—in love and life—was apparently assumed to be unimportant to the students (and the teachers) of a predominantly white school.

Certainly, as a student, I was not directed toward this book, which would have urged me more toward freedom and experience than toward comfort and security, but was directed instead toward a plethora of books by mainly white male writers who thought most women worthless if they didn't enjoy bullfighting or hadn't volunteered for the trenches in World War I.

Loving both these books, knowing each to be indispensable to my own growth, my own life, I choose the model, the example, of Janie Crawford. And yet this book, as necessary to me and to other women as air and water, is again out of print.* But I have distilled as much as I could of its wisdom in this poem about its heroine, Janie Crawford:

> I love the way Janie Crawford
> left her husbands
> the one who wanted to change her
> into a mule
> and the other who tried to interest her
> in being a queen.
> A woman, unless she submits,
> is neither a mule
> nor a queen
> though like a mule she may suffer
> and like a queen pace the floor

It has been said that someone asked Toni Morrison why she writes the kind of books she writes, and that she replied: Because they are the kind of books I want to read.

This remains my favorite reply to that kind of question. As if anyone reading the magnificent, mysterious *Sula* or the grim, poetic *The Bluest Eye* would require more of a reason for their existence than for the brooding, haunting *Wuthering Heights,* for example, or the melancholy, triumphant *Jane Eyre.* (I am not speaking here of the most famous short line of that book, "Reader, I married him," as the triumph, but, rather, of the triumph of Jane Eyre's control over her own sense of morality and her own stout will, which are but reflections of her creator's, Charlotte Brontë, who no doubt wished to write the sort of book *she* wished to read.)

Flannery O'Connor has written that more and more the seri-

* Reissued by the University of Illinois Press, 1979.

ous novelist will write, not what other people want, and certainly not what other people expect, but whatever interests her or him. And that the direction taken, therefore, will be away from sociology, away from the "writing of explanation," of statistics, and further into mystery, into poetry, and into prophecy. I believe this is true, *fortunately true;* especially for "Third World Writers"; Morrison, Marquez, Ahmadi, Camara Laye make good examples. And not only do I believe it is true for serious writers in general, but I believe, as firmly as did O'Connor, that this is our only hope—in a culture so in love with flash, with trendiness, with superficiality, as ours—of acquiring a sense of essence, of timelessness, and of vision. Therefore, to write the books one wants to read is both to point the direction of vision and, at the same time, to follow it.

When Toni Morrison said she writes the kind of books she wants to read, she was acknowledging the fact that in a society in which "accepted literature" is so often sexist and racist and otherwise irrelevant or offensive to so many lives, she must do the work of two. She must be her own model as well as the artist attending, creating, learning from, realizing the model, which is to say, herself.

(It should be remembered that, as a black person, one cannot completely identify with a Jane Eyre, or with her creator, no matter how much one admires them. And certainly, if one allows history to impinge on one's reading pleasure, one must cringe at the thought of how Heathcliff, in the New World far from Wuthering Heights, amassed his Cathy-dazzling fortune.)

I have often been asked why, in my own life and work, I have felt such a desperate need to know and assimilate the experiences of earlier black women writers, most of them unheard of by you and by me, until quite recently; why I felt a need to study them and to teach them.

I don't recall the exact moment I set out to explore the works of black women, mainly those in the past, and certainly, in the beginning, I had no desire to teach them. Teaching being for me, at that time, less rewarding than star-gazing on a frigid night. My discovery of them—most of them out of print, abandoned, discredited, maligned, nearly lost—came about, as many things of value do, almost by accident. As it turned out—

and this should not have surprised me—I found I was in need of something that only one of them could provide.

Mindful that throughout my four years at a prestigious black and then a prestigious white college I had heard not one word about early black women writers, one of my first tasks was simply to determine whether they had existed. After this, I could breathe easier, with more assurance about the profession I myself had chosen.

But the incident that started my search began several years ago: I sat down at my desk one day, in a room of my own, with key and lock, and began preparations for a story about voodoo, a subject that had always fascinated me. Many of the elements of this story I had gathered from a story my mother several times told me. She had gone, during the Depression, into town to apply for some government surplus food at the local commissary, and had been turned down, in a particularly humiliating way, by the white woman in charge.

My mother always told this story with a most curious expression on her face. She automatically raised her head higher than ever—it was always high—and there was a look of righteousness, a kind of holy *heat* coming from her eyes. She said she had lived to see this same white woman grow old and senile and so badly crippled she had to get about on *two* sticks.

To her, this was clearly the working of God, who, as in the old spiritual, ". . . may not come when you want him, but he's right on time!" To me, hearing the story for about the fiftieth time, something else was discernible: the possibilities of the story, for fiction.

What, I asked myself, would have happened if, after the crippled old lady died, it was discovered that someone, my mother perhaps (who would have been mortified at the thought, Christian that she is), had voodooed her?

Then, my thoughts sweeping me away into the world of hexes and conjurings of centuries past, I wondered how a larger story could be created out of my mother's story; one that would be true to the magnitude of her humiliation and grief, and to the white woman's lack of sensitivity and compassion.

My third quandary was: How could I find out all I needed to

know in order to write a story that used *authentic* black witch-
craft?

Which brings me back, almost, to the day I became really
interested in black women writers. I say "almost" because one
other thing, from my childhood, made the choice of black
magic a logical and irresistible one for my story. Aside from
my mother's several stories about root doctors she had heard
of or known, there was the story I had often heard about my
"crazy" Walker aunt.

Many years ago, when my aunt was a meek and obedient girl
growing up in a strict, conventionally religious house in the
rural South, she had suddenly thrown off her meekness and
had run away from home, escorted by a rogue of a man perma-
nently attached elsewhere.

When she was returned home by her father, she was declared quite mad. In the backwoods South at the turn of the
century, "madness" of this sort was cured not by psychiatry
but by powders and by spells. (One can see Scott Joplin's
Treemonisha to understand the role voodoo played among
black people of that period.) My aunt's madness was treated by
the community conjurer, who promised, and delivered, the desired results. His treatment was a bag of white powder, bought
for fifty cents, and sprinkled on the ground around her house,
with some of it sewed, I believe, into the bodice of her night-
gown.

So when I sat down to write my story about voodoo, my
crazy Walker aunt was definitely on my mind.

But she had experienced her temporary craziness so long
ago that her story had all the excitement of a might-have-been.
I needed, instead of family memories, some hard facts about
the *craft* of voodoo, as practiced by Southern blacks in the
nineteenth century. (It never once, fortunately, occurred to me
that voodoo was not worthy of the interest I had in it, or was
too ridiculous to study seriously.)

I began reading all I could find on the subject of "The Negro
and His Folkways and Superstitions." There were Botkin and
Puckett and others, all white, most racist. How was I to believe
anything they wrote, since at least one of them, Puckett, was
capable of wondering, in his book, if "The Negro" had a large
enough brain?

Well, I thought, where are the *black* collectors of folklore? Where is the *black* anthropologist? Where is the *black* person who took the time to travel the back roads of the South and collect the information I need: how to cure heart trouble, treat dropsy, hex somebody to death, lock bowels, cause joints to swell, eyes to fall out, and so on. Where was this black person?

And that is when I first saw, in a *footnote* to the white voices of authority, the name Zora Neale Hurston.

Folklorist, novelist, anthropologist, serious student of voodoo, also all-around black woman, with guts enough to take a slide rule and measure random black heads in Harlem; not to prove their inferiority, but to prove that whatever their size, shape, or present condition of servitude, those heads contained all the intelligence anyone could use to get through this world.

Zora Hurston, who went to Barnard to learn how to study what she really wanted to learn: the ways of her own people, and what ancient rituals, customs, and beliefs had made them unique.

Zora, of the sandy-colored hair and the daredevil eyes, a girl who escaped poverty and parental neglect by hard work and a sharp eye for the main chance.

Zora, who left the South only to return to look at it again. Who went to root doctors from Florida to Louisiana and said, "Here I am. I want to learn your trade."

Zora, who had collected all the black folklore I could ever use.

That Zora.

And having found *that Zora* (like a golden key to a storehouse of varied treasure), I was hooked.

What I had discovered, of course, was a model. A model, who, as it happened, provided more than voodoo for my story, more than one of the greatest novels America had produced—though, being America, it did not realize this. She had provided, as if she knew someday I would come along wandering in the wilderness, a nearly complete record of her life. And though her life sprouted an occasional wart, I am eternally grateful for that life, warts and all.

It is not irrelevant, nor is it bragging (except perhaps to gloat a little on the happy relatedness of Zora, my mother, and me), to mention here that the story I wrote, called "The Revenge of

Hannah Kemhuff," based on my mother's experiences during the Depression, and on Zora Hurston's folklore collection of the 1920s, and on my own response to both out of a contemporary existence, was immediately published and was later selected, by a reputable collector of short stories, as one of the *Best Short Stories of 1974.*

I mention it because this story might never have been written, because the very bases of its structure, authentic black folklore, viewed from a black perspective, might have been lost.

Had it been lost, my mother's story would have had no historical underpinning, none I could trust, anyway. I would not have written the story, which I enjoyed writing as much as I've enjoyed writing anything in my life, had I not known that Zora had already done a thorough job of preparing the ground over which I was then moving.

In that story I gathered up the historical and psychological threads of the life my ancestors lived, and in the writing of it I felt joy and strength and my own continuity. I had that wonderful feeling writers get sometimes, not very often, of being *with* a great many people, ancient spirits, all very happy to see me consulting and acknowledging them, and eager to let me know, through the joy of their presence, that, indeed, I am not alone.

To take Toni Morrison's statement further, if that is possible, in my own work I write not only what I want to read—understanding fully and indelibly that if I don't do it no one else is so vitally interested, or capable of doing it to my satisfaction—I write all the things *I should have been able to read.* Consulting, as belatedly discovered models, those writers—most of whom, not surprisingly, are women—who understood that their experience as ordinary human beings was also valuable, and in danger of being misrepresented, distorted, or lost:

Zora Hurston—novelist, essayist, anthropologist, autobiographer;

Jean Toomer—novelist, poet, philosopher, visionary, a man who cared what women felt;

Colette—whose crinkly hair enhances her French, part-black face; novelist, playwright, dancer, essayist, newspaperwoman, lover of women, men, small dogs; fortunate not to have been born in America;

Anaïs Nin—recorder of everything, no matter how minute;

Tillie Olson—a writer of such generosity and honesty, she literally saves lives;

Virginia Woolf—who has saved so many of us.

It is, in the end, the saving of lives that we writers are about. Whether we are "minority" writers or "majority." It is simply in our power to do this.

We do it because we care. We care that Vincent Van Gogh mutilated his ear. We care that behind a pile of manure in the yard he destroyed his life. We care that Scott Joplin's music *lives!* We care because we know this: *the life we save is our own.*